Humour, Comedy and Laughter

SOCIAL IDENTITIES

General Editors: Shirley Ardener, Tamara Dragadze and Jonathan Webber

Based on a prominent Oxford University seminar founded over two decades ago by the social anthropologist Edwin Ardener, this series focuses on the ethnic, historical, religious, and other elements of culture that give rise to a social sense of belonging, enabling individuals and groups to find meaning both in their own social identities and in what differentiates them from others. Each volume is based on one specific theme that brings together contemporary material from a variety of cultures.

Humour, Comedy and Laughter

Obscenities, Paradoxes, Insights and the Renewal of Life

Edited by
Lidia Dina Sciama

berghahn
NEW YORK · OXFORD
www.berghahnbooks.com

First published in 2016 by
Berghahn Books
www.berghahnbooks.com

Library of Congress Cataloging-in-Publication Data
Names: Sciama, Lidia D., editor.
Title: Humour, comedy and laughter: obscenities, paradoxes, insights
    and the renewal of life / edited by Lidia Dina Sciama.
Other titles: Humor, comedy and laughter
Description: New York: Berghahn Books, [2016] | Series: Social
    identities; 8 | Includes bibliographical references and index.
    Identifiers: LCCN 2015034272 | ISBN 9780857450746 (hbk:
    alk. paper) | ISBN 9781789200706 (pbk: alk. paper) | ISBN
    9781782385431 (ebook)
Subjects: LCSH: Wit and humor--Social aspects--Cross-cultural
    studies. | Comedy
Classification: LCC PN6149.S62 H835 2016 | DDC 306.4/81--dc23
LC record available at http://lccn.loc.gov/2015034272

British Library Cataloguing in Publication Data

A catalogue record for this book is available from the British Library

ISBN 978-0-85745-074-6 (hardback)
ISBN 978-1-78920-070-6 (paperback)
ISBN 978-1-78238-543-1 (ebook)

Contents

Illustrations

Figures

Tables

ACKNOWLEDGEMENTS

I am deeply grateful to Shirley Ardener, Elisabeth Hsu and Ian Fowler for their support and advice at the initial stages of this project. Joanne Eicher and Renèe Hirschon very kindly read an early draft of my Introduction and offered valuable feedback and encouragement, while comments by Berghahn's anonymous readers helped to strengthen the argument and clear up potential ambiguities. My warmest thanks go to my daughters, Susan Tapsell and Sonia Daniels, for their insightful comments and discerning criticisms and, not least, for their support during different stages of this work.

Taylor and Francis granted us permission to include Matthew Saxton and Ian Wilkie's Chapter, 'The Origins of Comic Performance in Adult-Child Interaction', first published in 2010 in their journal *Comedy Studies*. Berghahn Books allowed us to reprint Shirley Ardener's study of 'The English Christmas Pantomime' from *Changing Sex and Bending Gender*, co-edited in 2005 by Ardener herself and Alison Shaw.

Introduction

Lidia Dina Sciama

Anthropology is the science of the sense of humour. (Malinowski 1937)

In the end, this work, if we will carry it further, will make clear ... the nature and function of important aesthetic elements, naturally mixed ... with darker aspects of social life. Obscenities, satirical songs, insults against people, and ridiculous representation of some sacred beings, are also at the origins of comedy; just as the respect shown to Gods and heroes nourishes what is lyrical, epic and tragic. (Mauss 1968: 161)[1]

This volume results from a cooperative project to describe and analyse a wide variety of humorous experiences, expressions and texts in different social settings and contexts. While the main focus of the book is on anthropological aspects, it soon became clear that research on humour inevitably demands an interdisciplinary treatment. Indeed, contributors have drawn on the methods and theories of related disciplines; a strong emphasis on psychological and cognitive aspects of humour is thus variously combined in the different chapters with aesthetic, historical and philosophical considerations, and with the research methods of literary criticism, textual analysis and film studies.[2]

While each of the chapters contributes some theoretical insight and casts interesting light on earlier discussions, we did not attempt to reach a general and fixed agreement on the 'essential' nature of humour and, while well aware that the three terms in our heading 'Humour, Comedy and Laughter', may designate different realities, contributors to this volume have taken their connections at face value.

Theories of Humour

As Avner Ziv writes (1984: Introduction), humour appears to be highly resistant to a firm analytical definition: 'Nearly thirty years ago, no less than eighty definitions were put forth in the professional literature (Berger 1956) and since then another thirty have been added'. The OED simply defines humour as 'The quality of being amusing or comic, especially as expressed in literature or speech' and Merriam-Webster 'A funny or amusing quality, jokes, funny stories, the ability to be funny or to be amused by things that are funny'. A more extended definition of humour as 'mood, temper, feeling', and 'a message whose ingenuity or verbal skill or incongruity has the power to evoke laughter', also includes an understanding of humour as a form of communication – as we shall see, a fundamental aspect present in all the chapters in this book (www.wolframalpha.com).[3]

Humour is commonly associated with laughter, although the two are not always and necessarily interdependent: there can be humour without laughter, and conversely much laughter can be quite humourless. One difficulty is that laughter has been explained by ethologists in different and fundamentally contrary ways; for some, at the origins, the baring of teeth was a sign of hostility, while others, seeing it essentially as a form of smile, understand it as a sign of appeasement. Both laughter and smiling can express very different feelings: they can be bitter, arrogant, false, or apologetic and bashful; as Harbsmeier stated (unpublished paper, 2010), 'The Chinese … have a vast and subtly analytical vocabulary for laughter and smiling, each qualified and named according to the emotions which prompt or accompany them'. Most commonly, however, the feelings expressed seem to be simple friendliness, understanding and amusement. As Avner Ziv points out,

> Laughter is easier to define than humour, because we can see and hear it, and, although it can also be caused by physiological stimuli, like tickling, here too is a social element: you don't laugh if you tickle yourself and you don't tickle a stranger! Also we laugh more when we are with friends, than with strangers. It reinforces cohesion and reduces tension, thus creates a positive atmosphere. (1984: 9)

That view is now confirmed thanks to scientific research by neurophysiologist R.A. Provine and his conclusion that both chimpanzee and human laughter is '*decidedly a social signal with a social function*' (1996 and 2000, my italics). Quoting Provine (1996) in her chapter on 'Jungle Humour: Play in Wild Bonobos', Isabel Behncke describes laughter as 'A universal signal of wellbeing in a playful situation to help regulate and cement social interactions' (unpublished paper, 2010). On the subject of courting – as we shall see, central to several chapters in this book – Robin Dunbar explains,

> The evolution of the human brain was driven by the demands for sexual advertizing … the modern male has to keep his partner smiling. A property of smiling and laughter is that they are good at stimulating the production of endogenous opiates. Making a prospective mate laugh lulls them into a sense of security … [Opiates] are a crucial part in the mechanisms of bonding. (1996: 190–92)

Such attempts to define what it is that leads people to make others laugh and able to perceive humorous expressions and jokes as 'funny' are very usefully grouped under three main headings, as 'superiority', 'incongruity', and 'tension' (Smuts 2013). In addition 'Play theory' classifies humour as a form of play, or a disinterested and pleasurable activity considered to have strong adaptive value, and to be an important part in children's development of cognitive and social skills, as Wilkie and Saxton clearly illustrate (chapter 1 in this volume). Experiences of incongruity, superiority, tension relief, as well as a general view of humour as a form of play, are not exclusive, but, on the contrary, they may complement one another in explaining why a joke or event may lead to amusement and laughter.

However, a distinction remains between the laughter that may follow the perception of some amusingly absurd or incongruous remark or event, and the laughter directed at another's weakness and inadequacy. Many of those who have reflected on laughter have pointed out its potential for causing humiliation and pain – a view discussed by Plato and Aristotle and summed up in Thomas Hobbes' much quoted definition of laughter as 'Nothing else but sudden glory, arising from some sudden conception of some eminency in ourselves, by comparison with the infirmity of others, or with our own formerly', in keeping with his view of human nature as fundamentally cruel and competitive (Hobbes 1840). I shall return to that problem, but first – and without any hope of covering the vast critical literature on humour – I shall briefly sum up discussions by anthropologists, in particular Radcliffe-Brown, Malinowski, Gregory Bateson and Mary Douglas.

The first British anthropologist to write about joking – or, more specifically, 'joking relationships' – was A.R. Radcliffe-Brown: a joking relationship, he writes, is one 'between two persons in which one is by custom permitted, or in some instances required, to tease and make fun of the other, who in turn is required to take no offense'. The main example and topic of his analysis is the 'privileged familiarity between sister's son and mother's brother' observed in some African societies. Joking relationships are 'most widespread in relations by marriage' when the changed position of the two families in the social structure may lead to conflict and hostility, while 'conjunction requires the avoidance of strife'. Extreme mutual respect between the son-in-law and the wife's parents, most of all her mother, is therefore countered by 'the playful antagonism of teasing' (1968: 9).

Joking takes place between persons of similar ages, as it is usually the mother's younger brother who is involved; also cross-cousins like to tease and embarrass one another in jest when they meet, but they too are not supposed to take offence. In some parts of Africa, 'there are joking relationships that have nothing to do with marriage, as they can be between distinct tribes or clans'. Radcliffe- Brown thus describes joking as a form of adaptation, that is, a process by which 'an individual acquires habits and mental characteristics that fit him for a place in social life [and] ensures the continuance of a system' (1968: 90–94).

In light of the chapters in this volume, especially Ardener's and Sciama's on the vicissitudes and sometimes comical difficulties in courtship and marriage, Radcliffe-Brown's understanding of some of the sentiments involved – for example, 'a peculiar combination of friendliness and antagonism' between affines and the contrast between 'authority and a subtle undermining of respect' by the younger generation – do underlie much joking and humour in general. However, Radcliffe-Brown's critics rightly observed that his discussion is not so much about joking as it is about social structure and affinal relationships. Mary Douglas observed that 'He wrote on the subject of joking in a very dessicated perspective' (1975: 91), and indeed his analysis shows the limitations of a narrow functionalist approach whereby joking is understood as merely a way to avoid strife and keep the social system going, thanks to 'social behaviours in which conjunctive and disjunctive components … are maintained and combined' (1968: 95). Radcliffe-Brown's scant interest in individuals and his privileging of social structure over culture, which he defined as merely 'a characteristic of a social system' (1957: 106) really deprived his analysis of any deeper psychological insights or awareness of the aesthetic and symbolic potential of humour.

Just as in the 1930s, in Chicago, Radcliffe-Brown was promoting his view of anthropology as the 'natural science of society', anthropologists on both sides of the Atlantic were developing a strong interest in relations between culture and psychology. In England, Malinowski, as well as advancing the methods of anthropological fieldwork, developed and broadened the concept of culture, which he urged his students to analyse in a number of distinct aspects, including language, education, systems of knowledge, material culture, and above all psychology – as we have seen, essential in any attempt to understand humour. As Audrey Richards (1968: 22, 118–21) remembered, he had a strong interest in the psychoanalytical theories that flourished in 1920s and 1930s Europe, and, 'he carried that interest in his fieldwork'.[4]

At the same time American anthropologists, especially Boas's students and colleagues, were increasingly attracted to psychology, psychoanalysis and learning theories. Boas himself observed that 'An error of modern anthropology … [lay] in the overemphasis on historical reconstruction … as against the stress of the culture' in which people lived (quoted in Kuper 1973: 87). A key question in Ruth Benedict's *Patterns of Culture* (1959), based on her observation of the psychological traits of different Indian tribesmen, is how people adapt to the customs, life-styles and moral attitudes of their society – and the answer was to look at the different ways they were socialized. Also Edward Sapir, a close friend and colleague of Benedict's, inquired into relations of individuals and society, and found that deep-seated connections, a sense of belonging and a 'common sense' all developed through language learning – a process described by Wilkie and Saxton (chapter 1 in this volume) in their account of the way in which socialization proceeds hand in hand with the acquisition of language, with a capacity to communicate, and, of course, to appreciate humour and jokes within a given cultural group.

But the first anthropologist to conduct theoretical research on humour in a truly holistic way was Gregory Bateson.[5] Because of the great complexity of social relations, and the variety of cultural constructions, he thought that anthropology definitely required an interdisciplinary approach. His theory of humour is thus part of his wider research on the development of human cognition and communication. Some of his early thoughts on humour are recorded in a paper mainly based on discussions that took place at an interdisciplinary conference on 'The Position of Humour in Human Communication' (Bateson 1952). The meeting included a number of distinguished neurologists, cyberneticists, cognitive and clinical psychologists, as well as two anthropologists, Margaret Mead and Bateson himself, who, as 'presenter', was obviously taking the leading role in discussion. As the conference title indicates, it was generally assumed that humour is a form of communication, hence a strong emphasis on language and on implicit as well as explicit meanings. The connection between humour and laughter is taken for granted – their differences recognized – and the two terms then used interchangeably.

A starting point for Bateson's thoughts on humour was Russell and Whitehead's work on paradoxes, which, they found, were a major difficulty in their attempt to reduce all mathematics to logic.[6] Paradoxes may not in themselves be particularly funny, but they do create a sense of suspense or puzzlement comparable to that brought about by many jokes and riddles. Bateson's idea was that Russell and Whitehead's theory, developed to resolve problems in mathematical logic, could be applied to anthropological studies of communication, and especially humour. He emphasizes that messages usually carry a lot of implicit information; in particular jokes contain some information on the surface as well as implicit content in the background that usually becomes explicit when the point of the joke is reached and brings about laughter as 'a circuit of contradictory notions is completed' (1952: 2).[7]

An important aspect of joking behaviour is therefore the implied meta-message, or 'code', that indicates that such behaviour is indeed playful. 'Play', as a concept of greater generality (defined by Russell and Whitehead as of 'a higher logical type') than the names of the different forms and behaviours involved, thus designates the background – in Bateson's words, 'the ground' or 'mood' – for humorous events, and one of his most significant findings is that a failure to grasp such meta-messages and to recognize the different contexts of communication can lead to mental illness. Indeed, it was thanks to his understanding of Russell and Whitehead's insights into paradoxes and their relevance to the study of human communication that Bateson developed his influential theory of schizophrenia as sometimes a cultural rather than a solely genetic disorder.[8] But, although paradoxes and, I should like to add, contradictions, incongruities, nonsense, banter and so forth, are a problem for those who fail to grasp their nature, they are the prototypic paradigms for humour and jokes.[9]

As well as being a source of confusion and distress for those unable to understand their meta-messages and to grasp their contexts, paradoxes can provide an escape from the narrow boundaries of logic – they too, sometimes, a potential cause of madness.

As Bateson writes,

> These paradoxes, are the staff of human communication ... In ordinary life, as distinct from scientific talk, we continually accept the implicit paradoxes. Freedom to admit paradox has been cultivated in the therapy situation, but this flexibility exists between two people whenever, God willing, they succeed in giving each other a freedom of discussion. That freedom, the freedom to talk nonsense, the freedom to entertain illogical alternatives ... is probably essential ... In sum I am arguing that there is an important ingredient common to comfortable human relations, *humour* and that this ingredient is the implicit presence and acceptance of the paradoxes ... The alternative to the freedoms introduced by paradox is the rigidity of logic. (Bateson 1952: 3)

It is of interest that 'freedom' is repeated no less than six times! Logic cannot admit to life's changing realities, while the 'study of mind through a causal approach will lead us to accepting the paradoxes ... which are related to humour, and in general are related to mental health and human amenity' (ibid.: 3).[10] Commenting on Bateson's essay 'A Theory of Play and Fantasy' (1972), his daughter Mary explains,

> It is not merely bad natural history to suggest that people might or should obey the theory of Logical Types ... we believe that the paradoxes of abstraction must make their appearance in all communication more complex than that of mood signals, and that without these paradoxes, the evolution of communication would be at an end. Life would then be an endless interchange of stylized messages, a game with rigid rules, unrelieved by change or humor. (1999–2000: 192–93; see Hofstadter 1979: 11)

Indeed, humour and jokes are contingent: as we find in all of the chapters in this book, they are generally bound up with the times and places in which they are generated, although sentiments and imaginings about past or future times (Martinez, chapter 6) can also inspire jokes and bring about laughter.

I shall return to cognitive aspects of humour, but first examine Mary Douglas' essays (1975: 83–114), given that she too looked upon humour as liberating; while Bateson contrasts humour with the rigidity of strictly logical thinking and with an incapacity to accept the changing and contradictory nature of human realities, Mary Douglas sees humour and jokes as a counter to the constraints and formalities of social life. Both Bergson and Freud, according to Douglas, have in their different ways argued against rigidity (cf. Apte 1985). Bergson's reflections on laughter are in keeping with his belief in the superiority of intuition and spontaneity over logic, and of life over 'mechanism'. For Freud, as it brings unconscious thoughts and emotions to consciousness,

> A joke shows that an accepted pattern has no necessity ... It brings no alternative, only an exhilarating sense of freedom from form in general ... as it unleashes the energy of the subconscious against the control of the conscious ... For both the essence of the joke is that something formal is attacked by something informal, something organized and controlled, by something vital, energetic, an upsurge of life for Bergson, of libido for Freud. The common denominator underlying both approaches is the joke seen as an attack on control ... All jokes have this subversive effect on the dominant structure of ideas. (Douglas 1975: 95–96)

And, because different societies impose different manners and degrees of bodily control, social etiquette generally determines how much and how loudly people can give way to laughter. 'Some tribes are said to be dour and unlaughing. Others laugh easily' (ibid.: 84). For example, according to Turnbull, pygmies, who are freely mobile in the forests of Equatorial Congo, 'lie on the ground and kick their legs in the air, panting and shaking in paroxysms of laughter' (1961, quoted in Douglas 1975: 84). A similar difference, Douglas suggests, might be found in a comparison of jungle-dwelling chimpanzees with others inhabiting more exposed, and relatively more settled savannah areas.

Thanks to her interesting comparison of jokes with rituals, Douglas observes that both connect different symbols and concepts; but while in rituals they support each other, 'in jokes they disparage each other ... the rite imposes order and harmony, the joke disorganizes. ... They [jokes] do not affirm the dominant values, but denigrate and devalue. Jokes challenge ... A joke is by nature an anti-rite' (Douglas 1975: 102–103). Quoting Victor Turner (1982: 11–12) on the contrast between structure, which supports hierarchy and authority through a social system, and community, in which roles are not strictly defined and there is fellowship and warmth, Douglas observes that laughter and jokes express community: 'A joke represents a temporary suspension of the social structure' (1975: 107).

Here then we see that, while Bateson looks upon humour as a counter to rigid modes of thought, Douglas, developing Bergson's and Freud's arguments, concludes that jokes actually provide a form of critique and a potential escape from rigid structures, be they structures and forms of society, forms of thought that may restrict the potential for human communication and creativity, or, as for Freud, the domination of an oppressive superego.

Cognitive Aspects of Humour

'Didn't Frankenstein get married?'
'Did he?' said Eggy. 'I don't know. I never met him. Harrow man, I expect'.
(Wodehouse 1936)

> To call the social fact *total* is not merely to signify that *everything observed is part of the observation*, but also ... that in a science in which the observer is of the same nature as his object of study, *the observer himself is a part of his observation*. (Lévi-Strauss 1987: 29, my italics)

In this section, as my two epigraphs imply, I shall look further at cognitive aspects of humour, then discuss accounts of humorous and funny incidents that sometimes occur when people of different cultures meet – as Okely shows (chapter 2, this volume), an aspect of humour particularly relevant to ethnographers' accounts of their fieldwork.

As we have seen in Bateson's discussion, a 'sense of humour' implies both a capacity to understand a joke or comical event and a capacity to communicate a sense of amusement by some original, unexpected, or ironic observation, parody, bodily expression or turn of phrase. Making a joke, Köestler writes, is a creative act that requires intelligence and observation. There are, in his view, three main forms of creativity: that of the humourist, the scientist and the creative artist. The quality common to all three is 'the perceiving of a situation or idea in two self-consistent but habitually incompatible frames of reference' (1964: 95).[11] This section's first epigraph, for example, shows how a simple sentence can be amusing thanks to the contrast of different perspectives: Eggy's answer to Bertie's simple question, had Frankenstein got married, showing his naïve assumptions that Frankenstein was a real person, and that any man Bertie and he might have met would have been associated with a public school, is contrasted to the presumably wider perspective of the readers, who, Wodehouse assumed, would have known that 'Frankenstein' just referred to Mary Shelley's imaginary creature.[12] Comic creativity is thus a skill that depends on a keen understanding of social realities and a capacity to cast such realities, be they persons, situations or events, in some critical or whimsical way.

Examples of jokes and comic performances based on keen observation are reported in Keith Basso's *Portraits of the Whiteman* (1979). He introduces his book with quotations from two Native American writers, respectively Vine Deloria Jr. and Harold Cardinal. As the first writes, 'the humorous side of Indian life has not been emphasized by professed experts, yet every problem and experience has been well-defined by American Indians through jokes and stories ... the more desperate the problem, the more humour is directed to describe it' (Deloria 1969, quoted in Basso 1979: 4–5). And, as Cardinal stated, 'The biggest of all Indian problems is "the Whiteman"' (1969). Thus, to briefly paraphrase Basso's introductory remarks, 'the Whiteman' is an abstraction that Indian people use to confer order and intelligibility upon their experience of Anglo-Americans. Their portraits of 'the Whiteman' are actually different for different Indians, but the opposition 'Indian versus Whiteman' is fixed (1979: 5). Apaches partly solve, or learn to cope, with their 'Whiteman' problem by some humorous but insightful jokes and performances in which they portray Americans as incompetent and clumsy, ready to affect and take for granted a back-slapping, overly familiar friendship that does not actually exist; they talk too much, they say one thing and do another, and, worst of all, they boss people about and make them feel small – which is completely contrary to Apaches' strong emphasis on social equality. In this way, Apaches define what an Indian is not, or should not be, while their sketches and jokes are like a mirror in which Americans can see themselves portrayed.

The work of the humorist has also been compared to that of anthropologists: for example, Critchley (2002: 9–10), a philosopher, writes,

> A true joke … lets us see the familiar 'defamiliarized'.
> The genius of jokes is that they light up the common features of our world, not by offering theoretical considerations … but in a practical way … *they are a form of practical abstraction, socially embedded philosophizing.* (Ibid.: 87, my italics)

Critchley's observations thus come very close to those of anthropologists, who have reflected on humour in light of their fieldwork experiences. In comparing humour with anthropology, Henk Driessen (1997: 228–31) notes that 'defamiliarization and relativism make anthropologists open to seeing the funny side of their own society … more so than other professions'. Like Okely (chapter 2), he thinks that sociologists are dull and serious.

Comic incidents often do take place, especially on first encounters of ethnographers with the people they are setting out to study. There is some amusement in Evans-Pritchard's account of his arrival and fieldwork conditions among the Nuer in the 1930s, as he emphasizes the contrast between their customs and his own firmly British habits and expectations. His account of the way Nuer would 'from early morning till late at night' visit his tent uninvited to demand tobacco and to appropriate his game, on the ground that it was shot on their land, contains a great deal of insight into Nuer character, as well as Evans-Pritchard's ironical self-reflection. The main issue was his loss of privacy – an essential English value. 'The chief privation', he writes, 'was the publicity to which all my actions were exposed, and it was long before I became hardened, though never entirely insensitive, to performing the most intimate operations before an audience or in full view of the camp' (1968: 14–15). 'One is just driven crazy' by the Nuer's obdurate refusal to answer questions. 'Indeed, after a few weeks of associating solely with Nuer one displays, if the pun be allowed, the most evident symptoms of "Nuerosis"' (ibid.: 13).

David Maybury Lewis describes how, when he arrived in Shavante territory with his wife and one-year old son, a number of Shavante who had gone to the airstrip to help carry their luggage, had set it all down before the village chief, who expected the trunks to be open and their contents immediately distributed. Meanwhile, the guide who had accompanied him from Sao Domingos gave the men's council a detailed report on their two-and-a-half days' journey, expertly mimicking his clumsy Shavante and recounting everything he had said and done *en route*. This included the fact that one morning he could not find his packhorse because he had let it wonder away for miles over hard ground the previous night. 'The Shavante found this uproariously funny, and were obviously amused by my general ignorance and incompetence in their habitat'. Then, in order to make himself popular, he joined the men on their hunting treks and was found to be rather impractical and clumsy; he had to adjust to being 'cast in the role of camp jester, or perhaps mascot' (1974 [1967], introduction, no page number).

'In Bali', Clifford Geertz writes, 'to be teased is to be accepted'. On arriving in an isolated village to conduct fieldwork with his wife, he found that they were generally ignored, 'treated as non-persons, specters ... as if [they] did not exist, or anyway not yet' (1973: 412–16). That entirely changed after they decided to watch an illegal cock-fight – forbidden but integral to the villagers' way of life. As they were totally absorbed in the game when they were surprised by a large number of policemen, they decided to follow the villagers, who were dispersing and ended up being offered tea in a man's compound. Joined by the police, their host explained with considerable knowledge, that they were important people, anthropologists, fully cleared by higher authority. The villagers were amused and surprised that he had not himself explained his position, but they were happy he had shared their 'cowardice'. That incident put an end to their invisibility. 'Getting caught in a vice raid actually led to rapport...' (ibid.: 412–16).

Examples could probably be multiplied, but, Maybury Lewis comments, 'anthropologists are frequently reticent about the circumstances of their fieldwork. I find this regrettable ... it is time we abandoned the mystique which surrounds fieldwork and made it conventional to describe in some detail the circumstances of data collecting so that they may be as subject to scrutiny as the data themselves' (1974, no page number).

The great cognitive value of comical incidents and misunderstandings is clearly shown in Okely's chapter. As she writes, a reluctance to report the funny moments one may experience, especially at the beginning stage of anthropological fieldwork, is due to a tendency to exclude the autobiographical and the personal in the writing of ethnography (Okely and Callaway 1992; Driessen 1997: 228–31). That, she thinks, is a loss because not only the narration, but also systematic reflection upon comical moments, can be quite instructive, as well as amusing and encouraging to students. Indeed humour may develop precisely 'when cultural boundaries are crossed', and errors and misunderstandings 'may be resolved through laughter' (chapter 2) which may help to establish good field-work relations. When different people laugh together, mutual suspicion and reserve thus begins to give way to a positive sense of some common sentiments and outlooks.

Some shared knowledge and assumptions, whether based on a common background or creatively achieved, are nonetheless taken for granted for much humour to be fully understood and enjoyed. Indeed, an important cognitive aspect of jokes is their necessary connection with contemporary and past social realities. As we have seen above, in his contrast between logical and temporal thinking, Bateson points out the 'historicity' of humour and jokes: all the chapters in this book show that they are inevitably bound up with the times and places in which they are generated. Ian Rakoff's analysis of American comics (chapter 4) shows that they are actually part of the history of American social attitudes and prejudices, while Fiona Moore (chapter 5) tells us how the joking and banter of German bankers and their English colleagues in London are always constrained by awareness of a difficult past; while disposed to indulge in some office humour, they certainly show a keen sensitivity about the troubling history of the Second World War. Their joking itself, always ruled by caution and reserve, can be looked upon as a way of mutual learning which is instrumental to working together, as they turn embarrassment and ironical stereotyping into fun and solidarity.

As Ardener shows (chapter 7), pantomimes are anchored to their times through topical jokes and references to current social or political realities, local politics, gossip or scandal; not only the creators and performers of comic events, but also their audiences, are largely conditioned by changing tastes and times. It is of note that some comic products, like cartoons, films and drawings – among others, Donald McGill's bawdy seaside postcards, formerly dismissed as utterly vulgar and obscene – have recently been the subject of an exhibition, 'Rude Britannia: British Comic Art', at London's Tate Britain (9 June–5 September 2010).

Dolores Martinez's analysis of science fiction films also provides a commentary on aspects of modernity, with its hopes and its fears for the future. For example, comic renderings of young space scientists' ineffectual romantic enterprises, as well as differences in various remakes of the Frankenstein story, reflect apprehensions about masculinity and gender relations, in light of strong feminist power and scientific progress of in-vitro insemination, especially in 1970s United States. Changes in gender relations are also illustrated in the vernacular songs collected by Glauco Sanga, as they document social and family transformations in late nineteenth-century Italy, and they illustrate the misogynist attitudes of a conservative and narrow-minded peasantry to women's achievement of some measure of economic independence and personal freedom.

Goldoni's late eighteenth-century comedy, *Scuffles in Chioggia*, with its vivid representation of class relations and incomprehensions, is very much a product of its time, as it shows the sharp contrast between dialect and language speakers, and rustic versus urban culture. A noticeable difference in the responses of the people of Chioggia who inspired the play, from its first performances in the late eighteenth century to the present, clearly shows how sensitivity to ridicule can radically change with the passing of time and with changing circumstances.[13]

Elisabeth Hsu (chapter 3) shows that some ancient Chinese medical diagnoses, concerning the king's and the queen's complaints, are in fact ironical comments on the state of the country. Thanks to her painstaking linguistic detection and analysis, she finds that an awareness of the presence of comic elements can be a valuable key to unpacking the metaphors of an ancient text and it can guide the critic in her most subtle and original interpretative work. Most importantly, Hsu concludes that jokes and riddles that may superficially appear just as titillating 'sexual innuendo', condemned in the Christian tradition, 'are really about the ultimate mystery of life, the union of man and woman' and 'humour can broaden and deepen human understanding'.

Comedy

> The most promising advance in recent research ... has been the endeavour to isolate and conceptualize the time factor ... Maintenance and replacement [of society] ... are temporal phenomena ... These processes have biological determinants. One is the life span of the individual; the other is the physical replacement of every generation by the next in the succession of death and birth. (Fortes 1971: 1)

Succession to power and control by the young, as a phase in the life-cycle, with its attendant tensions and rituals, is very often the topic of traditional comedies and pantomimes. Indeed, an association, and sometimes a tension and contrast of humour and comedy with ritual and the sacred, noted by Douglas and Victor Turner (above) and subtly researched by Hsu (chapter 3), also characterizes the beginnings of European theatre. In the early Middle Ages all dramas, and especially comical performances, considered a continuation of pagan culture that potentially undermined the Church's authority, were strongly disapproved of and generally banished.[14] However, in time the Church asserted its control precisely by absorbing some theatrical elements into its ritual.

Antiphonal hymns for solo voices and choir thus became a starting point for dramatic dialogues, and, while early performances were based exclusively on sacred narratives, in the course of history they increasingly introduced secular themes. Partly through a need for wide spaces to accommodate their increasingly large audiences, performances had to be moved from the church to the village common, or to the town square, where, thanks to the Church's well considered syncretism, brief comical interludes, gags and dances were allowed between the scenes of liturgical dramas. The contrast between medieval gloom and a festive 'carnival culture' is eloquently described by Bakhtin in his book *Rabelais and his World* (ca 1940). As he writes, 'Nearly every Church feast had its comic folk aspects always marked by fairs, and varied open-air amusements, with the participation of giants, dwarfs, monsters and trained animals' (Morris 1994: 196).

Although condemned by the Church and even denied the Sacraments, the companies of mimes, storytellers, jugglers and minstrels who wondered around Europe generally aiming to reach the great Christian capitals of Paris, Rome and Santiago de Compostela in order to join their large festive gatherings, thus increasingly took part in those early shows that were eventually to develop into a great comical tradition. By the eleventh and twelfth centuries, when attitudes were changing, and distinctions were made between 'bad' and 'good' comic performers, some of the latter were actually employed by Church leaders to entertain and edify the large crowds who gathered at abbeys, sanctuaries and village fairs, by reciting some holy verse and recounting the lives of saints (Apollonio 1981: 69–79).

Some religious holidays thus gradually merged with ancient folk celebrations and seasonal festivals. Comparing this process to one of 'using old skins to contain new wine' a historian of the theatre notes that

> some dislocation of traditional customs and calendar dates occurred: some of the most cherished among them, however, obstinately refused to be accommodated. This is most noticeable in respect of certain spring and autumn festivals. (Wickham 1985: 61)

Most relevant from an anthropological point of view is the fact that such celebrations often included the ritual miming of death and resurrection – a recurrent archetypal pattern, most effectively described in Frazer's vision of the sacrifice of the 'Year-King' or God of vegetation, and analysed by anthropologists and literary critics.[15] In his extensive 'morphology of literary symbolism' Northrop Frye (1957: 105, 165–69) found that a death and rebirth cycle is present in almost all mythologies, and that, traditionally, different categories of drama, especially comedy and tragedy, were almost invariably associated with different times in the year's cycle. According to his theory of genres, comedy, associated with birth, is aligned with spring, summer with romance and autumn with tragedy, while death, associated with the final harvest in winter, is aligned with satire, with the underworld and the myth of Persephone. Seasonal comedies are therefore characterized by two time dimensions: the cyclical time of the seasons, like the repetitive sequence of generations and, by contrast, the linear long-term time of history.

Like Frye, Van Gennep (1997) and Frazer (1949), Bakhtin relates carnival to moments of crisis and renewal in nature, in the human life-cycle and in society; 'such moments', he writes, 'were the second life of the people, who for a time, during carnival, entered the utopian realm of community, freedom, equality and abundance'.[16] Bakhtin was well aware that in reality such feasts sanctioned the existing pattern of things and were just a temporary liberation from the hardships of poverty and social distinctions. However, in his view, the suspension or reversal of hierarchical precedence brought about a type of communication free from all the norms of politeness that would have been impossible in everyday life. As verbal etiquette was relaxed, insults and abusive language could be used even against the deity; the barriers between persons and social classes were weakened as they all took part in the Carnival drama of the death of the old world and the simultaneous birth of the new.

> Parodies and travesties, profanations and comic crownings and uncrownings humiliate and ridicule, but the Carnival is quite different from the negative parody of modern times ... Bare negation is completely alien to folk culture. It is a relativistic world, with no absolute denial – one in which the lower part of the body and its functions are associated with birth, prosperity and renewal. The body becomes 'enormous, exaggerated, grandiose' and is an image of fertility. Degradation, like indecencies and scatological humour bring people down to earth, but is at the same time an element of birth or rebirth: it is not destructive but regenerative. (1979: 200–208)

Underlying Bakhtin's vivid description of the 'carnival culture' is criticism of earlier scholars, who, in his view, did not sufficiently appreciate the dialogic nature of language or the significance of heteroglossia, that is, the presence of different forms of speech and different discourses within a given 'official' national language. Encounters and confrontations of different speakers with their diverse points of view, at times of street feasting, when boundaries are suppressed and inhibitions abandoned, usually reveal a tension between the state's centralizing tendencies and people's determination to maintain their identity and resist or oppose the state's authority and the overbearing attitudes of elites to their rustic or archaic speech. Indeed, linguistic differences often give way to much teasing and comical parodies (1981 [1934–1935]).

As we shall see, Venetians' mockery of Chioggiotti's dialect is one of the main themes in Goldoni's comedy I analyse in chapter 9. However, change in modern conceptions of humour – and, no less, in the street life of European cities – has brought a loss in the spirit of carnival, and in people's ability to communicate and express themselves in public. In looking at changes in scholarly attitudes to laughter, Bakhtin finds that in the pre-Romantic and Romantic period, when concepts of humour were based on 'narrow bourgeois aesthetics', no room was left for studying the market place and the aesthetics of laughter (Morris 1994: 195–96). He thus contrasts 'grotesque realism ... apt to free the conscience from the hypocritical seriousness associated with authority', and the 'Romantic grotesque' which he associates with fear, be it the fear of authority, of death and punishment in hell, or, as in the science fiction films analysed by Martinez (chapter 6), the terror of cosmic dissolution.

In light of Bakhtin's work, it is no coincidence that the pantomimes discussed by Ardener (chapter 7) are always performed during the Christmas season, while Goldoni's Scuffles in Chioggia (chapter 9) was first produced as part of Carnival celebrations in 1762. Indeed, although the dates are not strictly the same throughout Europe, where Christmas takes place at the end of December, and Carnival, with its masking and miming, its comedies and its mock execution of the Carnival King, is usually celebrated in early February, in the past all were associated with spring – or, more precisely, with the approaching end of winter, by all accounts a time of transition.

Bakhtin's association of carnival with the renewal of life is obviously in agreement with anthropological accounts of transition rituals. In his book on *Rites of Passage*, Van Gennep compares 'ceremonies pertaining to the seasons' with those performed at initiation rituals. As he writes,

> Often the expulsion of winter is a rite of separation, while bringing summer into the village [is] a rite of incorporation: in other cases the winter dies and the summer or spring is reborn. These rites … insure the resumption of animal sex life and the resultant increase in herds. All these ceremonies include both rites of passage and sympathetic rites … for fertility, multiplication, and growth.
>
> One of the most striking elements in seasonal ceremonies is the dramatic representation of the death and rebirth of the moon, the season, the year, and the deities that preside over and regulate vegetation … The idea is suggested or dramatized in seasonal ceremonies, rites of pregnancy and delivery. (1977: 178–79, 182)[17]

Frazer (1949: 28–38) also describes the way in which dancing and leaping high is thought to make grains grow high by imitative magic, and he quotes the chant 'We carry death out of the village and spring into the village' (ibid.: 308). During Carnival, in Italy's Friulan countryside, where I conducted fieldwork in the 1970s, the peasants would join a procession with their ploughs and other agricultural implements, while mimicking the movements associated with their use (Sciama 1977). After taking part in the jolly celebrations, a man who impersonated Carnival had to undergo a mock trial for his crimes and he was usually condemned to death. Before the execution, he was invited to dictate his will – generally in a comical vein, echoed by much joking and laughter from the bystanders – then, after a mock funeral, a large straw dummy would be burned in his place. A female equivalent, usually an ugly old 'witch', would similarly be burnt halfway through Lent.

Such winter festivals, with the mimicking of the death of Carnival as a scapegoat that takes away all the sins and excesses of the dying year, are mirrored in the plots of many a pantomime and comedy. Stripped of all detail and complexity, comedies usually begin with a problematic situation: a young couple are in love, but their union is opposed by either the young man's or the young woman's father, obviously reluctant to accept the limitations of old age and give up their position of authority and control. For example, Pantaloon, an ever-present character in Venice's *commedia dell'arte* (and usually the best-paid actor), was meant to represent a rich aging merchant, ridiculed because of his miserliness and his lasciviousness.[18] He usually appeared in the street, wearing a black mask with a suggestively large nose, and what looked like indoor clothes and slippers, with narrow red breeches that seem to be a caricature of young men's fashionable hose. By the end of the comedy, he was either defeated in his pursuit of a young woman, or he was circumvented and taken advantage of by a nimble and cunning servant, Harlequin or Brighella.

In the best of endings, he actually underwent a psychological change and, thanks to newly acquired wisdom, he accepted his daughter's choice of a husband, or his son's demands for greater independence, freedom to marry, and a more generous allowance.

Comedy thus challenges the balance of power in the relations of fathers and daughters or sons, and in general of youth against established society – in Meyer Fortes' words, the 'fundamental and difficult problems' related to the 'replacement of every generation by the next' (1971: 1; see also Okely on Masai rituals, chapter 2). But the rigid social rules upheld by the old, initially obstacles to the continuation and reproduction of life, are not hated; conflict does not lead to death, as it might in tragedy, but gives way to new insight and reconciliation. After a sequence of amusing, sometimes threatening, misunderstandings,

Figure 0.1: Conflict between old and young is a much favoured theme for comic writers and performers. Pantaloon is often represented as transgressive and lascivious, but very harsh towards his offspring. Here, in his role as a strict father, he is about to harangue his daughter, just as, unknown to him, she receives a message from her lover. (*Commedia dell'Arte.* Troupe Gelosi. In the collection of le Musée Carnavalet, Paris).

disappearances or confrontations, problems are resolved and the play usually ends in a wedding, with dancing and music.

Indeed, 'The theme of the comic', Frye writes, 'is the integration of society – incorporating a central character into it, and the mechanism that brings this about is marriage' (1957: 164, 166–70). A generally positive and benevolent view of society is represented as a parallel to the reawakening of nature and the animal world. As Victor Turner observes, although contemporary performances have become fully separate from religious practices,

> A sense of community and purification is still present in the best of experimental theatre ... Performances ... probe a community's weaknesses; call its leaders to account. ... [They] make explicit meanings that would otherwise remain implicit and little understood. ... in that way, also ludic and joking behaviours may be ethical features of cyclical repetitive societies. (1982: 11, 32)

As Turner's reference to 'cyclical repetitive societies' implies, Frye's theory of genres is of great interest for both literary texts and dramatic performances in traditional societies, but it may have little relevance for contemporary works, in which comic and tragic moments often mix and alternate. Post-modern critics, like artists and writers, have abandoned or altogether rejected a once conventional adherence to genre.[19] For example, while Goldoni's eighteenth-century comedy (see chapter 9) and the traditional English pantomimes analysed by Ardener (chapter 7) do conform to a comic style and are associated with the transition from winter to spring, in much contemporary drama, different genres are woven together and mixed. As Dolores Martinez shows, the science fiction films she analysed (chapter 6) always include and alternate serious and comic moments in a style that reflects contemporary realities and fears. As she explains, probably due to a deepening anxiety about the potential destructiveness of technology, in recent years few comedy science fiction films have been produced – and those mostly for children.

Is Humour Always a Good Thing?

> Human laughter is intimately linked with the accident of an ancient Fall ... In the earthly paradise ... joy did not find its dwelling in laughter ... it is with his tears that man washes the afflictions of man, and it is with his laughter that sometimes he soothes and charms his heart; for the phenomena engendered by the Fall will become the means of redemption. (Baudelaire 1956: 135)

Most of the authors I have quoted so far and, not least, the contributors to this book, write about humour as a positive aspect of human communication and a mode of interaction that can lead to amity. As Bateson and Mary Douglas have shown, humour can contribute to bringing about social and political change by implying criticism of society's rigid and repressive rules. However, aesthetic as well as moral aspects of humour have always been a concern to those who have reflected upon it. Baldesar Castiglione in his *Book of the Courtier* (1528) describes a quick wit and a capacity to amuse as desirable accomplishments, but, like Plato, Aristotle, Cicero and many others both before and after him – and unlike Bakhtin – he thought that jokes and humour are only enjoyable as long they are kept within the dictates of good breeding and *urbanitas*. A gentleman must never be raucous and vulgar and must 'in all circumstances maintain his dignity'; it is not right for him to try and make others laugh all day, or to do it 'in the manner of madmen and drunks' or 'in the way of those clowns and fools who are so popular at Italy's courts'. Style is then an important aspect of humour, and indeed Castiglione does admit that even some of Boccaccio's most scurrilous stories – like one about the way a priest contrived to make love to a farmer's young wife – are really quite amusing, because they are associated with witty dialogue and with truly clever and ingenious tricks (1947: 208; Boccaccio 1972: VIII, 2).[20] As a distinguished diplomat, Castiglione was supremely aware of the politics of joking, and he warned his readers that just as people 'must never laugh at those that are weak and vulnerable', equally they 'must bear respect to those who are powerful and universally loved … sometimes by jeering at such persons, one might acquire some dangerous enmities' (1947: 205, 209 and ff.).

A contemporary example is Basso's account of how an Apache woman, who saw her young daughter mimicking an American school teacher while she reproached her pet dog for biting her, warned the little girl 'it is dangerous to joke the Whiteman!'[21]

As we have seen above, Fiona Moore describes the way in which the German and English employees of a London-based German bank treat their joking with great caution and take care not to offend, so that an inevitable – and ultimately positive – joking activity is hedged round with rules concerning the extent to which mutual stereotyping and memories of the war-time past can be evoked or should be altogether avoided. Furthermore, as suggested by Castiglione, those making a joke must take account of office politics and hierarchy, because disrespect towards those in senior positions might bring about very unpleasant hostilities and tensions.

To safeguard their employment, the early writers of American comics described by Ian Rakoff had to choose carefully a safe path between social criticism and conformity, although in some instances, the strongly expressive visual medium offered some welcome opportunities for political criticism, especially in the 1950s, when a 'commie-hunting Senator, Malarky' was drawn as a swamp rat bearing 'a recognizable resemblance to McCarthy'. As Rakoff comments, 'How Possum got away with its scathing depiction of McCarthyism stands as a testament as to what one can get away with under the guise of humour' (chapter 4).

As Geertz writes, 'Fighting cocks, almost every Balinese … has said, is like playing with fire and not getting burned. You activate village and kingroup rivalries and hostility, but in play form, coming dangerously and entrancingly close to the expression of open and direct aggression … but not quite because, after all, it is "only a cockfight"' (1973: 440).

Unfortunately humour and laughter do not always amuse or express benevolence and warmth; not only can they offend against good manners but, when we laugh *at* rather than *with* others, they can be downright cruel and unpleasant. At its worst, humour can cause humiliation and shame, or indeed harm rather than assist a young person's learning processes, and, rather than encourage friendship and warmth, it can damage relationships. Many humorous events and expressions, as Ardener observes (chapter 7), can have 'an element of exposure'. Indeed, not all writers agree with a wholly sanguine view of humour. For example, Michael Billig (2005: Introduction) writes against the 'more good-natured, even sentimental, theories of humour that currently predominate'; calling into question the goodness of laughter, he challenges 'common-sense assumptions about the desirability of humour' and he draws his readers' attention to the 'darker, less easily admired practice of ridicule'. Humour, he writes, can be used to exercise authority and impose discipline (ibid.: 2).

The potential of laughter to hurt is also noted by those who ultimately give greater weight to its positive outcomes. Bergson pointed out that laughter always involves a momentary 'anaesthesia of the heart', a moment of detachment and standing back from a person or a situation, but the cruelties expressed in some jokes can be far more long lasting and damaging then he implies. For example, ethnic jokes, sometimes said to be good in strengthening people's sense of identity, can in fact be deeply offensive and divisive, while racist jokes and cartoons[22] can actually propagate negative stereotypes and keep alive prejudice. Laughing at others may indeed be evidence of that Hobbesian 'sense of superiority and triumph' so often cited in analyses of the most negative aspects of humour, especially when it turns to satire and sarcasm.

An important aspect of the psychology of humour and laughter is their association with fear: as Martinez shows in her study of science fiction films, producers deliberately introduce some comic incident just before a 'scene of pure terror' (chapter 6). And clearly suspense and fear are part of the thrill in pantomime as well, as the protagonists are threatened with some imminent disaster, while the gender ambiguity of heavily dressed and made-up characters sometimes does bring a few tears, as well as laughter, from children new to that form of entertainment.

In some instances comical figures carry sinister aspects or associations with life's sadness and poverty; by a truly interesting paradox, Harlequin, one of the most vivacious and popular characters in Italian *commedia dell'arte*, is surrounded with mystery, as his origin is associated by scholars with the chthonian world of the dead and with ancient beliefs about visions of the dead during the twelve days that followed the winter solstice (Ginzburg 1966: 44, 48–49).[23] Indeed, Harlequin was represented by the Church as a black-faced emissary of the devil and was generally associated with the fear of darkness and night and with the sounds of wind and howling dogs, especially in Italy's mountain areas. Punch, in Italian, Pulcinella, always at the receiving end of humiliations and blows by his betters, destined to reproduce (as is sometimes suggested, by parthenogenesis), and obviously hinting at a parody of some impoverished Neapolitans, is often cast as the exhausted and inadequate father of a very large family he is unable to feed. Only thanks to the actors' great skill can his endless misfortunes and discomfitures be represented in such a way as to bring about laughter.

Conclusion

The moral dangers of uncontrolled and cruel laughter are described by Critchley (2002: 64) who concludes that ultimately the best laughter is that addressed at oneself. By contrast, an American philosopher, Ted Cohen (1999: 10), finds that most humour has great potential for encouraging or even healing those who are suffering – and it may make the suffering more tolerable.[24] Similarly Peter Berger, and, not least, the contributors to this book, seem to have brought to light the positive emotional, as well as intellectual, aspects of humour.

It is of interest that Primo Levi, asked to write a personal anthology based on books he first read in his youth in order to bring to light 'the possible traces of what has been read on what has been written', included passages from his favourite comic writers, their names listed under the general heading 'the salvation of laughter'.[25]

The heartening, and possibly healing, quality of humour seems ultimately to prevail.

Notes

1 Translations from French and Italian are mine.
2 As Tim Ingold writes, 'I am an anthropologist: not a social or cultural anthropologist; not a biological or archaeological anthropologist; just an anthropologist...' (2011: Preface).
3 *Wolfram Alpha* also lists 'One of the four fluids in the body whose balance was believed to determine your emotional and physical state'. Chambers', a now old-fashioned twentieth-century dictionary first renders 'humour' as 'the moisture or fluids of animal bodies' then, as a secondary gloss, 'a mental quality which delights in ludicrous and mirthful ideas; playful fancy'.

4 Thanks to his interest in psychology, Malinowski emphasized that researchers should always take note of their individual informants' accounts and viewpoints. In his view, as Ericsen and Nielsen write, 'Institutions existed for people, not viceversa, and it was … ultimately their biological needs that was the prime motor of social stability and change … This was "methodological individualism" … in an academic climate dominated by Durkheimians, [like Radcliffe-Brown] it was not favourably received' (2001: 43–44).

5 After several fieldwork trips in New Britain, New Guinea, and Bali, and after the publication of *Naven* (1936), Bateson resided and worked in the US from 1940.

6 An example often quoted by mathematicians is Epimenides' paradox, 'All the Cretans are liars'. Because Epimenides is himself a Cretan, he too is a liar. But if he is a liar and what he says is untrue, the Cretans are truthful; but because Epimenides is a Cretan, and therefore what he says is true, in saying the Cretans are liars, Epimenides is himself a liar, and what he says is untrue. Thus, Bateson writes, 'we may go on alternately proving that Epimenides and the Cretans are truthful and untruthful'. The problem, Russell and Whitehead found, is due to the self-referential nature of the initial statement, 'All the Cretans are liars', which includes Epimenides' in the general class 'the Cretans'. Indeed paradoxes occur especially when a message also contains a message about itself. According to Russell and Whitehead's theory of language, paradoxes generated through self-referential statements can be avoided by arranging sentences in a kind of pyramid, according to their different levels of generality (Whitehead and Russell 1927).

7 Bateson concedes that jokes are not always literally 'paradoxes'; a joke is 'a paradox, or *something like it*' (my italics). He also notes that 'for some reason those who discuss humour from a scientific point of view always use dull jokes' (1952: 2). Groucho Marx acknowledged, 'Well, all the jokes can't be good, you've got to expect that once in a while'. However, his well known 'I refuse to join any club that would have me as a member' contains an unexpected paradoxical punchline that exhilarates the audience. The joke, a comical reversal of 'I would not, [even if I could] join any club that did not accept Italians, Jews, blacks, etc.', is clearly a comment on a sensitive social issue in 1930s New York. Harpo Marx joked, 'I am the most fortunate self-taught harpist and non-speaking actor who has ever lived'. But was it really lucky to have been too poor to have a music teacher, and to be told that his voice was so bad that he had better stay silent?' The idea of fortune is often treated ironically by Jewish writers. As Primo Levi writes, 'It was *my good fortune* (my italics) to be deported to Auschwitz only in 1944' (*Se questo è un uomo*, I, 5).
A poignantly paradoxical joke is 'We all have to die. If the rich could pay us poor to die in their place, we could make a very good living!'

8 Bateson's theory inspired R.D. Laing and the 1960s anti-psychiatry movement.

9 As Bateson wrote in his later reflections, 'Whether Whitehead and Russell had any idea when they were working on *Principia* that the matter of their interest was vital to the life of human beings … I do not know. Whitehead certainly knew that human beings could be amused and humour generated by kidding around with types. But I doubt whether he ever made the step from enjoying this game to seeing that the game was non-trivial' (1979: 129).

10 According to Hofstadter, paradoxes and contradictions, such as we find in many puns, puzzles and jokes, can be 'a major source of clarification and progress in all domains of life' (1979: 11).

11 Deleuze and Guattari's (1980) notion of language through the metaphor of the rhizome, a stem or plant that works through horizontal and trans-species connections, in contrast with 'arborescent' metaphors, may usefully describe the cognitive processes at the heart of humour. In their view, language is organized, like Freud's dreamwork, in accordance with the laws of condensation, displacement and compromise.

12 Another dimension to this joke is that for those who, whether rightly or wrongly, thought that Wodehouse was racist, or intended to represent Eggy as fashionably anti-Semitic, an implication that he thought Frankenstein was Jewish was based both on the name and the fact that Harrow was one of the first English public schools to have a Jewish house!

13 Some jokes do require a shared knowledge of the past. In my fieldwork island, Burano, I was puzzled as some women, when they couldn't decide what to cook, often laughed as they said 'Let us go to the friars!' (*andemo dai frati*). They explained to me that in the old days, when they were extremely poor, they would get the children into a boat and row to the nearby Franciscan monastery island, where the friars always kept a huge pot of soup, ready for anyone too poor to afford a meal. Memories of past poverty, now over, always brought a smile. But if the past was sufficiently close to cause hurt or offence, it had to be treated with care.

14 Tertullian (ca 160–226 CE) defined theatrical entertainments as 'false', 'sacrilegious' and 'demoniacal'. Actors were thought to be possessed by the devil (*De Spectaculis*: 195 CE).

15 The cycle of death and rebirth inspired many literary works, especially T.S. Eliot's 'Waste Land'. According to post-structuralist, deconstructionist and feminist critics, classifications by *genre*, and a strong focus on structural features, fail to account for the variety of plots and characters and tend to essentialize literary or dramatic works and to obscure their originality. I nonetheless find Frye's approach relevant in anthropological analyses, especially when dealing with traditional forms of entertainment, ritual and joking.

16 As well as carnival, there was the Festa Stultorum, or the Feast of Fools, the Feast of the Ass and the Risus Paschalis. Church Festas, as we have seen, always included amusements and fairs, as did the grape harvest.

17 In sixteenth-century Venice laughter at weddings was thought to encourage fertility; masked figures or mummers, representing ancestors anxious for the continuity of the family line, would entertain newly-wed couples with scurrilous songs (Sciama, forthcoming).

18 A figure parodied by Venetian renaissance actor and comedy writer, Andrea Calmo, in his madrigal: 'I am an old man in love / and with great pleasure / I make cheer and I sing and play the lute; / To my orchard I go / To gather figs / white, black and yellow / Then give them all as tribute / To the great beauty of Clare; / Who for love makes me pine / Wilt and despair' (1553: 49; my free translation). But Pantaloon has also been described as a prototype for Shylock (Moore 1949: 33–42): both are old,

rich and stingy, they come into conflict with their daughters or sons and are defeated. Although such themes are very widespread or even universal, a connection between Pantaloon and Shylock shows the latter's rootedness in Venetian custom and theatrical tradition. However, at the heart of Shakespeare's play is Shylock's ethnicity, and, although *The Merchant of Venice* is classified as a comedy, it is one in which the joke went badly wrong: the comic genre breaks down as tragic moments alternate with romantic and comic ones.

19   The progressive abandonment of adherence to genre is evident in a comparison of the chapters by Ardener and Sciama with Martinez's analysis of science fiction films, in which comic and serious parts are skilfully mixed and contrasted.

20   Castiglione concludes, 'It is more fitting to laugh at the faults found in persons not so unfortunate as to move one to compassion, nor so bad that they seem to deserve to be sentenced to death, nor so powerful that causing them even some slight anger may cause one great damage'. Given that proper caution is exercised, however, 'laughter exhilarates the soul and gives pleasure'; it takes the mind off 'the troubling afflictions and grievances of which our life is full. Laughter is therefore most welcome and those who can bring it about pleasantly at the right time are most praiseworthy' (1947: 208).

21   The difficult relation between respect and freedom of expression was tragically illustrated in January 2015, when Charlie Hebdo's cartoons, deeply offensive to Muslims, led to twelve people being murdered and to violent world-wide retaliation.

22   I would hesitate to call them humorous, although that may be their authors' intention.

23   One of the devils Dante encountered in Hell was called Alichino – according to Italian scholars, a name derived from French Hallequin, the diabolical leader in the mythical Wild Hunt (Dazzi-Vasta 1960: 268). In his reading of Inquisition trials, Carlo Ginzburg (1966: 44, 48–49) found that from time to time people claimed to have seen a procession of the dead led by a figure wearing multi-coloured clothes with a sword and a purse attached to his belt, in all ways similar to Harlequin. In the early days of *commedia dell'arte* Harlequin's slapstick acted as a magic wand that brought about a change of scenery.

24   The therapeutic potential of laughter is also confirmed by some doctors and psychotherapists.

25   Levi's book list includes works by Rabelais and Shalom Aleichem, as well as two late eighteenth/early nineteenth-century Italian satirical poets, Porta and Belli, who wrote in their dialects, respectively Milanese and Roman (1981: 1361–63). Other headings are 'the salvation of understanding', 'man's unjust suffering', and 'man's stature'.

References

Apollonio, M. 1981. *Storia del Teatro Italiano*. Florence: Sansoni.

Apte, M. 1985. *Humour and Laughter. An Anthropological Approach*. Ithaca: Cornell University Press.

Bakhtin, M. 1981 [1934–1935]. 'Discourse in the Novel', in M. Holquist (ed.), *The Dialogical Imagination*, transl. M. Holquist and C. Emerson. Austin: University of Texas Press.

————. 1979 [1965]. *L'Opera di Rabelais e la cultura popolare. Riso, carnevale e festa nella tradizione medievale e rinascimentale.* Italian translation by Mili Romano. Turin: Einaudi.

Basso, K.H. 1979. *Portraits of the Whiteman.* Cambridge: Cambridge University Press.

Bateson, G. 1952. 'The Position of Humor in Human Communication'. *Macy* Conference. pcp.vub.ac.be/books/Bates on/humour.PDF.

————. 1972. 'A Theory of Play and Fantasy', in *Steps to an Ecology of Mind.* New York: Ballantine Books.

Bateson, M.C. (ed.). 1999–2000. *Mind and Nature: A Necessary Unity.* (Foreword).

Baudelaire, C. 1956. *The Mirror of Art,* trans. and ed. J. Mayne. New York: Doubleday.

Belli, G. G. 1998. M. Teodosio ed. *Tutti i Sonetti.* Rome: Newton Compton.

Benedict, R. 1959. *Patterns of Culture.* Boston: Houghton Mifflin.

Berger, P. 1997. *Redeeming Laughter.* Berlin: Walter de Gruyter.

Billig, M. 2005. *Laughter and Ridicule: Towards a Social Critique of Humour.* London: Sage.

Boccaccio, G. 1972 [1349–1351]. *Decameron.* Milan: Mursia.

Bremmer, J. and H. Roodenburg. 1997. *Cultural History of Humour.* Cambridge: Cambridge University Press.

Calmo, A. 1553. *Le bizzarre, faconde et ingeniose rime pescatorie: nelle quali si contengono sonetti, madrigali, epitafi, disperate e canzoni.* Vinegia: Jovan Battista Bertagagno.

Cardinal, H. 1969. *The Unjust Society: The Tragedy of Canada's Indians.* Vancouver: Douglas & MacIntyre.

Castiglione, B. 1947 [1528]. *Il libro del cortegiano.* Florence: Sansoni.

Cohen, T. 1999. *Jokes, the Conditions for Understanding Them and Their Importance for Human Life.* Chicago: University of Chicago Press.

Critchley, S. 2002. *On Humour.* London: Routledge.

Dazzi Vasta, M. 1960. *La Divina Commedia.* Turin: G.B. Paravia.

Deleuze, G. and F. Guattari. 1980. *Mille Plateaux.* Paris: Edition de Minuit.

Deloria, V. 1969. *Custer Died For Your Sins: An Indian Manifesto.* New York: Macmillan.

Douglas, M.1975. *Implicit Meanings. Essays in Anthropology.* London: Routledge.

Driessen, H. 1997. 'Humour, Laughter and the Field: Reflections from Anthropology', in J. Bremmer and H. Roodenburg (eds), *A Cultural History of Humour from Antiquity to the Present Day.* Cambridge: Cambridge University Press.

Dunbar, R.I. 1996. *Grooming, Gossip and the Evolution of Language.* Cambridge MA: Harvard University Press.

Eliot, T.S. 1922. *The Waste Land.* London: Faber and Faber.

Eriksen, T.H. and F.S. Nielsen. 2001. *A History of Anthropology.* London: Pluto Press.

Evans-Pritchard, E.E. 1968. *The Nuer.* Oxford: Clarendon Press.

Fortes, M. 1971. 'Introduction', in J. Goody (ed.), *The Developmental Cycle in Domestic Groups.* Cambridge: Cambridge University Press.

Frazer, J.G. 1949. *The Golden Bough.* London: Macmillan.

Frye, N. 1957. *Anatomy of Criticism. Four Essays.* Princeton, New Jersey: Princeton University Press.

Geertz, C. 1973. 'Deep Play: Notes on the Balinese Cockfight', in *The Interpretation of Cultures.* New York: Basic Books.

Ginzburg, C. 1966. *I Benandanti. Stregoneria e Culti Agrari tra Cinquecento e Seicento.* Turin: Einaudi.

Goldoni, C. 1915. *Opere Complete di Carlo Goldoni nel Secondo Centenario della nascita.* Tomo XX. Municipio di Venezia, Istituto Veneto di Arti Grafiche.

———. 1951 [1787]. *Memorie.* Italian translation from French by G. Amoretti. Milan: Signorelli.

Goody, J. (ed.). 1971. *The Developmental Cycle in Domestic Groups.* Cambridge: Cambridge University Press.

Hobbes, T. 1840. *Human Nature,* in *The English Works of Thomas Hobbes of Malmesbury, Volume IV,* ed. William Molesworth. London: Bohn.

Hofstadter, D. 1979. *Godel, Escher, Bach: An Eternal Golden Braid.* New York: Basic Books.

Ingold, T. 2011. *Being Alive.* London: Routledge.

Koestler, A. 1964. *The Act of Creation.* New York: Macmillan.

Kuper, A. 1973. *Anthropologists and Anthropology. The British School 1922–1972.* London: Allen Tate.

Laing, R.D. 1960. *The Divided Self: A Study of Sanity and Madness.* London: Tavistock.

Levi, P. 1981. 'La ricerca delle radici', in M. Belpoliti (ed.), *Primo Levi, Opere,* vol. 2. Turin: Einaudi.

Lévi-Strauss, C. 1987 [1950]. *Introduction to the Works of Marcel Mauss.* Translation by Felicity Baker. London: Routledge.

Mauss, M. 1968. 'Parentès á Plaisanteries', in *Essais de sociologie.* Paris: Edition de Minuit.

Maybury Lewis, D. 1974 [1967]. *The Savage and the Innocent. Akwe Shavante Society.* Oxford: Oxford University Press.

Malinowski. 1937. In J. Lips (ed.), *The Savage Hits Back.* London: New Hyde Park Books.

Molinari, C. 1985. *La Commedia dell'Arte.* Milan: Mondadori.

Moore, J. R. 1949. 'Pantaloon as Shylock', *Boston Public Library Quarterly* 1.

Morris, P. (ed.). 1994. *The Bakhtin Reader: Selected Writings of Bakhtin, Medvedev, Voloshinov.* London: Hodder Arnold Publications.

Okely, J. and H. Callaway (eds). 1992. *Anthropology and Autobiography.* London: Routledge.

Porta, C. 1975 [1812]. 'Desgrazzi de Giovannin Bougee', in *Poesie.* Milan: Mondadori.

Provine, R.A. 1996. 'Laughter', *American Scientist* 84(1) (Jan.–Feb. 1996), 38–47. Sigma Xi, The Scientific Research Society.

———. 2000. *Laughter: a Scientific Investigation.* London: Faber and Faber.

Radcliffe-Brown, A.R. 1957. *A Natural Science of Society.* Oxford: Oxford University Press.

———. 1968. *Structure and Function in Primitive Society.* London: Allen Tate.

Richards, A.I. 1968. 'The Concept of Culture in Malinowski's Work', in R. Firth, *Man and Culture. An Evaluation of the Work of Bronislaw Malinowski.* London: Routledge.

Sciama, L.D. 1977. An Anthropological Reading of Ippolito Nievo's Narratives. (M/Litt. Diss. Oxford University).

————. 1992. 'Bembo's Acknowledgement of Tuscan Superiority in Language', in D. Chambers and B. Pullen (eds.), *Venice: A Documentary History, 1450–1630*. Oxford: Blackwell.

————. 2003. *A Venetian Island. Environment, History and Change in Burano*. Oxford: Berghahn Books.

Smuts, A. 2013. 'Humour', *The International Encyclopedia of Philosophy*. ISSN 2161-0002. <http://www.iep.edu>.

Tertullianus Q.S.F. 1961 [CE 195]. *De Spectaculis*. Italian translation by E. Castorina. Florence: Nuova Italia.

Todorov, T. 1984 [1981]. *Mikhail Bakhtin. The Dialogical Principle*, transl. Wlad Godzixh. Manchester: Manchester University Press.

Turnbull, D. 1961. *The Forest People: A Study of the Pygmies of the Congo*. New York: Simon & Schuster Inc.

Turner, V. 1982. *From Ritual to Theatre: The Human Seriousness of Play*. New York: Performing Arts Journal Publication.

Van Gennep, A. 1977 [1908]. *The Rites of Passage*. London: Routledge.

Whitehead, A.N. and B. Russell. 1925–1927. *Principia Mathematica*. Cambridge: Cambridge University Press.

Wickham, G. 1985. *A History of the Theatre*. Oxford: Phaidon Press.

Wodehouse, P.G. 1936. *Laughing Gas*. London: Herbert Jenkins.

Ziv, A. 1984. *Personality and Sense of Humour*. New York: Springer.

Lidia Dina Sciama studied English Literature in Venice at Ca' Foscari University and Cornell University in the US. She received her doctorate from the Oxford Institute of Social and Cultural Anthropology. She has lived in Italy, Israel and the US, where she taught Anthropology and Comparative Literature. She is a former Director, and currently a Research Associate, of Oxford's International Gender Studies Centre (IGS) and a member of Venice's Ateneo Veneto. Her publications include articles on women's crafts, 'Academic Wives' and Sport and Ethnicity. With Professor Joanne Eicher, she edited a book on *Beads and Beadmakers* (Berg 1998). Her monograph, *A Venetian Island: Environment, History and Change in Burano* (Berghahn, 2003) is based on long-standing fieldwork.

THE ORIGINS OF COMIC PERFORMANCE IN ADULT-CHILD INTERACTION

Ian Wilkie and Matthew Saxton

The Development of Smiling and Laughter

Newborn infants can smile, in the sense that the corners of their mouths curl up, just days after birth, but mostly this occurs when they are either very drowsy or even asleep. In the weeks that follow, infants begin to smile when awake, but in an indiscriminate way, at both people and things. It is not until about six to ten weeks of age that genuinely social smiling emerges (Emde and Harmon 1972); the baby responds to another person's smile with a smile of their own, and also begins to initiate smiling, in a process which only emerges through social interaction with other people. We know this from studies of blind infants, who often fail to progress spontaneously to social smiling (Fraiberg 1974). Once reciprocal smiling emerges, parents begin to feel notably more engaged, while the infant, in turn, begins to show signs of joy, a new emotion, when interacting with others. Soon afterwards, from twelve to nineteen weeks of age, laughter appears, generally in response to very active stimulation by the parent. For example, laughter can be induced by simple games of 'I'm gonna get you!' which might culminate in blowing a raspberry on the baby's cheek. Laughter can also be induced by a vigorous pitch or unexpected tone of voice. As it happens, CDS (child-directed speech), when directed at infants in the first year of life, sounds quite different from normal speech (Garnica 1977). A relatively high pitch is lent colour by exaggerated, swooping intonation contours, which are designed to grab the infant's attention. At the same time they can prompt delight and laughter in the child. Thus, Rasmussen reports of his daughter that at 'one hundred and sixty-two days old he could always make her laugh by asking: "Can you laugh a little at father?" pitching his voice on high notes' (Rasmussen 1920). Van Leeuwen describes the process of CDS, revealing many of the key features of proto-comic performative interplay, in a transcript of a mother interacting with her twelve-week old baby during a research project on 'toys as communication':

> Mother: 'What's that? … (excited high-pitched voice) What's thaaat?…'. She holds up the rattle and shakes it.
> Mother: 'Who are they? What are they? They are funny ones …'. She moves the rattle close to her ear again, shaking one of the characters and listening to it.
> Mother: 'This is a nice one … Oooh! This is a squeaky one!' She squeaks him again. The baby shakes her arms and legs vigorously and looks on intently.
> Mother: 'Oooh … (creating a voice for the alien) Ho-ho-ho. It's like a dragon'.
>
> (She continues, using the 'aliens' as puppets, creating sounds for them, making them wiggle, 'walk' across the baby's tummy, caress the baby's cheek, and so on). (van Leeuwen 2005: 84–86)

Surprise and Familiarity

From the very first, attempts to provoke smiling or laughter in an infant are characterized by an element of surprise. In this vein, Darwin relates his exchange with his 3½-month-old child who was 'exceedingly amused by a pinafore being thrown over his face and then suddenly withdrawn, and so he was when I suddenly uncovered my own face and approached him' (Darwin 1872: 289). Our response to being surprised in this way persists into adulthood, as we experience 'the physiological squeal of transient delight, like an infant playing "peek-a-boo"' (Critchley 2002: 10).

We see that an element of surprise is critical in triggering a comic response in both infants and adults. Comic triggers tend to be more vigorous than other forms of adult-child interaction, with parents engaging in exaggerated vocal play and facial expressions. A playful attitude is signalled by the introduction of absurdity and incongruity. This kind of early interaction is not only widespread but finds official sanction in advice dispensed by the National Health Service: 'Put out your tongue and make funny faces. Your baby may even try to copy you! … Your baby is learning all about expression, mood and communication' (Welford 1999: 124).

Surprise functions as a trigger for laughter, but not just any kind of surprise in any context. Arguably, an event is rendered both surprising and humorous by the occurrence of incongruity presented within a familiar setting. Sully observed the importance of surprise, rather than shock, more than a century ago: 'Provocatives [sic] of laughter … were sudden movements of one's head, a rapid succession of sharp staccato sounds from one's vocal organ (when these were not disconcerting by their violence) and, of course, sudden reappearance of one's head after hiding in a game of bo-peep' (Sully 1896: 407).

The infant as an audience for comic performance needs to feel secure with the performer, typically a parent or family member. Infant and parent are typically bonded by familiarity and feelings of positive affect, so the setting for early comic performance is generally ideal. In a similar way, the success of comic performance in adulthood is also predicated on familiarity with the performer. The audience must in some way recognize the comic actor or the character they play. Of course, many comic characters are created with the deliberate intention to caricature unattractive traits. In this vein, one might mention Basil Fawlty's irascibility, David Brent's insensitivity, Rigsby's cravenness, or Edina's rampant egomania. But personality flaws do not prevent one from liking either the character, or more subtly, the actor portraying the character. Thus, Thomson suggests that 'it is not simply that we like the actor in spite of the character, rather that, in defiance of our own moral judgment, we like the character because of the actor' (Thomson 2000: 131). Whether or not the audience likes the actor (or their character), a sense of familiarity with the performance is, arguably, essential. In the same way, the infant will only laugh when they are both familiar and comfortable with the performer. This is what Jean-Pierre Jeancolas refers to as the 'reassuring' element in comedy (Jeancolas 1992: 141). Accordingly, J.B. Priestley notes that 'The people to whom we are bound by real affection are always, to some extent, comic characters, and we begin to feel this in childhood. (We are always glad to see Uncle Joe or Aunt May but they can't help being rather funny)' (Priestley 1976: 9). Morreall notes that 'babies enjoy peekaboo only with familiar faces of people they feel attached to' (Morreall 1987: 135). By six months, infants begin to demonstrate an ability to distinguish between well-known versus strange faces (Sandstrom 1966: 173). And it is the familiar faces that evoke laughter.

If the reassuring context is absent, neither the young child nor the adult will be amused. For instance, the child's first encounter with a jack-in-the box is just as likely to terrify as to amuse, unless it is introduced carefully, with some preparation by the caregiver to ensure that the new object will be a source of fun. In essence, the child must learn that the toy is not threatening and is, in contrast, comical: the surprise which then ensues is more likely to be pleasant. Circus clowns also exemplify this point, inasmuch as many children seem to be scared by clowns – giving rise to the dedicated phobia known as coulrophobia. Perhaps the outlandish make-up creates an image of the human face that is excessively unfamiliar to young children. Events differ in their degree of novelty and hence in the extent to which the element of surprise they embody is amusing, rather than frightening. And often, the transition from comedy to alarm is quite subtle, as Hazlitt observed in 1885:

> If we hold a mask before our face, and approach a child with this disguise on, it will at first, from the oddity and incongruity of the appearance, be inclined to laugh; if we go nearer it, steadily, and without saying a word, it will begin to be alarmed ... it is usual

to play with infants, and make them laugh by clapping your hands suddenly before them; but if you clap your hands too loud, or too near their sight, their countenances immediately change and they hide them in the nurse's arms. (Hazlitt 1885: 5)

It becomes apparent that the manner of the interaction is as important as the action itself. We see this point confirmed in verbal as well as non-verbal humour. With puns or gags, the way in which the joke is told is essential in the realization of the comic potential. As the comedian Frank Carson would have it: 'it's the way I tell 'em'.

Incongruity

Incongruity is a fundamental feature of comic performance. And the element of surprise discussed above is an essential ingredient in the creation of incongruity. But so, too, is the familiar setting in which the surprise takes place. For an event to be incongruous, audience expectations must be confounded. It follows, therefore, that the ability to compare (however unconsciously) the expected with the unexpected is an essential ingredient in appreciating a joke or piece of slapstick (Morreall 1987: 130). For the infant, the ability to recognize the unexpected as the unexpected is therefore essential. In fact, research over the past twenty-five years has consistently shown that infants are attuned to unexpected events from the very first weeks of life (e.g., Cashon and Cohen 2000).

By the use of deception, infants can be presented with 'magical' events which defy the laws of physics or logic. For example, a drawbridge can be raised in front of an attentive infant, and, via illusion, can apparently 'pass through' a solid object (Baillargeon, Spelke and Wasserman 1985). On such occasions, infant behaviour betokens their sensitivity to the incongruity of the situation. They look longer or suck more vigorously on a dummy, and their heart rates increase when observing impossible events. This basic finding has been replicated dozens of times and the research method is now known as the 'violation of expectation' paradigm. It would seem that we are equipped from the very start with a key ingredient in the appreciation of comic performance: a sense of the incongruous.

Writing in the nineteenth century, Schopenhauer was well aware of the importance of incongruity in inducing laughter: 'The cause of laughter in every case is simply the sudden perception of the incongruity between a concept and the real objects which can be seen through it in some relation, and laughter itself is just the expression of this incongruity' (Schopenhauer 1909: 52). Similarly, Kierkegaard noted that surprise is present in any 'contradiction' that, in turn, leads to a perception of incongruity (which must contain its own innate truth or 'absurdity to itself' (Kierkegaard 1941: 460)). This perception then leads to laughter. But why should laughter be the response, when faced with incongruity? The answer to this question is much more mysterious, but the sense of relief, or release, which people feel when they 'get' a joke may hold the key, even for the infant:

> Research has shown we instinctively recognise these 'incompatible contexts' in the first year of life … research shows that if a mother crawls towards the edge of the cot the baby will laugh because it interferes with the convention that babies crawl, mothers walk … Laughter is essential because it provides a cognitive respite. (Hale cited in Skatssoon 2006)

The Here-and-Now

Adult-child interaction is rooted in the here-and-now. In fact, it might be argued that nothing else is possible (Saxton 2009). The typical one- or two-year-old is incapable of discussing ideas and concepts which are remote in time and space. Their interest is instead devoted to concrete actions and objects within their immediate orbit. In fact, five topics tend to dominate the conversation of very young children: clothes; parts of the body; family; food; animals (Ferguson 1977). An adult who attempted something more ambitious, say some treatise on stock market prices or global warming, would be met with a blank stare. The adult is forced to follow the child's interests and concentrate on matters of interest in the child's immediate environment. Comedians also often draw their audience into a world that is rooted in the moment, as noted by Bruce: 'Comedians drew on a repertoire of techniques which broke any theatrical illusion and rooted the experience in the here and now – they engaged directly with their audiences, ad-libbed, used catch-phrases and so on' (Bruce 1999: 83).

Language-based Humour

At the age of about twelve months, most children utter their first word and the subsequent shift into a world of language takes off with remarkable speed. By the time of the child's third birthday they can string multi-word sentences together. By the age of five, the typical child has a vocabulary of about 6,000 words and possesses most of the basic grammatical machinery for understanding and producing complex sentences (Saxton 2010). In tandem with this exponential linguistic growth comes a rising appreciation in the child for language-based humour. The development of a sense of humour seems to parallel the child's linguistic development (Morreall 1987: 217). In verbal language play,

> the sort of language play that leads to puns is thought to serve an important function in the development of a child's language and communication skills … the greater

source of pleasure seems to be the interaction with the carer or researcher … in this case 'telling' the joke … seems to make the children feel exhilarated at their new power to amuse their adult carer. (Carr and Greeves 2006: 31)

Children on the threshold of language take great delight in onomatopoeia, simple wordplay and puns (Moustaka 1992). We find here an echo in the use of catchphrases by many comedians: instantly recognizable triggers for a comic response. Dave Willis' 'way, way uppa kye' is particularly childlike and was, in fact, taken verbatim from an utterance made by his own son, Denny, when a young child (House 1986: 67). Tommy Morgan's catchphrase was similarly childlike, with onomatopoeic qualities: 'clairty, clairty', meaning 'dirty, dirty' (Irving 1977: 29). Arthur Askey's 'hello playmates' or Bernie Winter's 'hello choochy face' are further appeals to the childlike state. In a similar way, playground chants and rhymes, with their reliance on rhythm and vernacular language, are often resonant of comedians' catchphrases. In Scotland, for example, one finds so-called stottin rhymes, as in: 'Ruglen's wee roon rid lums reek briskly' (this translates as 'Rutherglen's small, round, red chimneys smoke copiously') (Mackie 1973: 102). In *Jokes and their Relation to the Unconscious*, Freud states: 'it is also generally acknowledged that rhymes, alliterations, refrains and other forms of repeating similar verbal sounds which occur in verse, make use of the same source of pleasure – the rediscovery of something familiar' (Freud 1964: 122).

The use of incongruity to provoke laughter shifts from purely physical events into the linguistic sphere during the pre-school years. For example, puns rely on incongruity in their manipulation of the phonological, morphological and semantic features of words. In consequence, 'a pun is a sort of jack-in-the-box' (Santayana 1896: 250). Jokes also depend on verbal incongruity: 'The punchline works by resolving the suspense of the story in an unexpected way. Your brain responds to this tiny paradigm shift by making a conceptual leap that mirrors the jump from perceived threat to no threat, with the same result – laughter' (Carr and Greeves 2006: 22). Undoubtedly, the level of sophistication witnessed in verbal humour develops gradually during the school years. It may be for this reason that Scottish educationalist and founder of Summerhill School, A.S. Neill suggested that: 'Few bairns have a sense of humour; theirs is a sense of fun. Make a noise like a duck and they will scream, but tell them your best joke and they will be bored to tears' (Neill 1916: 26–27).

Perhaps Neill should not have told these children his 'best joke'. Language-based humour is by no means beyond the grasp of even very young, preschool children. But it must be grounded in the experience and perspective of the child, not the adult.

Repetition

One of the most characteristic features of CDS is the occurrence of repetition. Both adults and children repeat both themselves and each other with very high frequency, especially between the ages of one and three years (Saxton 2010). Information is constantly recycled and re-presented, often with minor modifications, indicating that both the parent and the young child are highly sensitive to each other's contributions to the conversation. More broadly, verbal repetition is an example of imitation, which is a fundamental feature of social interaction. From the very moment of birth, neonates display the capacity to imitate facial gestures, including tongue protrusion and a wide O-shaped mouth gesture (Meltzoff and Moore 1983). It turns out that the human brain is equipped with so-called mirror neurons, directly associated with our ability to imitate (Rizzolatti and Arbib 1998). And of course, imitation and verbal repetition are staple components of comic performance. Making silly faces back and forth is not confined to interaction with young children. And Bergson argues that 'in a comic repetition of words we generally find two terms: a repressed feeling which goes off like a spring, and an idea that delights in repressing the feeling anew' (Bergson [1900] 1956: 54). In his consideration of comic performance within sitcom, Mills refers to the 'comfort of repetition' (Mills 2005: 140). Repetition also features in a very deliberate manner 'in French plays of the absurd, like Beckett's *En Attendant Godot* and Ionesco's *La Leçon* [and] doubtless take their inspiration from the Commedia tradition' (Styan 1975: 93).

Repetition is embedded in many of the rhymes and lullabies which are used to amuse young children, for example, 'eeny-meeny-miny-mo', 'one-two-three-a-lairy', and 'tinker-tailor-soldier-sailor' (Hoggart 1960: 49). And children take great pleasure in repeating enjoyable activities, like book reading, on occasion beyond the endurance of their parents. The use of repetition with children may well contribute to feelings of familiarity and security, which, as noted above, may create a backdrop for the introduction of surprise. In a similar vein, comedians' catchphrases imbue the audience with a sense of instant recognition and comfort. The radio comedy ITMA, during the Second World War, was famously littered with catchphrases:

> There was Ali Oop the peddler: 'You buy nice dirty postcard, very slimey, oh blimey'. There was Mrs Mopp the charlady: 'Can I do you now, sir?' There was Sam Scram the useless factotum: 'Boss, boss, sump'n terrible's happened'. There was Colonel Chinstrap the tippler: 'I don't mind if I do'. There was the salesman: 'I'll call again. Good morning. Nice day'. There was the diver: 'I'm going down now, sir'. There were many more: it sometimes seemed that every week Ted Kavanagh, who in all exceeded 300 half-hour scripts, invented a new catchphrase every week, and a character to go with it. (Halliwell 1987: 218)

Catchphrases continue to be very popular. The recent BBC comedies The Fast Show (1994–2000) and Little Britain (2003–2006) are popular with young audiences, in part because of their reliance on familiar catchphrases, identified with particular characters, repeated on every possible occasion. Meanwhile, young-child-specific shows such as The Teletubbies (BBC 1997–2001) and Tweenies (1999–2002) rely on repetitions and simple, nonsensical utterances to appeal to, and comfort, their target audience.

Nonsense

The oft-repeated rhymes and chants of childhood are often deliberately nonsensical. Against a background of conventional meanings and sentence forms, incongruity is introduced, in a linguistic form that echoes the incongruity of purely visual, event-based humour. The devices for making meaning, from infancy throughout childhood, include glorification in the use of bizarre words, turns of phrase or sounds, along with an enjoyment of conceptualizations that can be understood merely as silly or ridiculous. Children's nursery rhymes, chants, poems, songs and jokes all revel in such incongruities; an early example of nonsense is provided by Brown in his (possibly imagined, nonetheless illuminatingly detailed) description of Sir Walter Scott, playing with the seven-year-old Marjorie Fleming, in 1810:

> Having made the fire cheery, he set her down in his ample chair, and standing sheepishly before her, began to say his lesson, which happened to be – 'Ziccoty, diccoty dock, the mouse ran up the clock, the clock struck wan, down the mouse ran, ziccoty, diccoty dock'. This done repeatedly till she was pleased, she gave him his new lesson, gravely and slowly, timing it upon her small fingers, – he saying it after her, –
>
> > 'Wonery, twoery, tickery, seven:
> > Alibi, crackaby, ten, and eleven;
> > Pin, pan, musky, dan;
> > Tweedle-um, twoddle-um,
> > Twenty-wan; eerie, orie, ourie,
> > You, are, out'.
>
> He pretended to great difficulty, and she rebuked him with most comical gravity, treating him as a child. He used to say that when he came to Alibi Crackaby he broke down, and Pin-Pan, Musky-Dan, Tweedle-um and Twoddle-um made him roar with laughter. (Brown 1898: 205)

Comic performance aimed at adults can also embody revelry in the incongruities that language can present; double entendres, slang, puns and rhyme all demonstrate enthusiasm for playing with language and finding humour in confounding our linguistic expectations.

Superiority

One further standard ingredient often found in comic performance is a sense of superiority, which is enjoyed by the audience at the expense of the performer. As the great movie comedian Oliver Hardy noted, 'one of the reasons why people like us, I guess, is because they feel so superior to us. Even an eight-year-old kid can feel superior to us and that makes him laugh' (cited in McCabe 1966: 46). At the same time, there is an implicit collusion between performer and audience. The audience understands that displays of ineptitude and inadequacy are 'put on' for their benefit. Thus, W.H. Auden states in his 'Notes on the Comic' that:

> in appearance he is the clumsy man whom inanimate objects conspire against to torment; this in itself is funny to watch, but our profounder amusement is derived from our knowledge that this is only an appearance, that, in reality, the accuracy with which the objects trip him up or hit him on the head is caused by the clown's own skill. (Auden 1963: 373)

Charles Darwin also considered 'some sense of superiority in the laugher' to be an important ingredient in the humour we perceive (Darwin [1872] 1904). Once again, we find the foundations of adult comic performance in the structure of adult-child interaction. The acquisition of linguistic and social conventions by very young children depend on what Kuhl and Meltzoff (1996) call the 'hindsight basis' or 'I knew it all along effect'. In this regard, one might point to the fact that the comic characters enjoyed by young children are often incompetent, clownish figures like Rowan Atkinson's Mr Bean (ITV, 1990–1995). With his inability to perform even the simplest of tasks, the child enjoys a feeling of superiority over Mr Bean. They 'know all along' how to succeed where even concerted efforts by Mr Bean fail.

Conclusion

From the very first weeks of an infant's life, interaction with parents often constitutes a comic performance. Parents can make infants laugh by confounding their expectations within a familiar setting, via vigorous vocal or physical events. But it would be wrong to conclude that the infant spends a long apprenticeship as the audience, in thrall to the parent's 'turn' as performer. Long before the child's first birthday, we see signs of the child initiating the making of laughter. Thus, Piaget (1952) observed his ten-month-old son continually throwing a favourite metal toy into a basin to delight in the noise it made. The laughter provoked in this way was shared with the parental audience. Many of the elements of adult humour are witnessed from the very start in adult-child interaction. These include the elements of incongruity and superiority evident in slapstick and physical comedy. But incongruity and superiority can also be seen from very early on in adult-child humour based on language: verbal repetition, wordplay, nonsense, rhymes, jokes and puns. Hal Roach, the great silent movie comedy director, believed that 'one of the big secrets of successful comedy is relating it all to childhood' (Kerr 1975: 111). We would further refine this observation, by focusing on a very specific aspect of childhood: the quality of interaction between parent and child. As we have seen, several key features of adult-child interaction persist beyond childhood and can be identified in successful adult comic performance, based on the quality of interaction between comedians and their audiences.

Acknowledgement

This chapter is reprinted by permission of the publishers from Saxton, M. and I. Wilkie. 2010. 'The origins of comic performance in adult-child interaction', *Comedy Studies*, 1: 1, pp. 21–32.

References

Auden, W.H. 1963. *The Dyer's Hand*. London: Faber.
Baillargeon, R., E. Spelke and S. Wasserman. 1985. 'Object Permanence in Five-Month-Old Infants', *Cognition* 20(3), 191–208.
Bergson, H. 1900 [1956]. 'On Laughter', trans. C. Brereton and F. Rothwell, in *Comedy*. New York: Doubleday.
Brown, J. 1898. *Horae Subsecivae*. London: Adam and Charles Black.
Bruce, F. 1999. 'Songs, Sketches and Modern Life: Scottish Comedians 1900–1940', *Theatre Notebook: A Journal of the History and Technique of the British Theatre*, LIII, 2.
Carr, J. and L. Greeves. 2006. *The Naked Jape*. London: Michael Joseph.
Cashon, C.H. and L.B. Cohen. 2000. 'Eight-Month-Old Infants' Perception of Possible and Impossible Events', *Infancy* 1(4), 429–46.
Critchley, S. 2002. *On Humour*. London: Routledge.
Darwin, C. 1904 [1872]. *The Expression of the Emotions in Man and Animals*, ed. F. Darwin (ed.). London: John Murray.
———. 1877. 'A Biographical Sketch of an Infant', *Mind* 2(7), 285–94.
Emde, R.N. and R.J. Harman. 1972. 'Endogenous and Exogenous Smiling Systems in Early Infancy', *Journal of the American Academy of Child Psychiatry* 11, 77–100.

Ferguson, C.A. 1977. 'Baby Talk as a Simplified Register', in C.E. Snow and C.A. Ferguson (eds), *Talking to Children: Language Input and Acquisition*. Cambridge: Cambridge University Press.

Fraiberg, S.H. 1974. 'Blind Infants and their Mothers: An Examination of the Sign System', in M. Lewis and S. Rosenblum (eds), *The Effect of the Infant on its Caregiver*. New York: Wiley.

Freud, S. 1964. *Jokes and their Relation to the Unconscious* (volume VIII), Standard Edition of the Complete Psychological Works. London: Hogarth Press.

Garnica, O.K. 1977. 'Some Prosodic and Paralinguistic Features of Speech to Young Children', in C.E. Snow and C.A. Ferguson (eds), *Talking to Children*. Cambridge: Cambridge University Press, 63–88.

Grieg, J. 1969. *The Psychology of Laughter and Comedy*. Cooper Square Publishers Inc.

Halliwell, L. 1987. *Double Take and Fade Away*. London: Grafton Books.

Hazlitt, W. 1885. *Lectures on the English Comic Writers*. London: George Bell.

Hoggart, R. 1960. *The Uses of Literacy*. Harmondsworth: Pelican.

House, J. 1986. *Music Hall Memories*. Glasgow: Richard Drew Publishing.

Irving, G. 1977. *The Good Auld Days: The Story of Scotland's Entertainers From Music Hall to Television*. Jupiter.

Jeancolas, J. 1992. 'The Inexportable: The Case of French Cinema and Radio in the 1950s', in R. Dyer and G. Vinceneau (eds), *Popular European Cinema*. London: Routledge.

Kerr, W. 1975. *The Silent Clowns*. New York: Da Capo.

Kierkegaard, S. 1941. *Concluding Unscientific Postscript*. Trans D. Swenson. Princeton: Princeton University Press.

Kuhl, P.K. and A.N. Meltzoff. 1996. 'Infant Vocalizations in Response to Speech: Vocal Imitation and Developmental Change', *Journal of the Acoustical Society of America* 100(4), 2425–38.

van Leeuwen, T. 2005. *Introducing Social Semiotics*. London: Routledge.

Mackie, A. 1973. *The Scotch Comedians: From the Music Hall to TV*. Ramsay Head.

McCabe, J. 1966. *Mr. Laurel and Mr. Hardy*. Signet.

Meltzoff, A.N. and M.K. Moore. 1983. 'Newborn Infants Imitate Adult Facial Gestures'. *Child Development* 54(3), 702–709.

Mills, B. 2005. *Television Sitcom*. London: BFI Publishing.

Morreall, J. (ed.). 1987. *The Philosophy of Laughter and Humor*. New York: Albany.

Moustaka, K. 1992. 'Motherese: A Description of the Register Caretakers use to Address Children and its Relation to First and Second Language Acquisition', unpublished MA TESOL thesis. University of London.

Neill, A.S. 1916. *A Dominie's Log*. London: Herbert Jenkins.

Piaget, J. 1952. *The Child's Conception of Number*. London: Routledge and Kegan Paul.

Priestley, J.B. 1976. *English Humour*. London: Heinemann.

Rasmussen, V. 1920. *Child Psychology*. Part 1. *Development in the First Four Years*.

Rizzolatti, G. and M.A. Arbib. 1998. 'Language Within our Grasp', *Trends in Neurosciences* 21(5), 188–94.

Sandstrom, C. 1966. *The Psychology of Childhood and Adolescence*. Harmondsworth: Penguin.

Santayana, G. 1896. *The Sense of Beauty*. New York: Scribners.

Saxton, M. 2009. 'The Inevitability of Child Directed Speech', in S. Foster-Cohen (ed.), *Advances in Language Acquisition*. Palgrave Macmillan, 62–86.

———. 2010. *Child Language: Acquisition and Development*. London: Sage.

Schopenhauer, A. 1909. *The World as Will and Idea*, trans. R. Haldane and J. Kemp. London: Routledge and Kegan Paul.

Skatssoon, J. 2006. *News in Science: Why we Laugh at Slapstick*. 3 October 2006. ABC Science online: http://www.abc.net.au/science/news/stories/2006/1753373.htm

Styan, J.L. 1975. *Drama, Stage and Audience*. Cambridge: Cambridge University Press.

Sully, J. 1896. *Studies of Childhood*. Longman, Greens & Co.

Thomson, P. 2000. *On Actors and Acting*. University of Exeter.

Welford, H. 1999. *Ready, Steady, Baby: A Guide to Pregnancy, Birth and Early Parenthood*. Health Education Board for Scotland.

Ian Wilkie is a professional actor and a tutor in post-compulsory education at the UCL Institute of Education, London. He is currently undertaking research into comic performance at the University of Aberystwyth.

Matthew Saxton was a Senior Lecturer in Psychology and Human Development at the Institute of Education, London until 2011. His research interests are in the field of child language acquisition and include the role of input and interaction and their integration within theories of grammar development. He is the author of 'The Inevitability of Child Directed Speech', in *Advances in Language Acquisition*, edited by S. Foster-Cohen (London: Palgrave Macmillan, 2009) and *Child Language: Acquisition and Development* (London: Sage, 2010).

2

LEARNING FROM THE LUDIC
Anthropological Fieldwork

Judith Okely

Introduction

The demand for anthropological methods courses only occurred in the early 1990s. Before then, it seemed that the 'stiff upper lip' approach prevailed, at least in British anthropology. Thus the narratives of fieldwork, including the absurd and learning through mistakes, were only corridor talk. Often the most ludicrous or humorous incidents provided the best material for whispered, oral accounts. These were seen as only embarrassing, rather than vital insights into the acquisition of knowledge during fieldwork. Indeed, they revealed that it is precisely because cross-cultural, lived experience is unpredictable that the incoming fieldworker cannot know the rules and context in advance.

Regrettably, there has been pressure on academics to prove their worth only by appearing serious. Indeed, in some cultures, especially in English if not British traditions, intellectuals are dismissed by the derogatory label 'boffin', a term used by his 'superiors' to describe the tragic Dr David Kelly, after he challenged the Government's claim that Iraq had weapons of mass destruction. No wonder that the discipline of social anthropology kept as a dark secret its learning through the ludic.

By contrast, I have been deeply concerned with the specificity of anthropological fieldwork before I ever studied the subject. This was because participant observation fieldwork preceded reading any monographs.

Escaping the Limits of Cerebral Knowledge Alone

After graduating in Politics, Philosophy and Economics at Oxford, I accompanied my then partner Hugh Brody as honorary 'wife' to the West of Ireland

(Okely 2009). I escaped a library-bound form of knowledge, with tedious readings of discredited texts. My college politics tutor had insisted on repeated rewrites of essays on civil law, long deleted from the university syllabus and any final exam papers. Indeed Miss Crowe's 'privileged' Oxford tutorials had a ludic character. We undergraduates had to hop over her cocker spaniels' bowls of dog food, half spilt on grubby copies of *The Financial Times* all over the floor. A fellow student recalled, years later, how perhaps this tutor had a deliberate policy of censoring mini skirts. If so dressed, we were more vulnerable to fearsome sniffer dog attacks throughout the tutorial.

Now far away in Ireland, trying out fieldwork, I gloried in an alternative holistic form of knowledge, beyond solely cerebral interaction, through the whole body, and including what Malinowski famously labelled 'The imponderabilia of everyday life' (1922). We befriended Kate, a small farmer in Connemara. She asked us to help with the daily labour. Thus I learned how to walk a donkey to the Connemara peat bogs and load up turf as fuel into the baskets hanging either side of a seemingly compliant animal. Having set him on his way back to the farm, I presumed the donkey would continue over the hill as I lay down in the grass for a dreamy break, listening to the sounds of nature. But the first joke was played on me by the donkey. Once out of my sight, he also took a break and stood motionless and free: no slog home until this foreign woman arrived to give a gentle nudge and escort him all the way. Again my metropolitan naivety was shown up when I learned a song first heard in the rural 'isolated' pub. Back at the university and urban Belfast with Hugh, among academics, I offered to sing this 'traditional' song 'discovered' in the depths of Western Ireland. After my presentation, I was tactfully informed that it was the pop group The Dubliners' latest hit, to general laughter. Another sobering lesson through the absurd was learned when Hugh and I gave a lift to some local men hitchhiking on the road to the small town. It was customary to assist the car-less that way. But, far from any presumption of assisting 'isolated rural bachelors, ignorant of any distant metropolis', it transpired that these same sturdy labourers had built the London Underground's new Victoria Line. Thus day-to-day interaction, seemingly in distant places, and before the internet and streamed TV, this potential anthropologist was brought down to earth, not far from London pavements.

Any preconceptions nurtured by this novice graduate's own isolation were challenged through ludic lessons. Contrasts and comparisons were learned not with blackboard and chalk but through fieldwork fun, opening alternative worlds beyond the rigidities of class, nationality and hitherto disembodied academia. Grounded knowledge through human interchanges and the unexpected stream of events, namely participant observation, was offered through ethnographic fieldwork.

No Field Methods Taught

Returning from Ireland, eventually to enrol for a postgraduate Cambridge anthropology conversion degree, including a weekly course on Malinowski with the latter's former student Edmund Leach, I was puzzled as to the limits to the programme's range. In this 'Introduction' to the discipline, there were NO lectures on methods, no discussions of participant observation and fieldwork. Thus began a near obsessive focus on fieldwork practice.

Ironically, methods teaching in the social sciences became compulsory in the early 1990s. In the aftermath of Margaret Thatcher's attempt to abolish the Social Science Research Council (Okely 2013b),[1] we social scientists had to prove ourselves 'useful' by teaching 'transferable skills'. When Professor at Edinburgh University, and still faced with almost no texts, I embarked on what was to become an unpredicted number of years' work on the book *Anthropological Practice: Fieldwork and the Ethnographic Method*, now published (2012).

Dialogue Opens up Narratives of the Unexpected

Having transcribed and amended my university lectures on methods, I had a manuscript nearly ready by 1995, but in exchanging ideas with the anthropologist Brian Morris, I was transfixed by his narratives of fieldwork. He certainly had no investment in retaining the 'stiff upper lip' disguise in the name of an absurd notion of research and science as distant and planned, fixed trajectory. Originally my intentions had been to search through anthropologists' published prefaces and footnotes for lost anecdotes and accounts of fieldwork. But these were rare, irrelevant or non-existent. The enforced silence of the stiff upper lip was disguised as science or dismissed by other disciplines as merely 'anecdotal'. Brian found a tape recorder and, having scribbled down some questions for which I had found few answers in the literature, I recorded our dialogue. Four hours later, we turned off the recorder. This was to be repeated with over twenty anthropologists of some sixteen nationalities and who had done fieldwork around the globe from the late 1960s up to a year before the manuscript's completion (Okely 2012: 157–62).

Here I focus specifically on the theme of the ludic among the accumulated material, stretching through many hours. From the beginning, I have been sceptical, indeed angered, by the insistence that anthropological fieldwork should be reduced to formulaic training, including an advanced hypothesis, in a naïve imitation of what is believed to be science. Social anthropological fieldwork does indeed demonstrate aspects which we also find in orthodox scientific discovery, namely the role of chance, accident or serendipity. It was the pioneering Hortense Powdermaker who first drew my attention to the concept of 'serendipity' in her *Stranger and Friend* (1967). I have argued elsewhere that it is no coincidence that it was often women who were the earliest to publish autobiographical accounts of fieldwork. They, as the 'second sex', did not see it as loss of macho identity to reveal learning by mistakes (Okely 1992).

Despite the funding committees and bureaucratic demands for advance hypotheses, anthropologists cannot always stick to tunnel vision themes. They have to respond to what confronts them. Almost all the anthropologists I interviewed had to switch their focus and original advance plans once in the field. The way in which they switched often depended on accident. But they seized the chance. They often learned the rules of the culture when they innocently broke them. We learn through mistakes. We cannot predict in advance what these rules or their breaking may be. We may indeed learn through what emerges as the seemingly absurd.

Own Culture Recalled as Ludicrous

Granted we come to the field, whether we want it or not, with pre-existing assumptions. However much anthropologists may have wanted to escape and defy ethnocentrism, we are encultured in the imponderabilia of our pre-existing everyday. Even when we choose to study our 'own' culture, it is, as the cliché goes, a matter of 'making the familiar strange'. It may be that retrospective fieldwork in one's own past exposes the ludicrous. Here listeners, whatever their nationality, class or age, are incredulous at what was once seen as the elite education for upper-class English girls through to the 1960s. Recalling the long outmoded rules of my boarding school now exposes the bizarre, indeed ludicrous. For example, my sister's school friends secretly enrolled her for the Elvis Presley fan club. Innocently, she was summoned by our headmistress to her study and shown the seized material which she was immediately ordered to throw into the bin. This supremely powerful educationalist declared: 'You are fit only to dance at Hammersmith Palais!' seen as the glamorized meeting place for the lower classes.

Similarly, I was summoned to the headmistress and, despite the qualifications I had achieved and those I was expected to obtain, I was informed that I would be 'selfish to go to university'. I would be 'depriving a more worthy person of a place'. When I recounted this to my French teacher, who told me I should go to university, she warned: 'This will be our secret'. Already the class hegemony of my Isle of Wight boarding school had resulted in the teacher insisting that I, aged nine, change what I had been told in my previous Lincolnshire village school was beautifully looped handwriting. This had to be erased because the boarding school asserted it looked 'like the handwriting of a maid' (Okely 1996: chs 7 and 8). Class lessons such as these had long-term effects on some. Decades later at a school reunion, one of my contemporaries referred to another: 'She wrote to me on lined paper. I know when a friendship has to stop'. No wonder my article (ibid., ch. 8) was recently placed on a Harvard university psychology course. Thus the legacy of social class, through change from a previous hegemony, will in new times seem so ludicrously unbelievable.

Cross-Cultural Paradox

Beyond our 'own', (whatever that may be), culture, we are usually expected to make the strange familiar. We learn through mistakes. We learn when we make laughing stocks of ourselves. We learn when others laugh at our naiveties. Additionally, we learn when our experiences clash with advance expectations. Sometimes the ludicrous is apparent within a shared academic culture. Some jokes or paradoxes may only be understood within the discipline of anthropology and geography. One paradox, which I outlined at a distinguished lecture at the LSE (Okely 2010), was understood only by the four anthropologists present. They laughed out loud. The others in the audience, perhaps eighty sociologists and political scientists, did not get it. They sat silent. This concerned Professor Parry's ignorance of the word 'hypergamy' as elaborated below. If there had been Indian persons in the audience, they also would have laughed at the ludicrous case of Parry presenting a paper in Delhi about the practice of women marrying into a higher caste, while subsequently confessing to not knowing the familiar term for it: 'I had absolutely no intention of writing about hypergamy. It wasn't until right at the end of my fieldwork, when I gave a paper in a seminar at the Delhi School of Economics, that somebody said: "What you're describing is a system of hypergamy!" Which is a symptom of my appalling ignorance' (see also Okely 2012: 59).

Jokes through Contrast or Mockery

In the outline for this volume, there is a suggestion that humour or jokes can only be understood within a shared culture. I contend that humour can also be made apparent precisely when cultural boundaries are crossed. The clash of cultural understandings may be resolved through laughter. Of course laughter may also denote mockery and total sadism. Torturers may take pleasure in sadistic humiliation, as in the horrendous images from Abhu Graib, the prison in Iraq. The US personnel, as gaolers, had sick smiles on their faces as they inflicted suffering and terror on their hooded, naked Iraqi captives whom they also threatened with dogs. Here, the knowledge that for many Muslims the dog is a negative, polluting symbol was exploited by the alleged Judeo-Christian American soldiers. Again cultural inversion can be used as torturous entertainment for different believers. Rapists have also resorted to ludic strategies for humiliation and triumph:

something I witnessed in 1960s Oxford among some sexist male student contemporaries (Okely 2013a).

Some of the major themes which are almost universal, but specifically grounded and interpreted, arise from gender, sexuality and ethnicity, exploiting divisions of power and hierarchy. Other contrasts are found in cultural embodiment, what Mauss called 'The Techniques of the Body' (1935) which include skills, posture, movement and bodily attire. Contrasts and differences exist in belief systems, including notions of right or wrong, the cerebral and emotions, and finally distinctions of Man/Animal. Anthropologists need to learn the contrasts or similarities in all these categories. But as participant observers; they may not, cannot know these in advance. That is precisely why they embark on fieldwork.

Here are some examples, focusing on the ludic, from different fieldwork contexts. There are many other ways of learning. In this case it can be through paradox, the absurd, the inverse, the unexpected, or the subversive which can all lead to new knowledge.

Liminal/Reversal

There is an anthropological literature on reversals and what Turner (1969) has developed as the 'Liminal', or the 'twixt and between' status for neophytes in *rites de passage* which involve moving from one status to another. It is here that we find reversals of the norm. Melissa Llewellyn-Davies' film *Masai Manhood* (1975) records the neophytes in a ceremony preparing the passage from young man to elder status. Before emerging from the liminal state, they are visited by their mothers. As a symbolic break from the mother and movement to adult manhood, they are expected to indulge in mock obscenities with their mother, making her drink huge amounts of animal fat causing diarrhoea. The neophytes joke together while mocking their consenting and humiliated mothers.

Thus humour is found in a most sacred relationship, now symbolically broken, all performed as vital and within the specific culture. The mockery precedes the final parade of the emergent new 'elders', now around thirty years of age; finally permitted marriage, with locks all shorn. They are seemingly unrecognized by their own mothers: this bizarre claim had to be preceded by the ludic inversion of dependent son's respect for once nurturing mother. The mother is made to vomit after agreeing to be force-fed the indigestible by the now controlling son.

World Turned Upside Down

Barbara Babcock's *The Reversible World: Symbolic Inversion in Art and Society* (1978) gives crucial insights. Jokes may indeed be appreciated by complete outsiders, when the returning anthropologist recounts transformations demanded in the field. I have described the following reversal of expectations to an academic audience. It was even understood when I was called upon to address the President of Finland at the Annual Gypsy Lore Society conference in Helsinki. The local professor later thanked me for breaking the tension caused by the need for multiple security men in the hall.

By contrast, I doubt if it would be seen as a joke if recounted to English Gypsies. During the event for the Finnish President, I showed a photo of a Gypsy called Harriet who said she really liked the way I spoke. I must have, she said, had 'special elocution lessons'. I suspected some insincerity. I speak with an 'upper middle class accent' sharpened at my dreaded boarding school (Okely 1996). After several weeks living on the Gypsy site, I learned to speak as the Gypsies did, dropping any H and extending the vowels. Harriet came back from travelling some time later and heard me speaking. She said: 'Judith your speech 'as improved!' Thus it was the inverse of *My Fair Lady*, based on the George Bernard Shaw play *Pygmalion*. I had to learn to pronounce 'The Rain in Spain is falling in the Plain' in reverse, i.e. 'The Rieene in Spine is fawlin' in the Plieene'. This draws on the presumptions of social class in the English tradition, but even the multinational audience in Helsinki got the joke through paradox and reversal. When addressing an international audience in Romania in October 2013, I asked them if they had heard of the musical *My Fair Lady*. All hands went up and again this multinational audience laughed at my story. Thus some jokes can cross national boundaries.

Whereas an international audience may appreciate the musical *My Fair Lady* and my fieldwork comparison of having to learn a different cockney accent among the Gypsies, my account of the brutality of a boarding school imposing the confusion of changing a little girl's handwriting for class reasons has subsequently evoked only horrified gasps. Writing scripts or fonts may be creatively changeable, only if self adopted as avenue to multiple possibilities. Steve Jobs, founder of Apple Mac, a university 'drop out', sneaked back in for a course on calligraphy. Different scripts, for example Times, Calibri or Helvetica, would subsequently prove powerful in computer styles. What might have seemed ludicrously obscure helped unleash a multi-million brand.

Similarly, the unexpected, the unplanned, once accepted as creative inevitability in anthropological fieldwork, may in practice be the only means to new understandings. In some key instances, the anthropologist's identity and positionality cannot be changed but is open to culturally specific re-interpretation by his or her future hosts in the field. There are paradoxes, encountered by two of my interviewees, where the category of gender and that of 'race' or ethnicity come into play.

The Arrival of the Outsider

Mary Louise Pratt (1986) has explored the anthropologist's 'Arrival' as a literary trope in their texts. She did not, however, consider the effect of the arrival of the anthropologist as outsider on the people as hosts. Signe Howell, arriving in tropical forest Malaysia, found that whenever she approached people, they ran off screaming. She was relatively tall, compared to the Chewong. Unexpectedly, she was invited to join a family as adopted daughter. Eventually, Signe asked what had changed and, after some hesitation, they revealed that a man saw her bathing. Signe described how she was washing very modestly, under a sarong. But the man rushed back to the village, exclaiming: 'It's a woman! It's got breasts!' The family then felt reassured and safe with some universalized belief in women as 'weaker' and non-violent. Thus the familiar, now taken for granted, theorized distinction between sex as biological and gender as cultural did not apply. Her feminine upper body became the crucial reassuring key to access into the community.

In another example confronting insider perceptions of the outsider/stranger, the external 'race' difference of the anthropologist was predictably significant.

Louise de la Gorgendière, a white Franco-Canadian, having prepared for fieldwork in Ghana, chose a specific village for aesthetic reasons. The villagers appeared to be welcoming. After a week, they insisted she was 'a Confused Ancestor born in the wrong white body'. She had come back. When Louise asked why, they explained that she knew their names within a week and could speak their language. She explained she had learned it in advance in Canada, but this did not change their preferred identification. When I recounted this same narrative at a conference at Egerton University, Kenya, to an all-African,

Figure 2.1: Louise de la Gorgendière as a confused ancestor carrying a villager's baby.

non-anthropological audience, they also laughed at what they appreciated as ludicrously counter-intuitive. These Kenyans kept coming up to me, giggling and repeating the phrase 'Confused Ancestor'. Here amusement was shared at the paradox across cultures and nations within the African continent. Nevertheless, the majority of the audience was Christian with a few Muslims. They did not share the same beliefs about returning dead ancestors.

Another example recounts a different twist. In this case, the outsider would-be researcher was travelling through relatively unknown territory. Akira Okazaki, of Japanese nationality, had already lived with the Masai as a young man before ever studying anthropology. His subsequent journey across relatively new territory revealed the risks of venturing beyond the familiar and without back-up. In the midst of what could have been a life threatening accident, a chance encounter occurred, which can only be described as ludicrous. I present extracts of my interview with Okazaki:

> I had a terrible accident on the way to Sudan by motorbike. It was 1981. Civil war started in 1983. I was near Sudan in Turkana land in a very dry, arid area. My motorbike turned over. My left leg was like 'meat' under the motorbike. The engine was still running. The bike skidded 10–20 metres. I was frightened. There was no shade from trees – all small shrubs without leaves. It was 1 o'clock in the afternoon, the hottest time. I tried to put my body in the shade but it was difficult. Maybe this is the end of my life. That road was just a dirt track. Not a place with regular cars because very close to the border. Only someone venturing to other countries can pass there.
>
> I was waiting many hours. People were not around because there was a world cam-paign for the Turkana. The people were suffering from hunger. Many people were dying… A young man suddenly appeared – 17 or 18 years old, so thin, almost dying, very fragile, like a very old man. He was walking very slowly. He came over because I called out. I can't speak Turkana but I speak the Masai language. I showed him my leg and a lot of blood, meat and bones. He saw this and didn't move. Next moment he gestured that he wanted something to eat. I said unfortunately I didn't have anything to eat. Maybe something inside my bag, but I could not go over and open it. I said: 'I'm sorry. Please help me'. He again gestured. I said I'm sorry. He said OK and he went. Just bye-bye.

The starving man disappeared beyond the horizon.

Here is a tragicomic example of crossed encounter between a newly vulnerable stranger and a starving local, both missing a possible opportunity for mutual aid. It was so absurd as to be ludicrous. It had a final twist: in that, nearing sunset, a Land Rover appeared carrying people fleeing Rhodesia. They stopped to help Okazaki. One passenger, fortuitously a nurse, made a splint for his broken leg. They drove to a UN centre over the border into Sudan. Eventually Okazaki, in a complete reversal of fortune, was given a lift in a private plane flying to Nairobi. He was taken to a hospital for eventual rehabilitation. Thus a potentially grotesque tragedy had a happy ending for the anthropologist, but presumably not for the emaciated, starving Turkana.

Western or Non Western

For the cover of my co-edited book *Anthropology and Autobiography* (Okely and Callaway 1992), I deliberately chose the photograph volunteered by one of the contributors, Paul Spencer. This was to show the reversed gaze of a tall indigenous Sambura staring at the anthropologist, a relatively tiny white man, trying to push his Western contraption of a Land Rover out of a rut. Here the anthropologist willingly offered himself as a joke.

Sexuality and the Gendered Outsider

There are plenty of possibilities concerning sexuality played within the cultural group, but so often used against or to tease outsiders across cultures. Something universal also has specific gendered connotations. When living with the Gypsies, this non-Gypsy anthropologist in her twenties was asked by Gypsy men: 'If I handed you two hot pennies what would you do?' My naive answer: 'I would drop them'. Shrieks of laughter followed: 'Oh so you would drop your knickers to a man for just two pennies!' Thus the non-Gypsy woman is ludicrously seen to conform to the stereotype of being sexually available – a cheap whore indeed.

After a year's fieldwork with the Gypsies, I was sufficiently confident to turn a joke around, something which I have now regularly recounted. But it was also a necessary decision because I was still being used as outsider, this time to resolve an internal feud which had once led to murder. Someone started a rumour that I was pregnant by the most notorious Gypsy womanizer on the camp. The rumour-monger, a non-Gypsy woman whose Gypsy partner was in prison, wanted to divert attention from herself (Okely 2005). The story grew and grew. People were telling me that my alleged pregnancy by the Gypsy man was being reported in all neighbouring camps. One man suggested that the alleged father would be bringing his clothes and moving into my caravan. His wife, up to then my trusted friend, was ceasing to giggle at the joke, now well out of control. It was being used as means of censoring this man with a roving eye. Here the innocent anthropologist, as useful victim, had to take control.

I waited until there was quite a crowd and approached them, carrying a doll, wrapped as if in swaddling clothes. I complained that no one had helped me. I had given birth to a baby all on my own and demanded financial paternal support. I pointed to the womanizer as father of this 'baby'. Very quickly,

Figure 2.2: Paul Clough among the Hausa.

the group got the bizarre joke and shrieked with laughter. The youngest child smashed the doll, now a dead rival. As I had hoped, my joke followed the same trail as the earlier rumour. My extreme playacting ensured greater acceptance: 'Judith. You can muck in', they said.

Another example of sexuality being used by insiders to tease the identity of the stranger anthropologist is recounted by Paul Clough who did fieldwork among the Hausa in Nigeria. As a young unmarried white male Anglo-American, he proved an easy target for the African women. They would get him to sing 'The song of the Vagina' which they had made him write down. They would love his attempts to repeat, in Hausa, words and phrases with obscene innuendoes. 'They laughed at my mistakes' (Okely 2012: 134–35).

Bodily Movement and Posture

Bodily movement may be so internalized through cultural history that it becomes naturalized. Alternative bodily movement can be comical if unfamiliar and clumsy. In the field, the anthropologist adapts and is sometimes asked to dress like the local people. It is not necessarily, as someone once asked me, the case of a naive 'going native' in order to be invisible. I was indeed instructed to wear a dress over tight trousers and not to have tight sweaters. Fieldwork

Figure 2.3: Nancy suitably dressed alongside a Pashtun in Afghanistan.

becomes embodied. But here the anthropologist may become the object of humour if s/he cannot adapt, indeed not go fully native. Nancy Lindisfarne, doing fieldwork among Pashtun nomads in Afghanistan, was advised to wear the proper dress. But she was regularly teased because it was said she walked like a man, indeed a soldier. She could not adapt to the yards and yards of material required for the trousers. She also had to learn about wearing a veil: 'I was always being teased by how I wore the long black veil and by the fact that I walked like a soldier ... You had to hold your head in a certain way or the veil would fall off' (Okely 2012: 118).

Thus the outsider's difference, indeed bodily ungainliness, is a source of humour from within. Thanks to Mauss' brilliant essay (1935), it had long been recognized that early 'techniques' of the body depend on enculturation.

Bodily posture is indeed culturally specific. Margaret Kenna embarked on her first fieldwork on a Greek island as a young unmarried woman. She had to act primly. She spent more time with the older women to ensure the impression that she was not a loose woman. They could not understand why her parents had let her come alone. She explained that she was studying for a PhD. They concluded that her parents obviously had no money for a dowry so a PhD would be a vital substitute. Some years later, she returned as a married woman, thus proving their prediction. But they asked her why she always sat with her legs crossed. For her this was a sign of modest control. For them it was a sign of a prostitute who, by sitting in that position, was believed to twist the womb and avoid pregnancy. They did not laugh, but she appreciated the ludic or absurd in the misinterpretation of her behaviour, which was actually the opposite of their cultural norm (Kenna 1992).

Language Learning and Translations

Anthropologists' mistakes in language also elicit laughter from the host people. Helena Wulff's first fieldwork was among South London teenagers. As Helena was Swedish, English was her second language. She also had to become acquainted with street slang, beyond all the anthropological literature which she had read in advance. Sometimes she was pestered, so she learned that the best way to tell someone off was to use strong language, as did other girls. So she shouted to the young men to their delight 'Fuck away' instead of 'Fuck off'. It brought delighted laughter (Wulff 1988).

Irony is also found in the following account where the anthropologist has inside linguistic knowledge but can witness the paradox of interpreters. Traditionalists use the metaphor of the 'Armchair Anthropologist' before what I call the 'Verandah Anthropologist', where the early anthropologists, ignorant of the local language, depended on interpreters with select informants (Okely 2012: 17–19). In practice, interpreters may have long transformed and concealed feared outsider's stereotypes.

When in Malawi, Brian Morris, who was fluent in the local language, witnessed a Scottish biologist who flew in for a couple of weeks to find out about 'indigenous' views and uses of plant medicines. The local Malawi interpreter deliberately changed the herbalist's description of what each plant was for. One plant said to be for protection against 'spirit possession' was deliberately mistranslated by the interpreter into English, claiming it was used for a 'headache'. A very phallic shaped plant root was said to be for 'impotence', but the interpreter translated it as used for 'stomach ache'. He was well acquainted with Western stereotypes about his people, so concealed the local knowledge which might reinforce them. Witnessing the ludicrous, deliberate mistranslation, Morris respected the interpreter's choices and never once intervened. Meanwhile the Scottish academic appeared pleased and returned home. Perhaps he was to gain academic credit for publishing in a distinguished scientific journal article outlining 'first hand' original research on African medical beliefs.

In another example the anthropologist in search of the 'untouched', if not so-called primitive. Alan Campbell (1989) had obtained postgraduate funding to study the Wayapi in tropical forest Brazil in the early 1970s. It had been believed that this group of Indians had died out because they had last been recorded in the nineteenth century, but they were apparently suddenly spotted across the Brazilian border. After days of walking, Alan moved into deepest forest. Unlike the case of Signe Howell, the people did not run away screaming. They seemed curious. Alan had not been able to learn the language except for some limited vocabulary from the ancient records. He had to communicate and learn by gesture.

Eventually, to ease the communication, he brought out his Scottish mouth organ and started playing Highland music. Soon the Wayapi started singing back. They sang 'Jesus loves me'. Thus these so-called 'untouched' Brazilian Indians had long ago been 'contaminated' by missionaries. That first night was initially devastating. Campbell went to bed in a deep depression. But later he changed his mind. He realized the sounds were only phonetically repeated. The people did not understand the words, let alone the religious meaning. Campbell was later to discover that the Wayapi had always been present in the localities but had stood silently at the back when other known groups were at the front, visible to outsiders, including missionaries. These Wayapi had for years stood in the shadows and learned the tune and sound by rote. This is a delightful example of a group trying to make empathetic contact with the white stranger by selecting what they presumed he would appreciate most, namely 'his' own culture as a point of overlap, rather than difference.

Choice of Region and Topic

Humour can also be found within the broader academic anthropological context and in the choice, or indeed change, of topic. I found repeatedly how the anthropologists changed focus once in the field. They responded to what was there (Okely 2012: ch.3). It is methodologically and theoretically useless to start with a fixed hypothesis. But the way in which the anthropologists arrived at their topic is often humorous, indeed near farcical. When Evans-Pritchard asked a French anthropologist visiting Oxford where his student Malcolm McLeod might study witchcraft, he was advised to study the 'Asanti'. So McLeod did the required advance literature research on Ghana. Once in the field, he was, however, more drawn to the magnificent material culture. He changed his topic and was to become a leading expert on museum work with special reference to Africa. Years later, he encountered the same Frenchman back in Oxford and said he had not pursued his advice. But to Malcolm's amazement, the Frenchman insisted he had never suggested the Asante but the Azande (a people in an entirely different part of Africa). This was doubtless a Freudian mishearing, given that McLeod's postgraduate supervisor Evans-Pritchard, who asked the original question, was already a world expert on the Azande (Evans-Pritchard 1937; Okely 2012: 60).

Masquerade and Mimesis

Marek Kaminski, a stateless refugee in Sweden, needed to earn extra money as a penniless student while studying for a PhD in anthropology, and had a continuing commitment to fieldwork among Gypsies. He had already done work with Gypsies in Poland and Slovakia but now he could link up with Gypsy refugees in Scandinavia. Some of these refugees had devised a lucrative strategy of selling carpets door-to-door. Often of darker skin and hair, they passed as Pakistanis for greater 'authenticity'. When business was slow, his colleagues said:

> 'Marek today you are Pakistani'. I said: 'What do you mean? I don't look Pakistani. I have green, sometimes blue eyes and blonde hair'. My best Gypsy associate thought: 'Does it matter? The way you speak Swedish, you could be Pakistani or Turk'.

Kaminski found in the end that his customers were also mainly immigrants: 'I believe they already realized – how could I be Pakistani or Turk? They were trying to help me by buying those things'. Thus everyone recognized the ludic paradox, but played along with it.

I was also faced with paradoxes of identity when out 'Calling' with fellow Gypsies. Here my accent, despite my attempts at *My Fair Lady* in reverse, did not always succeed. In any case, unlike Kaminski, it was an advantage sometimes to be myself when I also called door to door. This time it was not usually to sell objects but to ask for 'Any old scrap, batteries, clothing, etc.'. Unlike my Gypsy co-workers, I was often asked 'What's it for?' I found myself talking to someone with the same accent. After several muffled answers, I said 'Save the Children Fund'. 'Oh', came the reply, 'I'm the secretary of the local branch'. I quickly mentioned a friend's address in a more distant town. Back in my van, I recounted the experience to Aunt Doll and Rena. They told me never to give a real address: 'We always say "3 Beech Drive". But that's a good answer'.

Just a few hours later, Aunt Doll was given a car battery. Due to its hazardous leaking acid, it was wrapped in protective newspaper. Before putting the battery in the back of the van, Aunt Doll screwed up the paper and pushed it in the neatly cut hedge of this manicured private estate. The house dweller was watching from afar:

> 'What have you done with the newspaper?'
> Aunt Doll: 'It's alright. I've put it in the 'edge'.
> House dweller: 'That's the trouble with you Gypsies. You live on dustbowls'.
> Aunt Doll: 'Madame. I'm not a Gypsy. I don't live on a dustbowl. I'm doing this for charity. I'm doing it for Save the Children Fund'.

The house dweller was thus silenced. I inwardly giggled, marvelling how my Gypsy companion swiftly incorporated an acceptable borrowed identity. Here was cultural creativity and ingenuity.

In most cases, nonetheless, it is the anthropologists who have to learn to imitate their hosts. They learn through their mistakes because they don't know the rules and practices. They then learn through their ineptitude. Their lack of skills can become a subject of much laughter and ribaldry among the locals. Paul Clough, in Nigeria studying agriculture, rented a field in order to grow produce. He did not know that it was already unsuitable land. A tree in the middle was inhabited by monkeys who devoured the produce. His 'harvest' was minimal and he, the 'expert white man', became a subject of ribaldry: 'When I took my crop to market I couldn't sell it. It was small enough to be carried on the back of my motorcycle. When I got back one of the villagers wouldn't stop laughing' (Okely 2012: 103).

In the case of my fieldwork in Normandy, I visited for the first time the head of the local village club for the aged.

This was Madame Grégoire. As entrée I went through the motions of an interview to establish my acceptable identity as an academic researcher. Such a role would have been unacceptable among the Gypsies. But I recognized that intellectuals in France, whatever the social class, were treated with respect. All this contrasted with my observations and first-hand experience of my 'privileged' boarding school and the English fear of, if not upper-class contempt for, 'boffins'. Madame Grégoire finally said she had to milk the cows. I accompanied her to the wintery, beamed barn. Hot air blew at us as she opened the doors. Inside were over a dozen cows. After she had hand milked a couple, I asked if I could have a go, thanks to my experience of direct participation in Ireland.

Here was a ludic event for both of us. Madame Grégoire chose the most docile cow named 'Mère No-No'. She had to introduce me to her: 'Mère No-No, c'est Judith'. The cow looked round. 'Judith. C'est Mère No-No'. Madame Grégoire gave me a three-legged stool and basic instructions. She disappeared, only to return with a flash camera. The sight of 'une professeure' 'stooping' to manual labour was so extraordinary that the gaze had to be turned back onto the stranger

Figure 2.4: Anthropologist and docile cow photographed by the farmer.

intellectual. I treasure that image, especially as I learned how difficult it was to extract any milk. By trying, as is the case with so many anthropologists in the field, we learn to appreciate others' skills.

Everywhere I went through that Normandy locality, it proved a marvellous story and entrée. In contrast, an eminent French anthropologist who had studied peasantry in her own country was incredulous when I told her I was milking cows. French professors, seemingly, did not do manual labour. The final irony was that I had to abandon my apprenticeship as I began to suffer from 'repetitive strain injury'. This condition was usually identified as the result of computer mechanical overload. By contrast, some Normandy locals explained that this was because I had not started milking in childhood, as they had. I wonder what my headmistress, who told my sister that she was fit only to dance with the working class, would have said.

To Conclude

The anthropologist crosses cultures or critically reassesses her own culture(s). The unexpected, the unpredictable, together with retrospective analysis, provide creative avenues towards greater knowledge. As Freud argued (1901), seemingly innocent jokes and so-called 'slips' of the tongue, cover hidden contradictions with profounder insights. We laugh at all this. But fieldwork as fun may prove to be very serious.

Note

1 'Hanif Kureishi claimed Thatcher had "no understanding of what a central place the arts have in British life" (Singing songs of rage, 9 April). She also had no understanding of the social sciences. Planning to close the Social Science Research Council, Thatcher commissioned Lord Rothschild to conduct an independent investigation. Unexpectedly, he concluded it would be an "act of extreme vandalism" to abolish the council. But Thatcher decreed the word "science" be deleted from the title. No paradox that her media organizer, Lord Saatchi, got a first-class social science degree and the MacMillan prize for sociology at the LSE'. Professor Judith Okely. Letter to *The Guardian*, 14 April 2013.

References

Babcock, B. 1978. *The Reversible World: Symbolic Inversion in Art and Society*. Ithaca: Cornell University Press.

Campbell, A.T. 1989. *To Square with Genesis: Causal Statements and Shamanic Ideas in Wayapi*. Edinburgh: Edinburgh University Press.

Evans-Pritchard, E. 1937. *Witchcraft, Oracles and Magic among the Azande*. Oxford: Oxford University Press.

Freud, S. 1901. *The Psychopathology of Everyday Life*. Translation by A.A. Brill (1914). London: T. Fisher Unwin.

Kenna, M. 1992. 'Changing Places and Altered Perspectives: Research on a Greek Island in the 1960s and in the 1980s', in J. Okely and H. Callaway (eds), *Anthropology and Autobiography*. London: Routledge, 147–62.

Llewellyn-Davies, M. 1975. *Masai Manhood*. Film. Disappearing Worlds.

Malinowski, B. 1922. *The Argonauts of the Western Pacific*. London: Routledge and Kegan Paul.

Mauss, M. 1935. 'Les Techniques du corps', *Journal de Psychologie Normale et Pathologique* 35, 271–93.

Okely, J. 1992. 'Anthropology and Autobiography: Participatory Experience and Embodied Knowledge', in J. Okely and H. Callaway (eds), *Anthropology and Autobiography*. London: Routledge, 1–28.

———. 1996. *Own or Other Culture*. London: Routledge.

———. 2005. 'Gypsy Justice and Gorgio Law: Interrelations of Difference', *Sociological Review* 53(4) (November), 691–709.

———. 2009. 'Written out and Written in: Inishkillane Remembered', *Irish Journal of Anthropology* 12(2), 50–55.

———. 2010. 'Crossing Borders', Obi Igwari Memorial Lecture. *The Association for the Study of Ethnicity and Nationalism (ASEN)*. London School of Economics (LSE).

———. 2012. *Anthropological Practice: Fieldwork and the Ethnographic Method*. London: Bloomsbury.

———. 2013a. 'Remembering 1960s Oxford: Sexual, Gender and Racist Divisions', Gender Week talk, St Hilda's College.

————. 2013b. Letter to *The Guardian*, 14 April.

Okely, J. and H. Callaway (eds). 1992. *Anthropology and Autobiography*. London: Routledge.

Powdermaker, H. 1967. *Stranger and Friend: The Way of an Anthropologist*. London: Secker and Warburg.

Pratt, M.L. 1986. 'Fieldwork in Common Places', in J. Clifford and G. Marcus (eds), *Writing Culture: the Poetics and Politics of Ethnography*. Berkeley: University of California Press.

Turner, Victor. 1969. *The Ritual Process*. London: Penguin.

Wulff, Helena. 1988. *Twenty Girls: Growing Up, Ethnicity and Excitement in a South London Micro Culture*. Oxford: Berg.

Judith Okely, formerly Professor of Social Anthropology, Edinburgh University, is an emeritus Professor of Hull University and Research Associate, School of Anthropology, University of Oxford. In 2013 she was Paul Lazarsfeld Guest Professor, Vienna University. Her publications include: *The Traveller-Gypsies, Anthropology and Autobiography* (co-edited), *Simone de Beauvoir: A Re-reading, Own or Other Culture*, and *Anthropological Practice: Fieldwork and the Ethnographic Method*. In 2011 she was awarded the seal of Pilsen City and an honorary medal of West Bohemia University, the Czech Republic.

3

HUMOUR AS A MODE OF COGNITION

Elisabeth Hsu

It is surprising how little has been written about humour in anthropology and how limited our understanding of this social phenomenon is. Irony, of course, has been an attractive theme for post-modern anthropology, as it once was for linguistic pragmatics, and the recent outburst of writings in Caribbean, Francophone and also in Chinese literary and cultural studies would suggest (e.g. Chey and Milner Davis 2011). The comic, however, infuses daily life in many more subtle and unverbalized ways. Humour is 'one of the few basic social phenomena which occur in all groups throughout the course of human history' (Mulkay 1988: 1).[1] The functions of laughter as social control have long been recognized by anthropologists and sociologists (e.g. Billig 2005) but, rather than elaborating on this well-rehearsed theme, this chapter will point to a cognitive component of humour to date not much discussed.

Experiencing a situation as comic is both a very personal and very social event, uplifting and infectious at once. In addition, as will be argued in what follows, the comic can enhance, broaden and deepen human understanding in that it allows us to perceive a situation from more than a single point of view. This is why kings had fools who were expected to tell the truth but in a way that would at the same time elicit a disarming smile. The comic does not merely reveal the known that cannot be said, like the Emperor wearing no clothes; it also provides a means of inquiry, or a mode of cognition, that enables one to dare to embark on an attempt to comprehend the unknowable.

When speaking of what their social world considers 'unknowable', people often assume a humorous tone. To investigate the 'unknowable' in a direct way would be inadequate, preposterous, even blasphemous, while a predilection for the comic goes hand in hand with an appreciation for tensions and surprise, ambiguities, multiple perspectives and a potential annihilation of oneself. Some people, more than others, are drawn to the unknowable. They are driven towards questions for which commonly there are no answers, some of them questions that tend to be addressed in the realm of 'religion'. Yet, as we will see, questions generally considered 'religious in essence' need not be dealt with merely in religious institutions and theology. They have been addressed – in a humorous tone – in genres as disparate as those of medieval grammar and 'wisdom' literatures, African political speeches and riddles and ancient Chinese historiography.

Redeeming Laughter

Redeeming Laughter was written in retirement by a sociologist, Peter Berger (1997), known for his 'inimitable live tone and chuckle'.[2] The book cannot be relegated to a specific discipline. Berger (1997: x) says he had to improvise as he went along. Philosophers had been 'of only modest use': he mentions Plato and Aristotle, Cicero, Erasmus, Descartes, Molière, Hobbes, Kant, Hegel, Kierkegaard, Bergson, touches on Pascal and Baudelaire, and among the more recent philosophers discusses Joachim Ritter, Francis Jeanson and Marie Collins Swabey.

Berger foregrounds the so-called incongruity theory, saying that the comic can 'pop out' of what appears to be an 'ordinary box', referring to *Doppelbödigkeit*: it can hint at another reality in a way that is unexpected. Hence the comic can be experienced as slightly threatening,[3] but it has a 'cognitive component', he says (ibid.: 33–35) that resolves the tension. Berger builds here strongly on Swabey's insight that recognition of the comic can enhance one's intellectual capacities.[4] This insight is key to the discussion that follows. The comic can widen one's horizon of understanding, Berger says (ibid.: 65–86), or it can deepen it, particularly when one experiences the comic, like the sacred, as providing an entry into another 'reality'. The experience of the comic is not merely an emotional process and a matter of social control, Berger notes, it pertains also to the intellect. 'The question is', as he puts it, 'just what this intellectual or cognitive contribution of the comic is' (ibid.: 32).

Berger poses the question succinctly but his answers are not entirely satisfactory. The limitations would appear to lie in his modernist understanding of humanity as is evident from the structure of the book. In a modernist way Berger segregates 'The anatomy of the comic' (Part I) from 'Comic forms of expression' (Part II), namely benign humour, tragicomedy, wit and satire, and his Cartesianism has him discuss biological and cultural aspects of humour in separate chapters: 'The physiology and psychology of the comic' and 'The social construction of the comic'.

The third and final part of the book, which is entitled 'Toward a theology of the comic', discusses holy fools, as known particularly from the Christian orthodox tradition, and their 'folly as redemption'. Experience of the comic is likened to moments of transcendence. Berger does not take recourse to the word 'spirituality' and he does not say that such experience tends to be relegated into the religious realm but his writing gestures towards it. He notes, for instance, that being 'earnest' as opposed to 'funny' is characteristic of a modern sensibility. Such a 'distinctively modern comic sensibility' is 'witty, sardonic, very much detached' (ibid.: 215). Yet, for Berger, the capacity for experiencing the comic is not merely a superficial and marginal aspect of human life. Quite the contrary: experiencing the comic is a profound human experience.

Berger ends with a comment on 'faith', and its contribution to cognition in that it introduces a novel epistemological perspective on the everyday. Faith provides a different, 'metaempirical' way, he says (ibid.: 213), of comprehending the human condition. (However, by calling it 'meta-empirical', Berger implicitly hints at a lack of empiricist vigilance among those living in faith. Once again he thereby demonstrates that he is a modernist.) With his seminal book on the experience of the comic Berger obviously points in the right direction. But we will depend on other thinkers to be guided more deeply into the issues at stake.

To summarize, *Redeeming Laughter* is central to this discussion of humour as its author, Peter Berger, does not reduce the comic to a structural functionalist analysis but provides a rich and insightful account of the experience of the comic and the moments of incongruity that it produces in a person and/or a social setting. However, what if Berger had not reduced pre-modern and, particularly, medieval scholarship to the writings of a few philosophers whom he brushed aside all too soon (ibid.: 33): 'In classical and medieval philosophy discussions of the comic are few and far between, and where they occur they tend to deal with the moral issue of laughter (usually in a pejorative mode)'. As for so many enlightened modernists, medieval scholarship is merely of the Dark Ages, and is therefore thoroughly misunderstood. Yet in the following section we will see that medieval scholarship, with its commitment to theology, commented on faith and the otherworldly with wit and profundity.

Virgilius Maro Grammaticus and Word Play

In her study of Virgilius Maro Grammaticus (seventh century CE), Vivien Law (1995) speaks of 'word play' rather than 'puns'. She does not explain why but one can easily guess: in common parlance today puns are associated with nursery rhymes and political satire. In other words, even for the medievalist, the word pun conjures up certain modernist associations. Puns belong for instance among the 'art of memory', which in medieval times consisted of very sophisticated techniques indeed (e.g. Carruthers 1990). In other words, puns are in a modernist's mind associated with either ephemeral, superficial and childlike ways of having fun or celebrated as a notable mnemonic technique now superseded by computer technology.

Vivien Law's take on word play and puns is different. She guides us through a reading of a treatise that was brought to her attention as a historian of linguistics because it presented itself as a Latin grammar. However, as the secondary literature on this treatise had already noted, it was a perplexing one. Some analysts doubted its author's command of Latin, which, as they said, should not be surprising in view of his peripheral provenance, Ireland; others questioned his knowledge of grammar. Vivien Law took a different stance in that she took Virgilius Maro's voice at face value: 'All we can do is to listen for hints from the author as to how to read his work. If their application provides a consistent reading, then we may be on the right track' (Law 1995: 11). However, the reader soon notes that this leads to the question: 'Which of his [Virgilius Maro's] statements are sincere, which tongue-in-cheek?' (ibid.: 11). We learn of his playful predilection for wisdom by 'simultaneously hinting at its presence and concealing its features' (ibid.: 35).

By treating punning as 'word play', Law foregrounds the notion of play. In contrast to humour, play has received due attention in the anthropological literature. Huizinga's (1955) *Homo Ludens* makes play to a basic human activity,[5] and Bateson (1972) underlines that adult human beings, as well as children, have play in common with animals. Accordingly, all ritual activity could be framed as a form of play. Indeed, as Kapferer (2004: 37–39) points out, we owe it to Victor Turner that we consider ritual today not merely a social form that consolidates power and the Durkheimian 'collective representations' but also as a form of action that provides a space for creativity and change. Rites are now seen as being 'technically' involved with 'self formation', they are 'pragmatically oriented' and both develop and exploit 'particular symbolic formations', so as to 'shape human perception and thereby transform experience' (ibid.). Insights like those of Bateson, Turner and Kapferer, derive from an anthropological analysis of ritual but they may as well apply to play and word play.

Virgilius Maro's word play then becomes comparable to the medieval commentaries on the 'wound of Christ', which, as Caroline Bynum (2011: 195–208, figures 44–48) shows, are manifest in paintings of the crucifixion, in stylized graphic emblems, in talismans and sculptures, woven into and printed onto textiles that were used in the context of birthing. The wound is here related to the death of Christ for the life of humanity. It conveys the hope of resurrection and the pain surrounding the processes of dying and birthing more generally. The wound of Christ is emblematic of the sorrows of the human condition and, by turning the slit of the wound from the horizontal to the vertical position, surely also of the joy of making life. The texts investigated, the drawings and sculptures, woven cloths and textile prints all seem to comment, from different angles, playfully, on the mystery of life as comprehended through the faith in the 'wound of Christ'.

To call these titillating approximations of the mystery of life, and its making, a form of 'punning' comes across as irreverent to the modern reader. However, this seems to be precisely what motivated their artful creation. This playfulness follows certain rules, as Law is able to demonstrate in regard of Virgilius Maro's exposition with great sensitivity and scholarly knowledge of the period. As the discussion of this medieval text proceeds, the reader finds herself embroiled in a detective story that rivals Umberto Eco's *Name of the Rose* which coalesced around the loss of Aristotle's second book of *Poetics* and – fitting to the discussion here – supposedly was on laughter. The difference is that Law's scholarly text is just as gripping and does not reproduce the usual modernist assumption about laughing in medieval times.

The goal of the scholar, Law tells us, was not to be reductionist and aim to find one correct interpretation through the exclusion of others. Rather, human understanding was thought to be enhanced and deepened, through a multiplication of interpretations. Importantly, those multiple interpretations should not be seen as paralleling each other, but as interpenetrating and interlacing with each other. Virgilius Maro's playful style leads us into an ever more complex and complicated world of thought experimentation, peppered with paradoxes hinting at the unfathomable: 'Far from being mutually exclusive, … various interpretations existed simultaneously, enriching the reader's understanding with their interpenetrating levels of meaning' (Law 1995: 4).

What is this word play all about, and why is it relevant to the discussion of humour? The answer lies in the genre with which Law eventually identifies this text. In this genre the voice alternates between tongue-in-cheek and matter-of-fact statements. It is brim-full with humorous word play. It plays on irony by stating the blatantly wrong and by overdoing what should be done (e.g. when authoritative texts are excessively quoted and exuberantly acknowledged). Law traces the anomalous structural elements to the medieval genre of wisdom literature.

To a modernist wisdom is an earnest and serious matter. Wisdom is considered one of the few aspects of human perception and cognition that – as contemporary psychologists found (Grossmann et al. 2010) – increases with age, in contrast to other capacities like hearing, seeing or memorizing that are well-known to decline. If anything, wittiness might be humorous. Wittiness in Oscar Wilde where language use becomes an intellectual game. Clearly, the wit and wittiness in a nineteenth-century author is not to be confused with the wit that the medieval wisdom literature aimed to cultivate. Virgilius Maro's parodies and word play were tongue-in-cheek but nevertheless all about wit and wisdom.

Wit in medieval times was about the comprehension of God and his world. Rather, wit referred to a faculty that could be enhanced through assiduous training. The conviction was that 'the daily practice of reading brings with it an increase in the acuteness of one's intelligence' (Virgilius Maro, cited in Law 1995: 41). The incongruities that philosophers and other authors dealing with humour have identified as one of its defining features abound in the word play of the medieval wisdom literature. They sharpen one's wit.

Puzzlement is Edifying

The idea that word play has a cognitive component is by no means limited to medieval Europe. James Fernandez (1980), who worked among the Fang in West Africa, speaks less of word play as a means of sharpening the acuity of one's wit than of its ability to be 'cosmogonic' in that it can 'edify' the collectivity of the listeners. The word play that constituted the sermons of the Bwiti movement leaders, and also the riddles of the Fang and Kpelle more generally, would result in what Fernandez called 'edification' – 'an emergent sense of a larger meaningful whole' (Fernandez 1980: 53).

The interpretive task, Fernandez suggested, consisted in providing context for the text. The meaning of the 'subtle words' had to be inferred from their cultural embedding and situational circumstance. The obligation to contextualize these words was much greater than textual interpretation generally requires, he maintained, because there is 'a lack of expository and didactic aids'. By speaking of 'a lack' he evidently aimed to make himself understood by a modernist audience, that of Western anthropologists, anticipating that they would consider the Bwiti sermons 'diffuse and spontaneous in the extreme' (ibid.). In his analysis, however, the sequence of images these sermons evoked – body images, forest images, suspended things images, food images, and the like – linked together cultural experiences from a whole variety of different domains. The sermons were 'cosmogonic', he explained, in so far as 'a cosmological integrity is suggested if not made explicit' (ibid.: 53–54).

(Anyone who works on literary Chinese texts of Chinese antiquity will recognize the peculiarities of the interpretive task that Fernandez refers to when emphasizing that word meaning depends on context. However, the suggestion that the constitution of word meaning by this constant back-and-forth movement between text and context has a cosmogonic function has to my knowledge not been emphasized in Chinese studies. Yet it is instantly appealing. In particular, it provides purpose to the editors who compiled texts from different provenances by juxtaposing them: they were involved in a cosmogonic activity!)

To explain in more detail the edification through puzzlement that these Bwiti movement sermons effected, Fernandez analyses word play in riddles. Riddles connect the phenomena of the world in two ways, he says. They play on, first, the metaphoric relation of a word (which emphasizes similarity) and, second, its metonymic relation (which stresses contiguity). Thus, if the riddle is: 'long legs, sharp thighs, no neck, big eyes', the feeling of edification in the answer 'scissors' derives from finding a common structure. This happens when metaphor is transformed into metonym, such that human body parts and scissors belong to one world. The transformation of contiguities into similarities, and vice versa, is according to Fernandez, who reminds us here of Levi-Strauss (1966), 'fundamentally edifying' (ibid.: 49–50).

Nowadays, one hesitates to analyse reasoning in terms of metaphors and metonyms if the people themselves do not use this framework (and its implied ontologies) to think and theorize about their verbal interactions. However, Fernandez's analysis is key to our line of argumentation here: if the comic arises from a sense of incongruity, then it is constitutive of the tension provoked by the riddle, which these processes of transformation into belonging to one world will resolve. An incongruity that is experienced as comic accordingly emerges as an intrinsic prerequisite for edification. This is a much more radical view of the comic and its relation to cognition than the medieval understanding fleshed out above. Rather than seeing in the comic merely a medium through which we can approximate ultimate mystery, we may think of the comic itself as constitutive of such ultimate mysteries.

The comic as intrinsically constitutive of edification throws an entirely different light on riddles with sexual innuendo. We might be inclined to write them off as 'dirty jokes',[6] and so may have some medieval scholars in the Christian tradition (Law says little on this). However, among the Fang and Kpelle, the riddles with sexual innuendo are really about the ultimate mystery of life, the union of man and woman that results in the creation of new life. Fernandez notes this in his appraisal of Köngäs Maranda's work on Finnish riddles: 'In a Durkheimian manner Köngäs Maranda suggests that the final referent for riddles is to some basic aspect of human behavior – a kind of language in which a group talks of its most basic social action – the union of man and woman' (Fernandez 1980: 48).

With this in mind, let us return to medieval Europe. There is a sculpture of the fourteenth and fifteenth centuries, where three penises carry a vagina in procession (Bynum 2011: 204). Clearly, it is a pun on the 'Wound of Christ'. However, why is it so bawdy? Bynum mentions 'mockery of pilgrim hypocrisy' (ibid.: 204) and notes that 'it was quite possible for medieval devotees and critics to see – and use satirically – the sexual overtones of devotional objects' (ibid.: 205). However, if we free ourselves from our prudishness and transpose Fernandez' insight into medieval Christendom, humour relating to sexual union takes on an entirely different value. Puns of the kind need not only be seen as objects of parody and satire, and ridicule that causes shame. Rather they are about an inquiry into an ultimate truth, the creation of life. To conclude with Fernandez: 'All this [word play] is rarely done in an explicit manner. "By indirections find directions out"' (ibid.: 50). Needless to say, this applies particularly to the ultimate mystery of human flourishing.

Shi ji 史記, Chapter 105: Beyond Political Satire

Equipped with the insights into humour of the modernist Peter Berger, the medievalist scholars Vivien Law and Caroline Bynum, and the social anthropologists James Fernandez and Köngäs Maranda, let us now revisit my published work on a Memoir included in the first dynastic history of China, the *Shi ji* 史記 (Takigawa 1932–1934), about an ancient Chinese physician, Chunyu Yi 淳于意 (Hsu 2010). The text caught my attention because it seemed to me formulaic. At the time I took formulaic linguistic expression as a sign that the physician who wrote the case histories, Chunyu Yi, had a sense of being 'systematic' and that he was thus far being 'scientific'. In each case history he prognosticated whether the patient would die or not, and if he predicted recovery, he provided treatment. All the prognostications he reported on were correct, and all his treatments effective. Chunyu Yi seemed to reason according to a certain rationale and presented meticulous detail but I could not understand it. The study I embarked on was in part detective work to decode, and an exercise in learning how to read the medical rationale in the twenty-five medical case histories that his Memoir contained.

I noted that certain linguistic expressions were recurrent and introduced specific themes, which I identified as relating to the name of the disorder, to its cause and to tactile qualities of pulse diagnostic investigation. The main argument of my published work was that in the first ten cases the names of the disorder were determined not so much by the cause of the disorder (as they are supposed to be in contemporary Western biomedicine), as by the tactile qualities that the physician felt when he examined the vessel/pulse (*zhen mai* 診脈). I demonstrated in each of the ten cases that the different qualities of the *mai* 脈 correlated, in an additive fashion, with each of the constituent components in the name of a disorder.

One of the implications of my study is relevant for the design of health care today: we do not need to spend most of our energy on improving expensive diagnostic devices in order to know what happened to a patient in the past. Rather, strategies of treatment matter and it is of utmost importance to identify the potential that the present holds for future well-being (among which the socially complex process of agreeing upon a 'cause' of an illness may belong). By engaging in a tactile diagnostic practice and claiming that touch attends to the present, I argued that the ancient doctor Chunyu Yi aimed to identify bodily processes of the present with a view to the future.

Why did I focus on cases 1–10? Their narrative structure and the medical rationale they contained was fairly consistent. Furthermore, they called for a humorous reading: cases 1–10 contained evident political satire. For instance, in eight out of ten cases, which mostly concerned the nobility of Qi 齊, 'wine and women' were mentioned as the cause of the disorder. This pointed to debauchery at the court of the famous and once powerful kingdom of Qi in Eastern China.

Considering that these medical case histories have been handed down to us today in a chapter of China's first dynastic history, it seemed likely that they had been included in this work to bring across a political message but coded in medical jargon.

Humour, I claim, in its various forms, is integral to several parts of this text; it may be situational or has been packaged into standard linguistic forms of word play. A careful reading of this word play can be used for text critical studies (see Hsu forthcoming), and makes it possible to reconfirm differences in narrative culture between cases 1–10 versus cases 11–25, the latter in all likelihood being edited by another editor than the first ten. This does not mean that cases 1–10 form a unity; they differ from one another in many ways that remain unexplained. Nevertheless, certain ordering features can be identified. For instance, they come in pairs: 1 and 2, 3 and 4, 5 and 9, 6 and 10, 7 and 8. Furthermore, all contain textual materials that can be shown to implicitly refer to a bipartite *yin yang* body as conceived in pre-Imperial feudal China, where sentiment and distemper among the nobility seem to have been of foremost concern to learned physicians (Hsu 2008–2009).

Thus, cases 1 and 2 discuss a disorder in the lower *yin* 陰 and upper *yang* 陽 parts of the bipartite *yin yang* body. In the extant *Shi ji* text these are disorders of the liver and heart respectively. Cases 3 and 4 form another *yin yang* pair, referring to a disorder of excessive coldness and heat respectively, which results in either a congealment or a heating of the bodily waters. Cases 6 and 10 also form a pair based on a third century BCE conception of the body, namely that a hard external form (*xing* 形) contains the elusive *qi* 氣 inside the body. Case 6 concerns a collapse of the form (*xing*), case 10 a *qi* amassment in the abdomen. In current Chinese medical terms, they can be characterized as a depletion (*xu zheng* 虛証) and repletion pattern (*shi zheng* 實証). The reading of cases 6 and 10 in their extant form is particularly difficult because they both are textual composites.

The cases that in my reading are most thoroughly infused with the comic are cases 7 and 8 and particularly, cases 5 and 9. Cases 7 and 8 form a pair in that they concern Qi nobility who die from constipation and diarrhoea respectively. It took me a long time to realize this, but when the penny finally dropped, I had to smile while sitting at my desk. In fact, this humorous interpretation reassured me that I was right, as now these two cases matched in tone the surrounding ones. However, unlike the others, the narrative in cases 7 and 8 is very repetitive and lacks the evocative imagery of the others. Moreover, cases 7 and 8 foreground divination methods for prognosticating death (as do the latter parts of cases 1 and 6), rather than reporting on successful treatment. In biomedical terms, cases 7 and 8 are about the digestive tract, rather than the urogenital system. Here the anthropology of humour reminds us that for some people dirty jokes can be about both, pooh and sex.

Cases 5 and 9 form a pair too in that they allude to a gendered *yin yang* body, and the humorous aspects in these two cases will preoccupy us in the remainder of this chapter. I have discussed these two cases already (Hsu 2007), and interpreted moments in them as containing the political satire with which the second-century BCE editor Sima Qian 司馬遷 seems to have imbued all of the first ten cases (Hsu 2010). However, in the course of reflecting on the anthropology of humour, I realized that these two cases differ from the other eight in that humour infuses them in each and every aspect. To be sure, there is word play that one can trace to an editorially introduced parody, and I will discuss it, so my former reading was not entirely wrong. However, the many comic moments that are constitutive of the two cases 5 and 9 would suggest that we are dealing here with an attempt to approximate an 'ultimate mystery' of the body politic and its perpetuation, namely the fecundity of royalty.

Speaking Tongue-in-Cheek about the Fecundity of Royalty

In the medical cases 5 and 9 (see translation in appendix) the discussion of the disorder's cause, name and treatment contains an instance of the comic. In both cases the cause of the disorder is given as sweating, which is somewhat surprising. Sweating is usually considered a symptom of a sickness, not its cause. To think of royalty dripping from sweat, like a peasant toiling his fields, creates an incongruity that was certainly meant to be comic. The activities royalty busied itself with were evidently hard work (*lao* 勞), and indeed the expenditure of sexual energies has been categorized as labour, *lao*, throughout the history of Chinese medicine to the present day. Accordingly, effecting a sexual union would be a rank-specific form of labour. The mood in which this is said is surely tongue-in-cheek, as though truths of the kind can be cognized only in this way.

In case 5, which concerns the queen dowager of Qi, the illness was caused by profuse sweating and a subsequent drying up due to an excessive exposure to *yang* and in case 9, the king of Jibei 濟北 suffers from what one would call today a *yang* depletion, due to an excessive exposure to *yin*. These *yin yang* bodies were presumably bodies that are easily affected by moral sentiment (Hsu 2008–2009) and the excessive *yin* and *yang* exposures are likely to have been erotic indulgences with the opposite sex. However, in the subsequent clause, after the one that mentions profuse sweating as cause of the disorder, additional information relating to an ecological aetiology is given, These added clauses explain that the excessive *yang* the queen dowager suffered from arose from exposure to sunlight and the king's excessive *yin* came from lying prostrate on the ground. They allude to an ecologically delicate body sensitive to sun light and earthy dampness by emphasizing the ecological aspects of the cosmological *yang* heaven and *yin* earth, and make the reading of excessive erotic exposure to the opposite sex seem unlikely.

However, the anthropology of humour, combined with the above text critical consideration, reinforce the reading of these clauses as commentatorial additions of a later period than that of the third and early second century BCE.

The disorder that the queen dowager suffered from is called *feng dan ke pao* 風癉客脬 and that of the king *feng jue* 風蹶. We do not know what these terms designate but I have approximated them in translation as meaning, in the case of *dan ke pao* 癉客脬, 'fatigue/lassitude is visiting the bladder' and, in the case of *jue* 蹶, 'numbness'. Furthermore, both have the prefix *feng* 風 which means 'wind'. I will return to *feng* later but let me here discuss *dan* 癉 and *jue*, as those terms are well-known names for disorders in the early and canonical medical literature. The word *dan* is a very old one, and refers to feelings of utter exhaustion and listlessness, and to a longing and lassitude that accompanies love sickness.[7] The word *jue* is old too, and refers to a situation past one's prime, an attenuation of one's strength or an 'inversion' of *yin* and *yang*. The terms *dan* and *jue* reconfirm – tongue-in-cheek – that royalty has overexerted itself and is in a state of utter exhaustion and impotence.

Likewise, the treatment that restored royalty back to health has a humorous note. The treatment can be read as being gender specific: the woman drinks a 'tea', the man a beer. The queen dowager recovers after drinking twice *huo ji tang* 火齊湯, which, in consideration of Yamada Keiji (1998), I propose to translate as 'a broth prepared through a careful regulation of fire'.[8] The king of Jibei recovers after drinking a *yao jiu* 藥酒, an alcoholic drink which presumably contained macerated medicinal drugs. In antiquity only kings and sages enjoyed the privilege of drinking *yao jiu*. Accordingly, this aspect of the medical treatment would have enhanced the king's royal status and social standing. The king had to drink three 'stones' of it, which according to a commentator was a great deal, but possible (3 x 20 litres?). Drinking such quantities of alcohol no doubt reconfirmed the king in his masculinity. The final cure was to wash out the excessive *yin* that lodged in his body. He did it, as it eventually dawned on me, by means of urination. The king's greatness was thereby once again reconfirmed, as in my reading, he did it by 'roaring' loudly (like a waterfall). The humour in the recounting of the king of Jibei's recovery is situational and not contained in a linguistic demonstrable form. So, for a textual scholar it is difficult to believe that my reading is accurate; all the more so, as commentators of the last 2000 years interpreted this corrupt passage in an entirely different way. However, from the perspective of the anthropology of humour it makes good sense.

In summary, cases 5 and 9 stand out in that they are suffused with a subtle humour. First, we pointed to the tongue-in-cheek remarks regarding aetiology: sweating from physical 'labour'. Second, we noted that the names of the disorders *dan* and *jue* both underline the plight of royals. Third, regarding the treatment, which was gender-specific, the king's treatment had a comic aspect which hyperbolically enhanced his masculinity and greatness. Evidently the two cases are thoroughly infused with the comic. Is this a parody of privilege? Yes, it certainly is, but it is not only that. The tongue-in-cheek manner of telling the plight of royalty was not merely a cynical comment on the feudal body politic in Eastern China but reminds us also of the medieval wisdom literature and the riddles among the West African Fang: humour is the requisite mode of cognition when it comes to a mystery of life such as, here, the fecundity of royalty.

Finally, the prefix *feng* (wind) occurs in the names of both disorders. To any reader since medieval times, *feng* instantly evokes the idea of madness, irregularity and irresponsibility. This is indeed what this prefix may have evoked in many a reader, particularly in Late Imperial China. If a king suffered from a disorder that was wind-induced, surely this meant that he was out of his mind and his kingdom in disarray. However, in Chinese antiquity the term *feng* also connotes regularity and recurrent seasonal change. It refers to age-old custom, regional climate and local conduct. In the manuscript texts from Mawangdui 馬王堆 and Zhangjiashan 張家山 from the second century BCE, rising heat in the *yang* brightness vessel (*yang ming zhi mai* 陽明之脈) resulted in madness. So in these third- and second-century BCE medical texts madness was not primarily thought to be wind-induced.[9]

In early China, the concept of wind had yet another connotation. Roel Sterckx comments: 'Perhaps the earliest occurrence of "wind" expressing mutual attraction between male and female species occurs in a passage in the *Zuozhuan* … Other texts link wind with the idea of "germination" (*meng* 萌), and present insects (*chong* 蟲) as the seminal essence of wind' (Sterckx 2002: 179).

So, the fecundity of royalty was here being likened to that of insects! From a cross-cultural perspective, it makes perfect sense that ancient Chinese royalty, just like an African village chief or a sultan of the Ottoman Empire, should be preoccupied with fecundity and the production of offspring (with the help of many wives). This is a serious and prestigious matter, but instantiating the unequal standing between kings and insects was surely meant to conjure up an incongruity that is comic.

Making Fun of Medics: The Editor's Parody

Yet another humorous element is packed into cases 5 and 9 but it is of a different order. It comes across as a joke. In order to get the point, it needs to be sketched out in the following few paragraphs. It is about this prefix *feng*, which means wind. In case 5 the name of the disorder is *feng dan ke pao*, in case 9 it is *feng jue*. It is made up of three constitutive nouns in case 5, namely *feng, dan, pao*, and of two, *feng* and *jue*, in case 9. According to the schema of the medical rationale I presented above, the three nouns in case 5 should correlate with three qualities of *mai* and the two nouns in case 9 with two qualities of *mai*. The qualities of *mai* I identified on the basis of text structural criteria are *feng qi* 風氣, *shi* 溼

and 'the opening of the major *yin*' in case 5, and *feng qi* and *zhuo* 濁 in case 9. In case 5 the *mai* feels *shi*, moist, and in case 9 it feels *zhuo*, murky. The *mai* that is moist (probably from perspiration) must have been indicative of the queen dowager's *dan* disorder of utter exhaustion and the *mai* that is murky presumably indicates the king's *jue* disorder, which, as established above, consists of an attenuation if not an inversion of his potency. In case 5, the moist is felt at a certain place, namely the opening of the major *yin*, and the *dan* disorder lodges (*ke*) in a certain place, namely the bladder called *pao* 脬. So, the 'opening of the major *yin*' probably correlates with *pao*, the bladder (this is a correlation that makes sense to anyone familiar with alchemical thought in China, where the major *yin* and the kidney/bladder both correlate with water and hence also with each other).

The difficulties in textual exegesis are at this stage not yet over. The problem that now arises is that neither the pulse quality *shi*, moist, nor *zhuo*, murky, is a standard one in the Chinese medical literature, past or present. One could stop the analysis here and say that everything is inconclusive and nothing more can be said with any reasonable certainty about this text. Or, one could argue, as I have done, that these pulse qualities were common medical terms in antiquity but fell into oblivion later in Imperial times. I have shown with regard to all *mai* mentioned in cases 1–10 that the different *mai* have an iconic-indexical quality that they share with the disorders they indicate.

In cases 5 and 9 the disorders in question are *dan* and *jue*. In order to make the *mai* that feels moist, *shi* (presumably due to droplets of perspiration on the skin), stand in an iconic-indexical relation to the disorder *dan*, one has to surmise that physical labour, which caused sweating, resulted in lassitude and longing. Once one has made this connection, the reading is plausible: the quality of *mai* is moist from sweating and due to the activity that caused the sweating the patient is now in a state of listlessness and utter exhaustion. The relation between the moist and the lassitude is indexical-iconic: both connote *yin* and immobility.

The pulse quality *zhuo*, which is given as a pulse quality in the extant text (not without causing puzzlement to the commentators), is a cosmological term, an opposite of *qing* 清, clear. The terms *zhuo* and *qing* are sometimes used in place of *yin* and *yang*.[10] We are here reminded that *jue* refers to an inversion of *yin* and *yang*, or an attenuation, in case 9, of *yang*. So, we can appreciate a possible indexical-iconic affinity between the pulse quality *zhuo* and the name of the disorder *jue*, insofar as both implicitly allude to a *yin yang* cosmology. So, by means of these complicated learned medical considerations we may now conclude, after a lengthy step by step procedure, that a moist *shi mai* may indeed have indicated *dan*-fatigue in the queen dowager and a murky *zhuo mai* a state of complete *jue*-numbness in the king.

However, when we look at the disorder name's prefix *feng* in cases 5 and 9, we find that it correlates in a very straightforward way with the pulse quality *feng qi*: a windy pulse indicates a wind-induced disorder. Vow, how simple: *feng* correlates with *feng*! We have just been preparing ourselves for yet another complicated exegesis and we find that *feng qi* indicates *feng*. This finding is a bit deflating. It surely must be a joke! It comes across as a parody of complicated scholarly medical reasoning. It is for this reason that I postulate that the prefix *feng* was added by an editor who used the term not in the sense it has had in medicine since medieval times but in the sense it generally had in antiquity: fecundity.[11]

Is it perhaps the case that *dan ke pao* and *jue* were medical terms that a physician used, and that we should read the extant text in a humorous way and interpret the prefix *feng* in the disorders *feng dan ke pao* and *feng jue* as a tongue-in-cheek editorial addition? Accordingly, there would have been a primary document written by a scholarly medical doctor, and the prefix *feng* would have been added by a historian-cum-editor who was just as learned, say Sima Qian, whose word play made fun both of royalty's preoccupation with fecundity and of inflated medical reasoning.

Discussion

Some people value in the humorous primarily the light-hearted and funny but the comic also contains within it a deeper cognitive component. We saw that Virgilius Maro Grammaticus' word play in medieval times centres on matters so profound that it is difficult to fathom them. The wit and wisdom he seeks is infused with creation's mystery and, ultimately, God. Similarly, the imagery that the sermons of the Bwiti leaders among the Fang in West Africa evoked was playful and spontaneous. And it was cosmogonic: the world it created provided a foundation for their social movement.

Finally, cases 1–10 in the *Shi ji*, chapter 105, had elements of the comic that have gripped my imagination for over two decades. Every summer I came afresh to them, I saw more in them. We need not deny that these cases which alluded to debauchery at court had an edge of political satire but the insight Fernandez gained vis-à-vis the riddles of the Fang and Kpelle draws attention to deeper aspects of humour. The sense of incongruity that they bring about often appears as the only way to approximate the ultimately unknowable, not least, the ultimate mystery of life and its making.

The anthropology of humour has provided a framework for making sense of my reading of Chunyu Yi's Memoir as imbued with sexual innuendo. In particular, cases 5 and 9, which tongue-in-cheek discuss fecundity, contain, as well as satire, deeper, previously unacknowledged meanings of the humorous.

Appendix

[Case 5]

The queen dowager of the King of Qi fell ill. They summoned your servant, Yi. I entered [the palace] to examine the *mai*. I said: 'A wind-induced condition caused by overexertion is visiting the bladder. One has difficulties with defecating and urinating, and the urine is dark.' Your servant, Yi, had her drink the broth prepared by careful regulation of fire. After drinking the first dose, she immediately could urinate and defecate. After drinking the second, the illness ceased. She urinated as before. The illness was contracted because while dripping with sweat, she went outside to dry up. In cases of drying up, having removed one's clothes, the sweat dries in the sunlight.

The means whereby I recognized the illness of the queen dowager of the King of Qi were that when your servant, Yi, examined her *mai*, and when I palpated the opening of the major *yin*, it was moist. In spite of this there was wind *qi*. The 'Model of the Pulse' says: 'In cases where when as one sinks [into the *mai*], it is very firm, and when as one floats [on the surface of the *mai*], it is very tight, the host of the disorder resides in the kidneys.' When I pressed onto the kidneys, it was the other way round. The *mai* was large, yet hurried. In cases when it is large, it is *qi* [coming] from the bladder. In cases when it is hurried, the interior has heat and the urine is dark, see Takigawa (1934, chapter 105: 31–32).

[Case 9]

The King of Jibei fell ill. They summoned your servant, Yi. I examined his *mai*. I said: 'A wind-induced numbness/inversion. The chest feels full.' Forthwith, I prepared a drugged wine. After drinking three times twenty litres, the illness ceased. He contracted it from sweating and lying prostrate on the ground.

The means whereby I recognized the illness of the king of Jibei were that at the time when your servant, Yi, palpated his *mai*, it was wind *qi*. The *mai* [coming] from the heart was murky. According to the 'Model of Disorders', if one excessively makes one's *yang* enter, then, while the *yang qi* is exhausted, the *yin qi* enters. If the *yin qi* enters and expands, then, while the cold *qi* ascends, the hot *qi* descends. Hence the chest feels full. As for the sweating and lying prostrate on the ground, when I pressed onto his *mai*, the *qi* was *yin*. In cases of *yin qi*, the illness must have entered and struck the interior. When one expels it, it reaches a degree of roaring water, see Takigawa (1934, chapter 105: 37–38).

Acknowledgements

This piece is dedicated to Vivien Law in memory of our bedside conversations in the winter of 1987–1988. I also thank Caroline Bynum for encouraging feedback.

Notes

1   Most authors writing on humour claim it is a uniquely human capacity, but ethologi-
    cal research on the Bonobo shows that they play, smile and laugh (Isabel Behncke,
    personal communication, 2010). Unmitigated anthropological thinking is bound to
    break down the boundaries between humans and animals (Ingold 2000).
2   See appreciative comments about the author on the book's cover page.
3   We are reminded here, with Desmond Morris (1967), that smiling is derived from a
    threatening grimace, i.e. a showing of one's teeth, to let the other know one's strength
    (the cognitive component), but only momentarily. Hence a smile is ultimately
    disarming.
4   Accordingly, she notes, 'comic laughter' should be distinguished from other types of
    laughter (e.g. ridicule, embarrassment, etc.).
5   Huizinga (1955) outlines three basic features of play: all play is 'voluntary'; it is 'not
    ordinary life'; it has its 'own course and meaning'.
6   Mulkay notes: 'Humor is often employed to deal with topics, such as sexuality,
    which are important, but which are also difficult to handle openly …' (1988: 120).
    As so many do, he underlines the social function of dirty jokes (their use for trans-
    mitting information and shaping gender relations), but misses out on the point
    made here.
7   This latter meaning is given in the *Book of Odes*, where in the extant text *dan* 單
    is written with a heart radical (Hsu 2010: 214), but before the first century to the
    second century CE the characters had no radicals.
8   Yamada (1998) considers *huo ji tang* a proto-type I decoction, i.e. a precursor of the
    decoction used in contemporary Chinese medical treatment which is prepared by
    simmering over a carefully regulated fire. Given that the first treatise on tea dates to
    the Tang dynasty (618–907), 'tea' has here rhetorical rather than referential mean-
    ings. So does the idiom 'wine and women' (see Hsu 2010).
9   This argument draws on Shigehisa Kuriyama, Chen Hsiufen and Mark Lewis, as
    detailed in Hsu (2007).
10 In contrast to the turbid-clear distinction that any medical doctor has been familiar
    with since late Imperial times, where *yang* is clear and *yin* turbid or murky, in ancient
    China the murky was *yang* and the clear *yin* (Hsu 2010: 135–38), as in idioms like
    zhuo yang (murky *yang*), which (like *zhuo yin*, murky *yin*, and *qing yang*, clear *yang*)
    is mistakenly given in inverted form in Hsu (2007: 123).
11 A supercritical reader may note that in case 8 the constituent *feng* in the name of
    the disorder (which is *dong feng* 洞風) also correlates in this simplistic manner with
    feng qi as pulse quality. However, here the connotations of *feng* are much the same as
    elsewhere in the medical canons. No fecundity is connoted.

References

Bateson, G. 1972. 'Metalogue: About Games and Being Serious', in *Steps to an Ecology of Mind*. New York: Chandler, 14–20.

Berger, P. 1997. *Redeeming Laughter: The Comic Dimension of Human Experience*. Berlin: Walter de Gruyter.

Billig, M. 2005. *Laughter and Ridicule: Towards a Social Critique of Humour*. London: Sage.

Bynum, C.W. 2011. *Christian Materiality: An Essay on Religion in Late Medieval Europe*. New York: Zone Books.

Carruthers, M. 1990. *The Book of Memory: A Study of Memory in Medieval Culture*. Cambridge: Cambridge University Press.

Chey, J. and J. Milner Davis (eds). 2011. *Humour in Chinese Life and Letters: Classical and Traditional Approaches*. Hong Kong: Hong Kong University Press.

Fernandez, J. 1980. 'Edification by Puzzlement', in I. Karp and C.S. Bird (eds), *Explorations in African Systems of Thought*. Bloomington: Indiana University Press, 44–59.

Grossmann, I. et al. 2010. 'Reasoning about Social Conflicts Improves into Old Age', *Proceedings of the National Academy of Sciences* 107(16), 7246–50.

Hsu, E. 2007. 'The Experience of Wind in Early and Medieval Chinese Medicine', in E. Hsu and C. Low (eds), *Wind, Life, Health: Anthropological and Historical Approaches, Special Issue, Journal of the Royal Anthropological Institute*, S115–32.

———. 2008–2009. 'The Sentimental Body: Outward Form (*xing* 形) and Inward *qi* 氣 in Early Chinese Medicine', *Early China* 32, 103–24.

———. 2010. *Pulse Diagnosis in Early Chinese Medicine: The Telling Touch*. Cambridge: Cambridge University Press.

———. Forthcoming. 'Humour in the *Shiji*: Word Play as a Text Critical Device'.

Huizinga, J. 1955 [1939]. *Homo ludens: A Study of the Play-Element in Culture*. Boston: Beacon Press.

Ingold, T. 2000. *The Perception of the Environment. Essays on Livelihood, Dwelling and Skill*. London: Routledge.

Kapferer, B. 2004. 'Ritual Dynamics and Virtual Practice: Beyond Representation and Meaning', in G. Lindquist and D. Handelman (eds), *Special Issue: Ritual in Its Own Right: Exploring the Dynamics of Transformation, Social Analysis: The International Journal of Social and Cultural Practice* 48(2), 35–54.

Köngäs-Maranda, E. 1971. 'The Logic of Riddles', in E. Köngäs-Maranda and P. Maranda (eds), *Structural Analysis of Oral Tradition*. Philadelphia: University of Pennsylvania Press, 189–232.

Law, V. 1995. *Wisdom, Authority and Grammar in the Seventh Century: Decoding Virgilius Maro Grammaticus*. Cambridge: Cambridge University Press.

Levi-Strauss, C. 1966. *The Savage Mind*. Chicago: Chicago University Press.

Morris, D. 1967. *The Naked Ape: A Zoologist's Study of the Human Animal*. London: Jonathan Cape.

Mulkay, M. 1988. *On Humor: Its Nature and its Place in Modern Society*. Cambridge: Polity Press.

Sterckx, R. 2002. *The Animal and the Daemon in Early China*. Albany: SUNY Press.

Takigawa Kametaro (ed.). 1932–1934. *Shiki kaichu kosho* (Examination of the Collected Commentaries to the *Records of the Historian*). Tokyo: Toyo Bunka Gakuin.

Yamada, K. 1998. *The Origins of Acupuncture, Moxibustion and Decoction*. Kyoto: International Research Center for Japanese Studies.

Elisabeth Hsu is Professor in Anthropology at the University of Oxford and Fellow of Green Templeton College. She is co-editor of *Plants, Health and Healing* (2010) and *The Body in Balance: Humoral Medicines in Practice* (2013), both with Berghahn, and author of *Pulse Diagnosis in Early Chinese Medicine: The Telling Touch* (2010, Cambridge University Press).

4

COMIC STRIPS AND THE MAKINGS OF AMERICAN IDENTITY

Ian Rakoff

Introduction

In the beginning they called them the 'funnies', then the 'continuities' and the 'dailies' but what this chapter is about is hardly a laughing matter. In their development, which closely paralleled that of American identity, comics (words in balloons with pictures in sequential frames) at the same time supported and exposed a plethora of discomforting attitudes and patterns of behaviour, particularly to do with ethnicity and gender. Indeed, alongside the racial and sexual differentiating are a slew of visions of Caucasian masculine superiority. For decades the comic entered the average American household daily, with impunity. It was, arguably, one of the most potent and influential art forms of the twentieth century. What follows is the evidence forming the basis for, and the clarification of, the moral culpability of the culture that affected the mentality of the American mind.

Outcault and his Ethnic Conundrum

In 1895 the comic strip arrived and before long the selling of newspapers became reliant on these strip cartoons because they taught the immigrant masses English, the language essential for citizenship. It was the era of frontier mentality. Capitalism was finding its feet. Mass communication was the preserve of newspapers; and the next best thing to the presidency was the press baron. Immigration was set to be the making of the nation and the primer was the daily comic strip.

R.F. Outcault (1863–1928) created *The Yellow Kid*, an urchin in a smudged yellow smock who made witty comments on current affairs. This 1895 seminal double-panelled narrative is considered to be the first American comic; indeed, *The Yellow Kid*, a seven-year-old urchin in a yellow, filthy ankle-length smock, gave rise to the term 'yellow journalism'. From early on the snobs were sharpening their knives, looking down on the nascent art form.

The newspaper strip that Outcault came up with was a synthesis of Hogarth's *Gin Alley* misery and Dickensian social realism. This colourful word and image strip swiftly acquired a huge readership. The competition between the press barons shifted to the embryonic 'continuities'. Astutely, the press barons Hearst and Pulitzer retained ownership of copyright until 1910 when Bud Fisher (1885–1954), the author of *Mutt and Jeff* (1907–8), outmanoeuvred them with a minor duplicity. Wanting to elevate his social standing and win over the snobby 'better people', Outcault created *Pore Li'l Mose* (1900–1902), the fanciful adventures of a Victorian boy. However, *Mose* was black and the strip folded after a year. Taking the same idea but relocating the young boy to a white suburb, brought Outcault a lot of money; *Buster Brown* (1902), a whimsical child, with curly golden hair and reeking of privilege, was syndicated around the world.

By the first decade of the new century the grid formation of assembled rows of panels – having appeared intermittently since early *Yellow Kid* – was flourishing and well into its stride but the hoi polloi still wanted nothing to do with the comics. The social stigma, the prejudice attached to comics was well entrenched.

Winsor McCay – Fantasy and Perspective

In 1905 Winsor McCay (1869–1934) converted his nightmares into *Little Nemo in Slumberland* (1905), a comic fantasyland in colour on a weekend page. The exquisitely rendered adventures ended daily with *Nemo* tumbling out of bed roused by his mother's waking call. *Nemo* might be admirable art but the African stereotyping was distasteful. The depictions which the Victorians revelled in were gussied up with caricatures that set the standard for twentieth- century illustrative art and seeped into the minds and attitudes of the majority of people. *Little Nemo* covered the spectrum of prejudice and crass naiveté, from over-sized lips to obese chiefs in grass skirts with top hats practising cannibalism. Nevertheless, McCay's sequential sense heralded the grammar of the cinema. The exemplary narrative flow stood apart for years. Later, Alex Raymond's *Flash Gordon* might have been successful but it never matched the graphic vision of *Little Nemo*. *Flash* was inescapably trapped in the static illustrator tradition, often coming across as wooden. The 1930s serials and films interpreted *Flash Gordon* with risible parody. McCay was a pioneer of animation, making houses fly and dinosaurs dance.

Herriman – Genius without Peer

How *Krazy Kat* (1913–1944) lasted as long as it did is amazing. On the surface it seems too inaccessible to be recognized for what it is, superficially *Krazy Kat* resembles scribbles on a notepad gone berserk, the *Kat*'s got squiggles and sharp angles up against curves in the wrong places, and dialogue askew. Compare it to the mechanics of an impressionist painting; if you stand too close it becomes nothing more than senseless splashes and splotches. One needs the correct distance and the right frame of mind, then it falls into place; with *Krazy Kat* the curtain is lifted on the eternal triangular psychodrama locked in the dark recesses of the mind, as violence, jealousy and betrayal are portrayed as ordinary fare with a lightness of touch. With perverse pleasure the audience pry into the affections and obsessions of the emotions being paraded across the stage and from frame to frame as a dog, a cat and a mouse.

Krazy Kat survived only because of the newspaper mogul W.R. Hearst. Low circulation figures did not warrant its continuation but Hearst kept publishing *Krazy Kat*. What was behind it all? It dealt with psychology on a level that comics never did. The interior that's what it's about. But the comics don't go there, or are not supposed to. How does he feel about being a she? Who is she? What is she and what is he? And mostly what does he feel about her and she feel about him? What does the one left out want, and who deserves what? Those are the conundrums of the three characters, without mentioning indeterminate race. Nothing seems to matter as questions are asked but not answered; mesmerized, you sink into a plot which is mired in chaos at the end of the page. The action is located in a quixotic, ever-changing surreal landscape resembling Coconino County [Kokonino Kounty], Arizona. The genders are as blurred as the topography and the races are indecipherable, governed by witless authorities who can see nothing beyond the horizon. It is as impossible to decipher the mysteries of *KK* as it is to know what any dog, cat, mouse – or, indeed, another human being – is actually thinking. Nothing changes and everyone is interchangeable.

Bergman films also plumb the depths of interior psychology, dissecting and wringing out the emotions. Bergman's films go inwards, as deep as any academic theorist or novel might dare to venture and where few filmmakers are able to go. What Bergman creates is a living, moving cinema ruled by the violence of the heart and the anxiety of the mind, with the sense that there is more going on inside than outside. I would suggest that Bergman was a peer of *Krazy Kat*.

Krazy Kat creator George Herriman (1880–1944) never appeared in public without a hat. The newspaper industry was predominantly Caucasian and Christian, and Herriman's features hinted at otherness. On his birth certificate he was registered as Creole of Greek parentage. The otherness might have been reflected in his hair. Could anyone fault him for hiding something which could make him a target for prejudice? I don't think so. To get into, never mind get on in, cartooning, colour prejudice might easily have scuppered his chances, whether or not he was a brilliant talent; therefore, he kept his hat on because his hair was slightly crinkled which, combined with a Mediterranean complexion, was highly suggestive of otherness. It's a tragic reflection of those times. However, no matter how comparatively liberal the law, colour prejudice still persists robustly.

Mutt and Jeff – First Comic Strip Millionaire

One of the funniest strips of the early twentieth century was Bud Fisher's *Mutt and Jeff* (1907–8) – social realism though with stylized figures and influenced by vaudeville. In those days all syndicated comic strips were owned by the parent newspaper. No matter how often a strip was published (syndicated) the rights remained with the publisher, Pulitzer or Hearst mostly. Late one night Bud Fisher (1885–1954) strode over to the printing presses saying he needed to make a minor alteration to the plates. The next day 'Copyright 1907 by H. C. Fisher' appeared in small print in a corner of the daily strip. When Fisher transferred to a Hearst newspaper his previous publisher continued the strip with a different artist, as was customary. However, the signature proof of copyright left the publisher without a leg to stand on. The newspaper was legally obliged to stop publishing *Mutt and Jeff* as drawn by another artist. The precedent for copyright was secured and Bud Fisher was set to become the first comic strip millionaire.

There was something subversive about Bud Fisher which provides a clue as to how he went on to tackle the most contentious issue in 1910. The former world heavyweight boxing champion Jim Jeffries was coming out of retirement. Chronic gamblers Mutt and Jeff were crossing America to get to the title fight; day by day they progressed with little fuss. Balding little Jeff advanced cautiously while gangly Mutt blustered on thoughtlessly with an overdose of gusto. Ethnicity entered and left the frame often puzzling and questioning racism despite the humour accentuating racial stereotype. Initially one was often unsure as to what Fisher's daily strip was getting at.

The strip was so funny that one was tempted to forgive it anything, which is tantamount to declaring that humour can transcend anything and that laughter is the most contagious of all responses. Nevertheless, the implications of *Mutt and Jeff* seemed too farfetched to be credible and it was a delicately drawn fine line that Bud Fisher was precariously perched on. With hindsight one might see the Fisher approach as a pre-emptive strike, should the situation turn to litigation. Given the racist resentment prevailing since Jack Johnson won the world title in 1908, the journey to the fight of the century was nothing short of miraculous. The fever of the nation was aroused.

In their personal exchanges, Mutt and Jeff combined gambling with sadomasochism; in other words, between Simon Legree and Uncle Tom, or between

Figure 4.1: Usual stereotype, but bringing wit and colour into the funnies whereas others balked at any race presence. © by Star co. © Fisher circa 1910. Mutt & Jeff, post Johnson vs. Jeffries.

the big bully and the benign victim. Often it was small Jeff's slowly engaged but sharp intellect that won the day. The race issue slipped in repeatedly, with the big bigot Mutt versus the little egalitarian Jeff. Jack Johnson's propensity for flashy sports cars, combined with his penchant for white women and his often cruel sentiment in the ring when he prolonged knocking out opponents when he could do so. This sentiment of racial revenge enraged the colour conscious white promoters of race hatred. Many of Johnson's ilk were unhappy about their champion, feeling that his behaviour set back the cause of integration by years. The fight of the century, as the match was termed, was getting closer. Jim Jeffries, the undefeated retired world champion (1899–1905), was stepping back into the ring to uphold the supremacy of the white race.

Mutt and Jeff trudge onwards, doing odd jobs, pleading, prepared to do anything to make it to the ringside, despite being penniless. In race confrontations brassy Mutt comes a cropper whereas Jeff is rewarded for his natural anti-racist stance. Nonetheless, the reader does not believe they will make it. Whenever they appear to be making headway, something goes wrong. They lose their train tickets and get thrown off the last westbound train. They hitch a ride but thanks to Mutt's bigoted big mouth, they are dumped in the middle of nowhere. The luckless pair plod on hampered by the weather and Mutt's inept sense of direction: 'Followed daily, week after week, month after month the undaunted twosome pursue their seemingly hapless course, never doubting that somehow or other, despite the odds, they will get to watch the fight of the century'. They reach the stadium without tickets or money but Jeff is a cousin of the challenger, the Boilermaker. Mutt anticipates sitting with the hoi polloi but is ensconced

Figure 4.2: Jeff hides out in a bar.

as the only white man present in a packed stand. Curiously, the reader is not taken into the actual fight and at no time is it suggested who might win. The Boilermaker was knocked out in the fourteenth round, and Johnson's victory prompted riots and lynching. Jeffries dismissed the claim that in his prime he would have defeated Johnson; his praise for Johnson was unstinting.

The daily strip continues with the post-fight social perspective. Waiters and other menials made fortunes betting on Johnson and left work. Penniless Mutt blacks up in order to land a job as a waiter; embarrassingly, his first customer turns out to be Jeff. Desperate for money to get home Mutt enters a bar wearing a card in his hat announcing 'I bet on Jack Johnson' and aggrieved rednecks beat him up. In the following daily Mutt secures the Johnson card across Jeff's forehead and forces him into the next bar. But this turns out to be a black bar. Jeff emerges with a black friend and money to get home to the east coast. In Texas Johnson was arrested on a trumped up charge. Out on bail, he skipped the country and stayed in self-imposed exile for seven years. Johnson was demonized as a mindless brute but a contemporary sound recording reveals a suave intelligence.

The 'Great White Hope' did appear after the Johnson reign, but in the 'funny' papers rather than in the flesh: *Joe Palooka*, world heavyweight boxing champion. There was plenty to say about race attitudes surrounding *Palooka* but it was off the page, and concerned the author's friendship with Joe Louis and Sugar Ray, two of the greats! What isn't funny is what happened to the creator and his ghastly last round. Before we conclude the saga of the greatest fists in comic strip history, in the mid-1950s, we review racial interpretations in the decades between Jack Johnson and the end of Ham Fisher's *Joe Palooka*.

White and Black – Conforming and Non-conformity

In 1915 Henry Ford manufactured his one millionth motor and a few years later America saw the publication of the appropriate black-and-white daily strip. Frank King's *Gasoline Alley* (circa 1918) transformed the mundane, unthreatening day-to-day suburban existence, imbued with quiet heroism, into art. The car takes the lead, steered by amenable Walt who is available for both sides of any argument. Overweight Walt is the embodiment of what the strips aspired to: to offend no one, to show the impartiality of the American identity, to alienate nobody. It made perfect marketing sense. Comic strip creators were probably the wealthiest literati artists in American history during the first half of the twentieth century. The delicate art lay in sitting on the fence without seeming to do so.

The storyline meanders on, in a low-key way, until the adoption of a foundling, Skeezix, abandoned on Walt's doorstep in 1921. Then the strip takes off with a vigour that just avoids being puerile, with sporadic outbursts of drama. A highpoint of the 'continuity' is the arrival of a nurse, Rachel, who dispenses wisdom and perspicacity. The action of *Gasoline Alley* stretches over the decades in real time. After twenty years the foundling Skeezix is twenty years old. The mechanics of Nurse Rachel's appearance is similar to that of Richard Hannay in Alfred Hitchcock's film *The 39 Steps*, made in the mid-1930s, and also the opening of Milton Caniff's strip *Steve Canyon* in the late 1940s. Frame by frame we view parts without seeing the whole image, metonymy divided into four frames to a row.

With Hitchcock it is a sleeve, a shoulder, a pipe, someone greeting the advancing lens, a door being opened until finally we meet the coat, hat and pipe all in one: it is actor Robert Donat playing Richard Hannay. Steve Canyon's entry in the strip of his own name probably pays homage to Hitchcock, using the identical process. Writer/artist Milton Caniff might well be the finest exemplar of cinema in the comic book format. (Orson Wells was an admirer of Caniff.) Nonetheless, neither Caniff's nor Wells's metonymy is as effective as Rachel's entry in *Gasoline Alley* in 1921. The strip (spread over two days) resonates with more gravitas than Hitchcock or Caniff because there is a motive behind the withholding of the revelation. It involves far more than merely the art of structure and editing.

Forced to engage with fatherhood, Walt the bachelor wants a nurse. Rachel, who has answered the advertisement, is a big matronly woman seen at first from behind, then from the side. Her features are obscured firstly by a broad hat as she walks in, then by the hood of a baby carriage and then by a kitchen cabinet door. When she is finally revealed, as she removes her hat and turns, we see that Rachel is black, a racial stereotype in keeping with the *Little Nemo* depictions in the first decade of the century.

To begin with Rachel the nurse features substantially in the strip and then, without any explanation, she is transformed from nurse to servant. Wide syndication was of paramount concern to the merchandising conscious Frank King. The majority taste governed the ratings and required that the strip, in order to garner mass appeal, be a bastion of Caucasian conformity, which meant bowing to popular prejudice. The stereotype ruled. King was very interested in marketing figurines and bric-a-brac from the *Alley*. His commercial aspirations were extensive and grew as the strip became more widely syndicated.

A Sensitive Star on the Black Horizon

In the late 1930s, the first African American woman cartoonist and formidable beauty, Jackie Ormes (1911–1985), began her cartooning career, during which she tackled contemporary issues generally ignored in white comic strips. By the 1950s, major problems – such as pollution, environmental waste, injustice and prejudice – featured in her stories, and she stood firm when bullied by McCarthy's witch-hunting House Committee. She began with topical, raunchy gag panels. In the late 1940s her comic strip *Torchy in Heartbeats* was widely circulated in the black press. Her stories were adult oriented, open, honest, enthralling and fast paced. The sophistication of her narrative – often displaying the unfair plight of womanhood – was readily published in the black press, whereas, such material would probably not have been accepted in white newspapers. It was the black environment she described, but it differed little from the white environment; the settings and values were unquestionably American. She was accepted and she thrived but only in a segregated section of the world. The passions that film *noir* alluded to *Torchy* had on the page.

As a recognized celebrity Ormes mixed with stars like Count Basie and Duke Ellington. She too was a star. She launched a line of black dolls and designed their clothing. The dresses began as paper cut-outs adjacent to her cartoons but soon spilt over into the life-size world. *Torchy* crossed the colour line; a little white boy balks at being friendly with *Torchy*, as his parents have forbidden him to mix with anyone from that other place and she is black. Ormes tackled ethnicity issues without shoving anything in the reader's face or laying the blame on anyone. Had *Torchy in Heartbeats* crossed over into the white press, it would surely have contributed in a major way to the floundering American identity.

The Most Successful Syndicated Strip

There was no real answer to Jack Johnson until in 1928 when the fists of the blandest clean-cut hero *Joe Palooka* came to dominate the strip: the 'Great White

Hope' found his feet not on a real life canvas but during the late 1920s in the 'funnies'.[1] Ham Fisher, the writer/artist of *Joe Palooka*, was a fervent fight fan and he acquired an uncanny knowledge of the lore of the square ring, and thus created a proletarian fable. In the sports-crazed 1930s, his work compared favourably with the boxing journalism of Liebling, who coined the phrase 'the sweet science', with Budd Schulberg's *The Harder They Fall*, Nat Fleisher's boxing bible, *Ring Magazine*, and Robert Wise's film *noir The Set-up*. Ham Fisher's strip made readers feel involved and smile, if not laugh. He had a down-to-earth sense of story and a carnival of off-the-wall subsidiary characters. Previously, sports strips had failed. The spirit of Jack Johnson put the kibosh on any boxing 'continuities'. Even after he became a thing of the past Johnson continued to haunt social attitudes.

After getting *Palooka* into a few local papers in 1928 Ham Fisher persisted in punching above his weight and within a couple of years *Palooka* was coasting towards national syndication. The word *Palooka* is derived from Greek slang; it conjures up the image of a shuffling, punch-drunk veteran with cauliflower ears and slurred speech, the very opposite to the blond-haired clean-cut Joe Palooka. The strip originated with the *ingénu* store assistant, Joe Palooka, who is being outwitted by some conmen. They leave the store without paying. The outraged owner, Knobby, hits the roof. Joe charges out and Knobby witnesses Joe catching and beating up the thieves. Knobby persuades the reluctant Joe into becoming a professional boxer, with Knobby as his manager. Joe hates having to fight.

The widespread appeal of *Joe Palooka* was partly due to the idiosyncratic characters surrounding Joe, contrasted by Ann Howe, his blonde fiancée, who was bland, tepid, proper and stiff. She never altered not even when she became amnesiac after a plane crash. Her father was a wealthy cheese tycoon. Between blond Joe and blonde Ann the strip was awash with clichés and accompanied by an array of quirky and often shifty characters, with a certain Damon Runyon type wittiness and Brooklyn patois. Beneath the humour the strip was uncannily real, which might explain why it had such allure. It was also suffused with conformity: there was nothing in it which might rock the boat and Joe's patriotism was unquestionable. For a while, it was actively non-racist and incorporated a black character, Smokey, probably influenced by there having been two black world boxing champions. However that was to change.

As he become increasingly successful, Ham Fisher employed more assistants but kept on drawing the faces of all the characters. World boxing champions Joe Louis and Sugar Ray Robinson asked why Joe Palooka had only fought white opponents, to which Fisher answered that he couldn't draw a black person being beaten up, and Palooka had to win. To make up for the lack of any black opponents Fisher brought 'corner man' Smokey into the limelight. In 1938 when the heartbroken Joe fled the States to join the French Foreign Legion, Smokey went with him, as a genuine friend and equal. It was an exemplary anti-racist declaration.

Lost in the desert, they become prisoners of a portly Sheik who is a boxing fan. When Joe breaks his right hand in a bare-knuckle contest with the ferocious Assassin, Smokey remembers Joe's left uppercut in Seattle. The Assassin is knocked out and they win their freedom. When it is time for their departure from the hidden kingdom Joe advises Smokey to stay behind, telling him that he would have a better life in the desert kingdom than he could ever have in America. Loyal Smokey refuses to abandon his friend and they leave together, accompanied by the kidnapped heiress who has fallen in love with Palooka.

The drawing of Smokey was a ludicrous stereotype: thick lips and huge eyes with a rotund figure. The acceptance of such derisory caricature only began to wind down with the Second World War, the last segregated American war. In the approach to the Second World War Smokey was drawn taller, he lost his rotund shape and his thick lips, and the colour of his skin got lighter. By the time the war started Smokey was skinny and almost white but not enough for the segregated armed forces. Unlike the French Foreign Legion in 1938, Joe Palooka could not enlist and go to war side by side with a black companion. Joe signed up for Uncle Sam without Smokey. Instead he was accompanied by one of his most dubious friends, Jerry Leemy, a sharpie spiv from Brooklyn.

In 1943 Joe was on a North Africa goodwill tour, revisiting the desert kingdom of Ibi ben Abou where Joe had defeated the Assassin, thanks to Smokey. Now there was no Smokey. Instead there was Jerry, the big-mouth spiv from Brooklyn, a Caucasian. He had been with Joe and the Serbian guerrillas, fighting the Nazis in Montenegro; indeed, many newspaper strips supported the war effort in theory, but few were on the frontline like *Joe Palooka*. A return match with the Assassin is arranged with the proceeds going to the Red Cross. Since 1938 the Assassin has been taught the Queensbury rules by a German. A boxing ring is erected on the ground. Joe gets in with boxing gloves which are soon discarded. The starved, bestial Assassin wears spiked cestuses. Joe artfully ducks and the Assassin almost breaks his hands on the iron posts holding up the ropes. The shark-eyed neighbouring sheik, secretly a Nazi, is thwarted by Jerry.

In the 1940s Fisher developed diabetes and other ailments which left him more querulous. By that time, *Joe Palooka* was being syndicated in around 600 to 900 newspapers, not including overseas ones, while other statistics suggest a national daily readership of a 100 million in 4000 newspapers, Fisher was earning around $250,000 a year, with additional income from *Palooka* marketing, wireless and film. By either assessment *Joe Palooka* might have been the most successful of all the strips and was certainly the one which resonated most strongly with the national consciousness, together with Harold Gray's *Little Orphan Annie*.

How Palooka got Killed off

Something had been niggling at author Ham Fisher for years. At stake was the credibility of one of the foremost giants in the comic strip industry.

In the one corner was Al Capp, the fresh-faced raconteur with a scathing tongue, creator of *Li'l Abner*. In the opposite corner was Ham Fisher, the famed master of fisticuffs, creator of *Joe Palooka*. In 1933 Al Capp had assisted Fisher on a *Joe Palooka* hillbilly story. On leaving Fisher's studio, Capp took the idea with him and the following year launched his own hillbilly strip, *Li'l Abner*. Many of the characters (Daisy Mae), places (Dogpatch), events (Sadie Hawkins Day) and the loveable Schmoo entered the nation's psyche, getting some of the loudest laughs in strip history.

Ham Fisher's resentment over *Li'l Abner's* success increased as the strip's popularity grew. Had he tackled the situation immediately he might have stood a chance of winning a case for plagiarism, but by the 1950s it had become an ongoing, unresolved battle and Fisher saw defeat looming. Ridiculed by laughter and driven into his corner, the desperate Fisher pondered the last round, his final chance in the ongoing battle. In his frenzied state he doctored Capp's original *Li'l Abner* artwork: mouths were converted to vaginas and noses to penises. However, the courts rejected the crudely rendered, pornographic alterations and so did the Society of Cartoonists who saw nothing funny in them and evicted Fisher from the society. Ham went to the studio of his assistant Moe Leff who he had purloined from Capp, and shot himself. The strip died with the author.

Battling Kelly's Satirical Laughs

How *Pogo Possum* got away with its scathing depiction of McCarthyism stands as a testament to what one can get away with under the guise of humour. The humour is not quite as immediate or as graphic as Al Capp's but it digs deeper, has greater social relevance and enjoys a closer relationship with contemporary bluster. One could say that *Pogo* was the favourite of the political intellectual class, not only wrapped in wit but also oozing charm. It is a beguiling venture and one which it is almost impossible not to become entranced by. The Okefenokee Swamp where the strip is located is a long way from Dogpatch and even further from Disneyland.

The anthropomorphic strip features Albert, a sleazy alligator, and Pogo, an uncorrupted, ingenuous possum, as well as an assortment of habitués of the Okefenokee Swamp, who are a parody of humanity at its most absurd. Deftly woven into the intricate but flawless tapestry are characters such as the commie-hunting Senator Malarky, a swamp rat with a recognizable resemblance to McCarthy, Castro and Khrushchev. The comic was so eclectic that it was impossible to nail down, or maybe McCarthyism was too humourless to realize how unfunny the intentions behind *Pogo* were. Nevertheless, Kelly did appear in front of a House Committee on Juvenile Delinquency.

Pogo's characters enter and leave frame puffed up as if stepping on and off a stage. The names tell all: Dr Howland Owl, with his wizard's hat and scholarly glasses, struts about and indulges in crack-brained experiments; P.T. Bridgeport, the bear, tries to promote mind-boggling schemes; Beauregard, the retired blood-hound, epitome of veterans everywhere, constantly retells his wartime exploits; Churchy-la-Femme the turtle pokes about into everyone else's business; while Porky the porcupine shyly avoids all contact. By the 1950s, *Pogo* was met with laughter, but in the early 1940s it had an inglorious start not dissimilar to that of *Buster Brown* in 1901 when ethnicity was also at centre stage. Socially conscious and politically aware, Walt Kelly's strip got off to a creaky start. It fluctuated on the sidelines and nearly faded away when towards the end of the decade it became the darling of the thinking classes and inherited the mantel of the emotionally conscious *Krazy Kat* (George Herriman had passed away in 1944, taking his dystopian *Kat* with him to the grave).

The colourless landscape of the Okefenokee Swamp was hardly free of prejudice. Seldom had a more inappropriate name resonated so loudly. Initially the benign fur-ball lead of the strip was named Bumbazine, and it was failing badly. Only when the strip was renamed *Pogo* did it take off: Bumbazine sounded black and Pogo sounded white. It is of interest to recall that in 1902 the failure of black *Li'l Mose* was replaced by the success of the white *Buster Brown*.

The Sailor Man and the Poseur

Another funny contributor to the patina of the American identity was the one-eyed sailor who was a misshapen, spinach-guzzling precursor to the superhero, and who resolved every argument with 'I yam what I yam' and a terrific punch.

Perhaps the funniest 'funny' and one of the longest lasting strips was *Popeye*, originally, and at its most masterful, written and drawn by Elzie Crisler Segar. It was, more accurately, a brief continuity until the curt gags were extended into long-running stories beneath the masthead of *Thimble Theater*. Ever belligerent, squiffy-eyed Popeye, with his upside-down arms and muscles bulging in all the wrong places and girlfriend Olive Oyl, with equally spindly appendages, was the star in the firmament of popularity, outdoing even *Mickey Mouse* according to a 1930s children's survey.

Popeye artefacts and spinoffs became the largest licensing property of King Features (a unit of Hearst Corporation) for two generations. *Popeye's* market appeal owed a great deal to Wimpy, the masterly moocher and at times almost a co-star to the one-eyed sailor.

The *Popeye* characters were consistently well conceived, villains and heroes alike. The postures and shapes looked different but were of a type. There was an unfaltering homogeneity and a graphic style had been achieved. Olive Oyl, the imperfect companion, was demanding, and not above betrayal and deception. Wimpy, the overweight incorrigible human scavenger with an insatiable stomach, was an unapologetic scoundrel. Popeye might have been the star of the panoply of characters but Wimpy was an unforgettable close second.

The combination of distinctive graphics, excellent dialogue and inventive wittiness with an insatiable penchant for the prowess of spinach all swirling round Popeye's anti-social and rebellious stance, was unbeatable. Popeye the humorous subversive delighted in the virtues of his own absurdity. As an individual, the sailor man is on a par with Carl Barks' equally scandalous *Donald Duck*, the most anarchic, side-splitting character of them all. The American identity has a great deal to thank *Donald Duck* and *Popeye* the sailor man for. The ever hungry Wimpy lends himself to a host of literary comparisons, including Micawber, Sancho Panza, Papageno and Pangloss. It's no wonder that the Wimpy figurine sold so well. Whereas Popeye might stand alone at a lofty height, a sliver below is the lying Wimpy with his unpolished, philosophical observations, a proletarian moralist who sees truth as an alien concept. 'I yam what I yam and that's all I yam', Popeye asserted repeatedly. But it is the Wimpy dialogue that has reverberated most ardently:

> Thank you too much. … Let's you and him fight. … Come up to my house for a duck dinner – you bring the ducks… Will you join me in a lunch – on you…? Would you know where I could find $100,000…? Nice weather we're having, we're having…. You must have me confused with somebody, my name is Jones, I'm one of the Jones boys … I would gladly pay you Tuesday for a hamburger today…

Popeye was not able to fly but when he punched, the recipient could fly though brick and stone. Morally, Popeye was true to himself; buffeted by the bigotry of society and the snobbery of the times, his heroic mien was unshakeable and his stance incorruptible. He would bring a seemingly indestructible bully to submission by allowing his attacker to batter away as much as he wanted without defending himself. When the bully collapsed from exhaustion the undamaged sailor struck and he did more for spinach than anyone else.

When Popeye sailed onto an island and met a local tribe, not only were they stereotyped but they were doubly battered and abused by *Thimble Theatre* humour and by the sailor's unparalleled violence. Occasionally the sailor's stance and opinions altered, grudgingly, but towards the black stereotypes that crossed his path he was consistently vile, indefensibly so, even though this may have been in keeping with the tenor of the times.

Rude, Crude and Very Funny

In the department of the bizarre none can surpass the widely distributed, under-the-counter obscenities, the infamous *Tijuana Bibles* (aka the Eight-Pagers). With no artistic merit, boasting crudeness and revelling in irreverence, these dirty gems must have been an absolute joy in the Depression years. No big name in the movies, politics or comics was safe from the scurrilous *Bibles*, which were explicit and incredibly witty. Conscientiously crude, they were the equivalent of lavatory wall doodlings dedicated to debunking the famous. Gandhi and Winston both got taken down with equal indifference. Mickey even did it with Minnie Mouse and Popeye certainly went at it with Olive Oyl. Pants went down and skirts went up with great rapidity, accompanied by pleasurable exclamations. Even laconic Wimpey got it in somewhere with a pithy narrative and gymnastically inspired postures. What transpired between Little Orphan Annie and her dog Sandy is simply not repeatable.

This is hardly the forum to discuss whether they were purely pornographic or worthy erotica, for that would entail a long debate. The presentation always adhered to the sequential grammar of the comic strip, reduced to a regular series of eight equally sized frames printed on cheap card, stapled together, and tiny enough to be concealed in the palm of one's hand. Despite some feverish attempts at prosecution no one was arrested for producing the *Bibles*. They appeared everywhere, vanished and reappeared somewhere else, in the same smudged, thin cardboard format. Then suddenly the fad had passed and what remained became museum pieces and collectors' items.

Not a Laughing Matter – White Hope Usurps Africa

Although no contender for the humour strips, the impact of *Tarzan* on the American identity is undeniable and must be mentioned. What Rider Haggard launched, Edgar Rice Burroughs consolidated. *Tarzan*'s largest exposure after the novels and the movies was probably the comics. Was Tarzan the embodiment of American manhood, the benign colonial supremacist? What a concept, the white hero casting a shadow of superiority over the unenlightened continent! The cultural vacuum of hatred produced by Jack Johnson was responsible for innumerable manifestations of racism but one of the worst can be attributed to *Tarzan*, one of most potent of the contemporary works of fiction inspired by the climate of racism circa 1912 during the reign of the first African-American world heavyweight title holder, in effect creating the 'great white hope' lording it over black Africa, a seriously displeasing, provocative and insulting conceit that still flourishes with little apology and continuing insensitivity.

This is hardly part of the story of the funnies that brings about laughter, so we'll leave him hanging on the vines and move on, bearing in mind what a major impact *Tarzan* had on white male identity. What *Tarzan* did generate in the comics that was highly regarded is the art. Hal Foster, the earliest of the major *Tarzan* artists, was the most liked by author Edgar Rice Burroughs: sleek and fanciful, his drawings were undeniably brilliant but Tarzan's white supremacy was an uncomfortable prelude to the rise of Nazism.

The next impressive *Tarzan* artist was Burne Hogarth who in the 1940s presented luscious jungle greenery never surpassed, and muscular torsos that earned him the sobriquet of the Michelangelo of comics, but his vicious racism remains unparalleled. However, the artist who escaped the inherent racism of the concept and artfully delivered an authentic vision of Africa was Jesse Marsh, whose chunky figures and total absence of caricature or stereotype presented a decidedly inoffensive, heartening narrative of the continent, imbuing it with an uncanny sense of equality.

The Wittiest Superhero of Them All!

Drawn with exquisite simplicity of line, the immortal hero *Captain Marvel*, derisively named the Big Red Cheese by his brilliant arch enemy the mad scientist Sivana, came a cropper after a decade of attack from *Superman*. The accusation of plagiarism was a false beast if ever there was one; *Captain Marvel* and *Superman* were entirely different, apart from a few similarities. The truth resided in the marketplace where *Captain Marvel* proved superior. Amongst the Superhero comics, *Captain Marvel* comics towered over the rest in terms of moral integrity, ranking alongside the non-super *Joe Palooka* strip. Both involved plagiarism. The *Marvel Family* lost a plagiarism case to *Superman* and ceased publishing in the mid-1950s. The author of *Joe Palooka* (Ham Fisher) accused his ex-assistant (Al Capp) of plagiarism. No one believed Fisher in court and in the comic book society and he committed suicide. In one incident the wittier one was accused but won through; in the other the wittier one lost.

After that cursory history of mid-1950s jurisprudence, let's tackle *Captain Marvel Adventures* (1951: 113). America is awash with suspicion, fear and paranoia. The terrifying spectre of McCarthy's anti-communist witch-hunt casts its shadow everywhere. It takes a lot to frighten Captain Marvel but that's what happened in the town of Perfection. What Captain Marvel abhorred was actually democratically legal, and he never broke the law. This was the conundrum. He resolves the problem with strategy, brilliant in its absurdity. The town of Perfection had democratically reconstructed itself on the Greek ideal. The Civic League had voted in favour of a set of standards, which meant that anyone of difference was evicted from town. Citizens who were too fat or too thin, too short or too tall, those who fell below the acceptable standard, were hounded out of Perfection.

Captain Marvel was irrefutably perfect in looks, height and build, which is why he was invited to be honorary Mayor for a day. Upon assuming his new position, he uses force to punish anyone below his standard, which of course is everyone. His absurd behaviour almost results in the destruction of the town and the Civic League backs down; they see the error of their ways and the evicted populace is welcomed back. Bigotry has been outmanoeuvred. This exquisite gem sneaked by under the radar, with little fanfare and without drawing the attention of the witch-hunters.

From the Female Point of View

The original *Wonder Woman*, circa 1942, although created by a man, is regarded as a bulwark of feminism. It was devised to counter the male superhero genre. *Wonder Woman* defines the plight of women. It is a serious adventure comic with a bubbly chorus of college girls, never short on humour and cheeriness. The Holliday girl gang provide the warmth needed to balance the strength and acumen of the heroically powerful *Wonder Woman*. Gloria Steinem wrote that the Amazonian heroine imbued her childhood with a sense of female identity. The idea behind the comic was to tap into the unexploited market of young girls. This was achieved but the strip also appealed hugely to young boys. Previously, in the culture of comic books and the syndicated strips, females existed only on the periphery: this was predominantly a male domain.

One of the earliest female newspaper strips, *Brenda Starr*, appeared in 1940 and was written and drawn by Dale Messick; it was an adventure drama with a flair for fashion. Brenda got into scrapes and out of them again with ingenuity and a dash of quirky romantic involvements. *Brenda Starr* was expected to fail but didn't; in fact, it competed successfully in the male market. Her adventures were enlivened by the ardent but absent St John who sent her black orchids and suffered from a 'secret disease', a mystery never to be revealed. Not since the art deco clothes displayed in George McManus' 1920s and 1930s strip, *Bringing up Father*, had dresses been so stylish and in vogue.

Whereas the *Brenda Starr* strip oozed femininity, delicate in line and intent, her contemporary, *Miss Fury* by Tarpé Mills, was not so restrained. *Miss Fury* was as sexually provocative as that era could bear. Violence, sadomasochism, action and thrills were the hallmarks of the *Miss Fury* Sunday pages. Branding irons, spike-heeled boots, vicious women's fights, with clawing and eye-gouging, appeared when Marla Drake dropped her everyday identity and squeezed into her sleek black leopard skin suit to go into action against gangsters and Nazi spies; an air of sadism wafted from the pages. Her passing in the late 1940s was deplored by aficionados of the bizarre.

Wonder Woman was authored by William Moulton Marston, the psychologist who invented the lie-detector. He wrote the comics which were chunkily drawn by H.G. Peter, and he saw the venture as an opportunity to explore male-female relationships and to put forward his views on gender. Whereas Gloria Steinem praised Wonder Woman as a role model for girls, Dr Wertham's *Seduction of the Innocent* vilified the heroine for corrupting the youth with sadomasochism and bondage. This biased, fanciful book became the basis for the ruination of the comic book industry in the mid-1950s. In contrast, *Wonder Woman* converted rather than destroyed and set about improving a world torn apart by the hatred and wars of men. She decried the idea of a woman submitting to anyone or being groomed for victimhood. Great Hera!

Race and Humour in the Duck World

For years writer and artist Carl Barks worked without public acknowledgement. *Walt Disney* insisted on only his name being on everything. Nonetheless, *Donald Duck* and *Uncle Scrooge* were both clearly superior to the other habitués of the *Disney* barnyard and the public wanted to know who the real creator was. Who was the Duck-man? Who was the anonymous writer/artist of the miserly Scrooge and his wayward, anarchic nephew, Donald? The untameable Donald and the money-mad Uncle Scrooge flourished in their own anthropomorphic universe. Scrooge was the richest duck in the world. No one else understood the philosophy of capitalism better. So many clamoured to know the Duck artist's identity that Uncle Walt eventually relented: the one and only Duck artist was Carl Barks.

What was it that so endeared the world of ducks to such a vast readership? Barks transformed the pedestrian Donald Duck into wild, rebellious anarchy and created three nephews who were constantly try to save him from himself. There was no depravity Donald would not sink to – he would steal and lie shamelessly – but there were also no limits to the humane heights he could ascend to. In the hands of Barks, the Duck family, with its humour and prescience together with the excellence of the art, transcended all other *Disney* products. *Scrooge*'s vistas and perspectives were of a quality seldom seen in comics since the early twentieth century with *Nemo in Slumberland*. The most fantastical schemes were devised to part Scrooge from his capital, often secretly plotted by his dastardly nephew. Scrooge humiliated Donald, made him squirm, beg and weep and still refused him the mingiest of loans. Scrooge whines. What does his nephew think? That he's made of money?

The character of Donald Duck is a study in madness and the same might be said for Scrooge. One is deranged from not having money and the other lives in fear that someone will steal his money. In their mutual untrustworthiness,

Donald and his uncle understand and 'trust' each other; theirs is an eternal human condition.

The 1952 *Omelet* story begins with Donald's girlfriend Daisy asking why they must drive through a harmless-looking small town in disguise. Daisy hears how Donald's business dream became a nightmare. With manic intensity Donald had charged ahead with his plan to make a fortune out of eggs. Everything went wrong for Donald; he bought chickens that laid no eggs and then shed their feathers, smothering the town. People panicked and, thinking it was snowing, prepared for the unseasonal winter. The bald chickens broke free and ran amok, resulting in chaos and damage everywhere. Finally the chickens did lay eggs and once they'd started, they didn't stop. The hilltop storage bins burst and the town was submerged in scrambled egg. The people set fire to the egg lake, renamed the town Omelet and ate the giant omelette.

In his aging years Barks was knocked off kilter by worldwide fame. Declaring himself to be an artist, he spoke disparagingly of comics and launched a painting career which never took off. He produced lithographs of the Ducks but they weren't narrative or sequential and they weren't in the format where he excelled, particularly in his masterly pagination. His talent did not transfer beyond the comic book page. Does Barks' behaviour not relate to what America might well be? Suddenly cast centre stage, while too underequipped to comprehend?

The Duck-man was not as sophisticated as his comic art suggested. This was evident in his infamous 1949 *Voodoo Hoodoo*. Expertly rendered, it presents an artfully composed amalgamation of the stereotypical clichés about Africa. A curse intended for Scrooge is delivered to Donald by a zombie. Exaggerated features, poison darts and miniaturized people abound as the wily nephews manage to get the shrinking curse lifted. *Voodoo Hoodoo* makes an equally vile racist companion to *The Adventures of Tintin in the Congo* (1931), which met with similar opprobrium.

Superheroes Coming of Age

The newspaper strip was a product devised for the whole family. There was no niche market; one size fitted all. Along came *On the Road* in the 1950s and *Easy Rider* in 1969. Social relevance soon entered the comics. Times were a-changing. The award winning comic book series *Hard-Traveling Heroes* was introduced by Dylan's lyrics from *Blowin' in the Wind*, 'how many times can a man turn his head and pretend he just doesn't see?'

A victim of a housing scandal confronts *Green Lantern* and asks

> ... how on a planet someplace you helped out the **orange skin**... and you done considerable for the **purple skins!** Only there's skins you never bothered with! The **black skins!** I want to know... **How come?!** Answer me that, Mr. ***Green Lantern!***

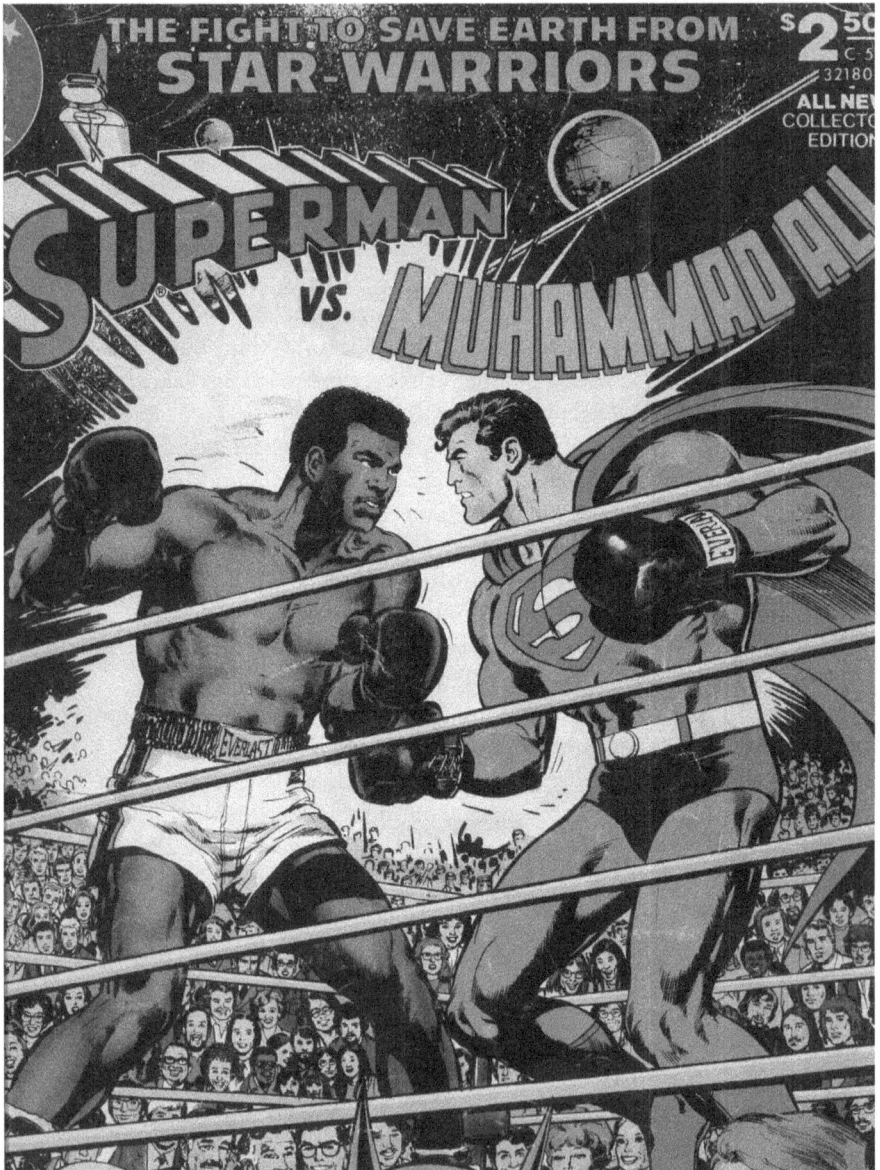

Figure 4.3: Muhammad Ali vs. Superman.

Shamefacedly *Green Lantern* admits he can't.

In 1978 the same writer/artist team, Denny O'Neil and Neal Adams, created *Muhammad Ali vs. Superman*. Earth is threatened with annihilation; a challenge is issued. Superman is trained by Ali. As a team they take on the green alien giant and prevail; through impersonation, a change of skin colour and lots of words. We are left in no doubt as to who is the greatest of them all.

In Summing Up

We began the twentieth century with the first medium to enter so many house-holds and witnessed the teaching of English through the comic strips. We saw strips dominated by white males. Ethnics and women stayed in the background. The foreground was fully occupied by white homogeneity. One might say that comics were proletarian; they certainly did not emerge from the elite classes. Consequently snobbish assessments of funnies, continuities or strips, together with derision and disapproval, were always plentiful and still are.

Let's discount noisome attitudes and assume that comics are coming of age or on the point of being considered on an equal footing with other media, and ask the question: did America produce a Tolstoy, Dickens or Cervantes, a Zola or Pushkin? Perhaps *Gatsby* was too privileged and Dreiser too rarefied, dos Passos not quite there, and Steinbeck too down in *Cannery Row*, too sub-proletarian?

Maybe America and the comic strips could never quite stand up to repa-ration or a Truth and Reconciliation Commission. Slavery and the plight of the Native American Indian still have to go a long way to be resolved in the national psyche. But the comics culture did produce Harold Gray's *Little Orphan Annie*. Maybe it is to *Little Orphan Annie* that we should look as the great American novel and perhaps it might be an accurate summing up to say the American national identity nestled somewhere between *Donald Duck* and Muhammad Ali.

A 1959 *Pogo Possum* page provided a pithy definition which became justifiably famous: 'A comic strip is like a dream ... a tissue of paper reveries ... it gloms an' glimmers its way through unreality, fancy an' fantasy'.

Conclusion

It should be borne in mind that America and England both impinged on my thinking in equal measure under the governance of apartheid South Africa on the battlefield of prejudice. The aim here has been to highlight that what was characterized as innocent nostalgia was, in fact, insidious fare. The accusation is that this was racism and misogyny which still continues under the disguise of harmless humour.

Note

1   Jack Johnson (1878–1945) was the first African American to hold the heavyweight
    championship title (from 1908 to 1915). White fans of boxing were enraged and the
    phrase 'The Great White Hope' referred to their expectation that a new white star
    would eventually defeat Johnson.

References

Barks, Carl. 1989. *Walt Disney's Donald Duck in Voodoo Hoodoo*, no. 238, 1949 (writer
    artist), *The Carl Barks Library of Walt Disney's Comics and Stories in color No. 22*, Reprint
    edn. Prescott, Arizona: Gladstone.
Batchelor, D. 1990. *Jack Johnson and his Times*. London: Weidenfeld & Nicholson.
Binder, Otto. *Captain Marvel Adventures*, vol. 19, no. 113, Oct., 1950 (C C Beck art,
    Captain Marvel and the Imperfect Perfection).
Blackbeard, B. and R. Marschall (eds). 1985. *The Complete E.C. Segar. Popeye. volume
    three, Sundays 1934–1936*. Thousand Oaks, CA: Fantagraphics Books.
Fisher, Bud. 2007. *The Early Years of Mutt & Jeff by*. New York: NBM.
Fisher, H. 1949. 'Joe Palooka', *Sunday Mirror*, 20 March 1949 (publishers doctored reissue).
———. 1992. *Joe Palooka*, Reprint edn. Classic Comic Strips. (Reprint 1938 in the
    Foreign Legion.)
Fleischer, N. and S. Andre. 1981. *A Pictorial History of Boxing*, Rev. edn. London:
    Hamlyn.
Goldstein, N. 2008. *Jackie Ormes: the First African American Cartoonist*. Ann Arbor, MI:
    University of Michigan Press.
Gray, H. 1970. *Arf! The Life and Hard Times of Little Orphan Annie 1935–1945*.
    New Rochelle, New York: Arlington House.
Herriman, G. 1990. *The Komplete Kolor Krazy Kat*, volume 1 (1935–1936). London:
    Titan Books.
Horn, M. (ed.). 1999. *The World Encyclopaedia of Comics*, Rev. edn. Philadelphia: Chelsea
    House.
Kelly, W. 1992. *Pogo, volume 1*, Reprint edn. Seattle, WA: Fantagraphics Books.
Kelly, Mrs Walt and B. Crouch, Jr. (eds). 1985. *Outrageously Pogo*. New York: Simon &
    Shuster.
King, Frank O. 1921 and 1922. *Walt & Skeezix*. 2005. Montreal: Drawn & Quarterly
    Books. NB: Originally syndicated in newspapers as *Gasoline Alley*.
Li'l Abner Comics, Feb. 1949, vol. 2, no. 9 (issue 69) (basis of allegation before
    doctoring).
Mills, Tarpe. 2013. *Miss Fury. Sensational Sundays 1941–1944*. San Diego, CA: IDW
    Publishing.
O'Neil, Denny (writer) and Adams, Neal (artist). 1978. *Superman vs. Muhammad Ali. All
    New Collector's Edition.*, Vol. 7, C-58.
Sagendorf, Bud (writer artist). Nov.-Jan. 1949. *Popeye*.

Additional References

MEN OF TOMORROW Geeks, Gangsters, and the Birth of the Comic Book by Gerard Jones. William Heinemann, 2004.

Palestine by Joe Sacco (Fantagraphic Books, first appeared in 1993); *Maus a Survivor's Tale* by Art Spiegelman (Pantheon Books, 1986).

PERSEPOLIS the story of a childhood and the story of a return by Marjane Satrapi (Jonathan Cape, 2006).

Watchmen by Alan Moore and Dave Gibbons writer and artist. Titan Books, 1987.

Ian Rakoff's involvement with cinema started in Africa on *The Hellions* by Ken Annakin. His flight from apartheid brought him to Chelsea, documentaries and then features. McGoohan's cult series *The Prisoner* transformed his career. He edited Frears' rebellious *The Burning*, then Anderson's Palme D'Or winner, the rebellious *If...*, and subsequently *O Lucky Man!* Other directors include Nicholas Roeg (the never completed *Glastonbury*), John Boorman (*Deliverance*), Robert Altman (*Images*), Alberto Ferro (*Sensations*), Jan Troell (*Flight of the Eagle*), Hugh Hudson (*Lost Angels*). His focus changed with the sale of 16,000 comics. *The Rakoff Collection* is now housed in the National Art Library at the V&A Museum. He has done a series of lectures on ethnicity and gender in newspaper strips and early comic books.

5

JOKES WITHOUT FRONTIERS, WAR WITHOUT TEARS
Humour, Stress and Power in an Anglo-German Bank Branch

Fiona Moore

Introduction

This chapter considers the use of humour as a means of alleviating stress, of strategic self-presentation and micro-political negotiation in the London office of a German bank. Looking at jokes, spontaneous performance, and business-related cartoons such as *Alex*, it considers the way in which that humour stems from the tensions arising from the nature of transnational banking and from the well-documented ambivalent relationship between the British and the Germans.

The uses of the symbolic presentation of self as a means of negotiating power relations has been well established, from the work of Goffman in the 1950s, elaborated upon by Bloch's work on politics and the use of symbols to restrict discourse in the 1970s, and later by Sperber and Strecker's respective works on symbolism. However, although Goffman acknowledges the use of humour as a form of tension relief in socially charged situations, there has been little work on its use as a means of self-presentation and of negotiating power relations. A study of the London branch of a German transnational bank in the early 2000s indicates that humour is a strategic tool for negotiating relations between different ethnic groups in the organization. The chapter concludes by arguing for further research in anthropology and sociology on the ways in which humour is used as a means of strategic self-presentation and cross-cultural negotiation.

Literature Review: Humour, Power, Identity

Identity and Self-preservation

Many anthropologists have considered the links between symbolism, strategy and power, and how this is expressed through communication, stories and performances. Sperber (1974) argues that the key aspect of symbols is their multivalency, i.e. their ability to simultaneously hold multiple meanings for their perceiver. Ivo Strecker (1988) builds upon this and considers how the way in which people strategically present themselves and interact with each other, the impressions which they hope to give out and/or undermine, all form part of the way in which power is negotiated in society; he argues that much of this presentation is symbolic, allowing people to play with the different meanings of symbols, interpreting and reinterpreting them strategically. Bloch (1974), similarly, considers how the way in which speeches and ritual events are phrased and structured involves the restricting of discourse in favour of those controlling the event in question, employing the interpretation of symbols. As jokes and humour usually involve stylized, symbolic displays where multivalency is key to the nature of the expression (the pun, for instance, trading on the double meaning of a word in the sentence), they can thus be considered a specific form of symbol for analytical purposes.

As regards identity, I will therefore take an approach based on the work of sociologist Erving Goffman, which has been a key influence on research on identity, self-presentation and power in organizations (see Burns 1992). Many of Goffman's works focus on the ways in which people define themselves; he describes how individual and corporate actors select between expressions of allegiance to maximize their benefits in particular situations (1956; 1961: 101; 1963: 243). Actors, he says, may define themselves predominantly according to a connection with one group, but within that there is a constant interplay of allegiances to many groups, with different ones prioritized in different situations according to which the actor feels best suits their aims (1961: 143). While Goffman has been accused of verging on rational action theory, people do use symbolic self-presentation strategically to some extent; one might also argue that to act strategically is not necessarily to act rationally, or even consciously (Burns 1992: 119; Jenkins 1996: 70–71). One must also note, as Goffman does not, that it is not just that we present ourselves strategically, but that at the same time our self-presentation is being interpreted by, and incorporated into the strategies of, others (Jenkins 1996: 58). Symbolic self-presentation will thus be considered as a part of negotiations for power and status in the organization, and jokes will now be examined in this context.

The Role of Jokes

Where humour has been considered in the context of symbolic self-presentation, however, it is mainly in terms of its role as tension-reliever. Goffman's study of surgeons briefly discusses how jokes are used to defuse fraught situations (1961: 50, 122–24). However, there is also evidence that jokes can be used in much the same way other symbol-heavy performances are, as means of negotiating power relations and status in groups. Strecker (1988) tells of a woman using a humorous allusion to a well-known folk story to gently dissuade a potential suitor. More pertinently to the subject of this chapter, Hughes' (1994) essay on humorous images of Germans in British media shows how jokes and cartoons expressing German stereotypes are used not only to elucidate and relieve tensions, but also to draw ethnic boundaries, defining and reinforcing images of 'The German' in the British consciousness. Ramsden's *Don't Mention the War* (2006), a more complex book-length study of representations of Germans in British popular culture from 1900 onwards, includes jokes and humour in exploring the ways in which different images of Germanness have been used to attack, defend and build symbolic links with Germany by British writers, artists and journalists.

I would thus contend, combining literature on humour with the literature on symbolism, power and self-presentation, that jokes and humour, as well as entertaining and relieving tension, are a means of defining and negotiating identity for their performers and audiences. I will now consider this in light of a case study of the London branch of a German bank.

Background to the Study

This project is based on an ethnographic study which was carried out at a German multinational bank between January and June 2000, with follow-up work done between July 2000 and January 2001, as part of an eighteen-month study of a German bank branch in London and in its Head Office in Frankfurt. While the material is now over a decade old, contextualizing material has been added to explain situations which have passed out of the popular consciousness, and the nature of humour in organizations has changed little if at all.

The material on which this chapter is based consists of, firstly, six months' worth of observation of and participation in the office environment, which involved coming in to the bank every working day and having access to a desk in a shared office, the canteen and other basic staff resources, and meeting rooms in which to conduct interviews. The location of the desk changed three times, allowing me to see different parts of the organization in action.

My position with regard to the bank was as an outside consultant to the London branch, brought in to advise, based on my interview results, on the impact of the implementation of a matrix integration programme (which will be discussed in more detail below) on Anglo-German relations in the branch. I was expected to submit a report at the end of the first six months detailing the issues in this area which had arisen from the matrix integration, and suggesting solutions. Interviewees were thus aware that the results of their interviews might find their way – albeit anonymously – into the final report; I have tried to compensate for this by evaluating each interviewee's answers in the context of their political agenda with regard to the bank and the matrix integration programme, and thus to factor their individual biases into the report.

ZwoBank London

'ZwoBank', the organization in which the field research took place, is a Frankfurt-based universal bank which, while it was one of the largest banks of its kind in Germany and maintained an above-average number of foreign branches, was fairly limited in its international operations, a not-atypical state of affairs in German banking (as noted in Ebster-Grosz and Pugh 1996). It had maintained a presence in London since the early 1970s, with a full branch being opened in 1981. The longest-serving employee (a senior manager) had been with the London branch for fifteen years at the time of the study, the shortest-serving (a trainee) three months. The branch had about 160 staff members, including trainee, temporary and service employees (the latter frequently being on contract from other organizations). Of these, about one-third were German, Swiss or Austrian, one-tenth non-German foreign staff, and the rest originated from the United Kingdom. Contrary to the traditional pattern for German overseas bank branches, in which the German personnel tend to be concentrated in the upper echelons (Arthur D. Little Ltd. 1979: 73), the Germans were fairly evenly distributed throughout the bank. The focus of the bank as a whole is on the German market, with the London branch's main function being to serve its clients' overseas offices.

The jokes that will be considered here are those which took place in the London branch office, during informal meetings and casual social interaction; gossip and joking between participants, ranging from mild to salacious or taboo humour depending on how well the participants knew each other, often seemed to be as essential as was the actual work. Jokes, albeit of a somewhat milder sort, were also used in more formal meetings in order to break the ice; here, however, their use was restricted to the presenter (although occasionally mild to biting sarcasm would be used by the more senior questioners). Humorous images of national affiliation and globalization would thus be expressed in the same forum as the more serious, 'official' ones, and also in a milieu in which power relations are expressed. Significantly, much of the joking revolved around the supposed 'character traits' of English and German 'business cultures'; others revolved around transport and communications equipment, transnational issues such as the Euro conversion, and relations between branch and Head Office. We shall thus consider here two of the main genres of jokes, both of which link into power relations in the office: work-related and ethnic humour.

Just Having a Laugh: Humour in the Office

Work-Related Humour

In the office, transport and communications equipment formed a continuous topic of discussion, and additionally a source of humour. Jokes of this sort often occurred as a result of the failure of one such piece of equipment. As a multinational corporation cannot operate without these, joking about them both relieved tension resulting from the accident and asserted the importance of such items of technology in representing the office's culture and 'business culture' in general (Goffman 1961: 122–24); no magazine aimed at businesspeople goes for long without running a piece on the vagaries of trains, planes and computers. Consequently, joking about travel and technology reinforced the importance of transnational and global practices to business, as both are dependent on international communications and transport technologies. They also, as a result, confirmed the place of the Germans as a transnational elite, as the German expatriates are the employees most closely linked with such items of equipment through their role in bridging the gap between Head Office and the London branch. Jokes about office equipment and means of transport thus seem to reinforce power relations and inter-ethnic boundaries in the office.

However, such jokes also provided a means of expressing diverse allegiances at once. For instance, symbols relating to transport could be used to denote Germanness, as punctuality is regarded by many, Germans and non-Germans, as a German obsession (Lawrence 1980: 147). Since many expatriates made frequent use of the cheap Stansted–Frankfurt daily flights, it could also be associated with one cohort at the expense of others. Alternatively, joking about the fitting of the Euro key to the office's computers, which evokes associations of banking and international finance, also connected with discourses about Germany, as the British associated the Euro, and the European Union, quite strongly with Germany, viewing it as the key economic and political driver of the EU. Joking about communications and transport technology, then, was not so much a means of expressing or defusing power relations between global and local as it was of forming connections between them.

Jokes were thus a way of presenting particular groups in complex ways, and at the same time expressing areas of tension within the organization. Staff from the dealing room, for instance, came in for a lot of teasing related to their reputation as 'cowboys', rich and risk-taking but none too intelligent; this did not, however, simply reflect the tension regarding the prestige afforded the dealing room at the expense of other departments, but also reflected the fact that the dealers are the source of much of the humour in the branch, and are considered to be 'good sports' willing to laugh at a joke on themselves. Similarly, an English mainte-nance man, asked how he had got rid of a mouse spotted in one of the kitchens, joked 'I raised its rent'; this does not only express ambivalence about the high rents in the City, but also sends up the euphemistic nature of business jargon and portrays ZwoBank itself (through the image of the mouse) as helpless in the face of the fluctuating City real estate market. Joking thus seems to be more complex than simply reflecting tensions or defining intergroup relations.

Ethnic Humour

Nationality-related humour largely seemed to revolve around the tensions of a multicultural workplace in which one ethnic group appears to dominate. One common joke, for instance, involved someone responding to a question in a foreign accent or using a foreign idiom, as when Greta announced in a loud voice that she was going down the street for a *sarnie* (English slang for sandwich). One might also say something similar about the following casual exchange between two British older males, upon hearing a nearby group speaking German:

A: There's too many Germans in the bank.
B: If it isn't Germans, it's people talking German.

Both of these appear to express Anglo-German conflict within the workplace, or possibly to be exposing a site of tension in a 'safe' way through joking (see Strecker 1988: 110; Goffman 1961: 122–24). However, while both examples seem to express hostile power relations between English and German, they also call into question the whole notion of Germanness. In the first instance, the sarnie joke was subsequently taken up by an American in the same office who overheard the exchange, redefining the putative group boundary from German/English to non-English/English. The second instance, also, redefines the butt of the joke not as Germans, but as people speaking German, which, in ZwoBank, would include at least some native English speakers. Furthermore, the joke is made with the unspoken knowledge that the speaking of German has a different meaning for other groups. Ethnic jokes are thus also as much a form of combination and boundary-crossing as they are a form of conflict and renegotiation, suggesting not so much divided groups as of different ways of being 'local' and 'global' within a broader social remit.

There is also, however, the case of 'wartime' jokes. This is a type of British humour which relates either to Nazism and the Second World War, or to the Anglo-American 'wartime' genre of films, television programmes and popular novels (such as *Colditz*, *Secret Army* and *The Great Escape*), which present fiction-alized accounts of the Second World War, often with stereotypically-rendered German villains (Beevor 1999; *Der Spiegel* 1998; see Davies 2000 for an example of this genre's use in a British workplace). In the joking sessions in offices, in which employees make fun of each other's personal traits, portrayals of German managers and staff members can draw on 'wartime' film clichés and images, albeit seldom in the presence of the subject of the joke. Again, the most obvious explanation is that joking is a form of resistance by English employees, or a form of contestation over power in the workplace.

In ZwoBank, Nazis were seldom referred to even in humorous interactions between English and Germans, but people were not unaware of them, nor nec-essarily averse to using these images. To cite one of the less offensive examples, when a client turned out to have the same name as a character in a popular British 'wartime' comedy, *Dad's Army*, catchphrases from it were bandied about, and imitations of 'wartime' stock film characters periodically surfaced during joking sessions. The sports-focused nature of the City also meant that whenever there was a Europe-wide football championship, chants and songs relating to the 1966 England victory over Germany, which often referred to the Second World War as well (one chant, for instance, began with the words 'Zwei World Wars and Ein World Cup'; another, conflating fictionalized images of Germans with military history, involved singing the theme from *The Great Escape*), could be heard in the offices. Such images also crop up in 'respectable' City newspapers, albeit often in a jocular way, as when a headline in the business section of the London Metro read 'Germany Poised for Blitz on C&W'. Even in bank branches in which there is a good relationship between English and German employees, then, jokes relating to the Second World War and Nazis can be heard, confirming the above hypothesis.

While the Germans with whom I spoke did not openly discuss these jokes, it was plain that they were not unaware of them. When I asked both expatriates and local hires whether they had encountered any preconceived notions about Germans in the UK, most took me to mean prejudices (*Vorurteile*), even though I used the more neutral phrase 'preconceptions' (*vorgefaßte Meinungen*). One of the two who said that they had never encountered such stereotypes later said that she had misinterpreted the question. Furthermore, all Germans who had been in the UK for more than a year admitted, in private, to having encountered stereo-typing of this sort, albeit normally outside the workplace. Even in non-hostile situations, then, people are aware of negative, anti-German humour.

Significantly, though, this humour was only used in particular contexts. Jokes about the Second World War only occurred in mixed or English-only groups, never in one-on-one Anglo-German interactions. Furthermore, the people who initiated this sort of joking were usually young English men, and therefore the humour has connections to the British 'lad culture' of the late 1990s, incorporating frequent stylized displays of xenophobia which, at the time, did not necessarily denote feelings of prejudice on the part of the speaker. The jokes were also used in different ways in each context; in mixed groups, they were never explicitly linked to Germanness or used in reference to German colleagues. In English-only contexts, with the rules being slightly more relaxed, such jokes were often made and linked to colleagues, with the thrill of addressing a taboo subject. When I unthinkingly made a facetious reference to Nazis in the presence of Tom, a Germanophile, while setting up for an interview, he coldly said 'We don't say things like that around here'; in the same office, however, I would hear open discussions of 'wartime' films in less formal English-only contexts, even some involving Germanophiles. Finally, the same 'wartime' images also had a connection to a well-known episode of the popular British comedy *Fawlty Towers*, in which the protagonist Basil Fawlty, played by John Cleese, assaults German guests at his hotel with a ludicrously over-the-top impression of Adolf Hitler; as the incident is clearly played to show Fawlty as an insane xenophobe and his guests as decent, well-meaning people, the use of 'wartime' images can also be taken in some contexts as ironic references to British insularity. The German-as-Nazi image thus crops up in City humour in a conflict-based way; however, its use in restricted areas, and the potential for irony, suggests that there is strategy involved in its use, and it is not just simply a question of conflict and consensus.

The Germans were also not above derogatory ethnic humour against the British, for instance, referring to Mad Cow Disease in such a way as to imply either that a colleague has it (frequently with a gendered element; female managers were particularly prone to being referred to as 'the Mad Cow'), or that the British in general are incapable of coping with a crisis. Stereotypical images of the British as effete socialites or as antediluvian union leaders would also emerge in all-German conversations. As with the 'wartime' jokes, furthermore, these were not only in mono-ethnic contexts, but were generally made in German, so as to further ensure that the humour remains private (although, again, the British are not unaware of the genre). Ethnic humour is thus not simply the private revenge of an oppressed group, but a means of building ethnic solidarity for both linguistic groups in the organization.

One can even go further and say that humour actually crosses and effaces the distinctions between groups. For instance, while much humour revolved around stereotypes of Germans as efficient and work-obsessed, none revolved around German foods, Germany itself, or other symbols of Germanness which my German interviewees cited as important, other than those that also tied into images of Europe and of the corporation in question. Also, such jokes seemed to

build group solidarity as bank employees as much they seemed to define separate conceptions of German and English, as they could also be taken to reduce
cultural differences to the level of eccentric traits. The Nazi-joke genre is more
problematic; however, the fact that such jokes were avoided in mixed contexts
but deployed in English-only ones suggests that they are used to build solidarity
on different levels. An English person can build solidarity with German colleagues by not making the jokes in their presence, but with British colleagues by
making them in private contexts; the Germans, for their part, return the favour
by limiting their Mad Cow Disease jokes to particular settings. Tom's ostenta-
tious concern about the political implications of 'wartime' humour might thus
have been intended to emphasize to me, an outsider to the organization, that he
wanted to be seen as sympathetic to the Germans within it. Ethnic jokes can thus
build solidarity at the same time as they divide groups.

Cartoons

This multivalent quality is also reflected in the two most popular cartoons in
the City, *Dilbert* and *Alex*, both of which revolve around white-collar individuals employed by an information technology firm and a bank respectively, and
which frequently appear on slides shown in meetings, office doors and the sides
of computers. Dilbert, on the face of it, is a site of elite-subaltern protest, as
it derives its humour from playfully exposing inefficient management practice
and incomprehensible workplace jargon; it is a common half-joking aphorism
in business that the level of employee dissatisfaction in an office can be mea-
sured by the number of Dilbert cartoons in the leisure areas. However, much
of its popularity stems from the way in which the cartoon's creator, Scott
Adams, a businessman in his own right, taps into the concerns of people on
all levels of the multinational corporation. His parodies of business literature,
e.g. *The Joy of Work* (Adams 1998) and *The Dilbert Principle* (Adams 1996),
are published by a press which specializes in actual management-development
works, again blending anti-establishment humour with an establishment pre-
sentational form. Dilbert cartoons are also as likely to crop up in a manager's
PowerPoint presentation as on a staff member's cubicle. Dilbert thus simultaneously expresses protestation against and affirmation of the social mores of
business in diverse ways.

Alex is equally complex, but in the opposite way. On the face of it, the cartoon
is very much a reflection and vindication of the City establishment, revolv-
ing around a successful London businessman scoring points off the uncom-
prehending world around him. However, the cartoon is at the same time a
sendup of money- and self-presentation-focused City attitudes: a typical cartoon
(29 July 1999) depicts a businessman who was the subject of a documentary

raging at the filmmakers, not for portraying his marital and social indiscretions, but for showing him recommending a stock which subsequently proved to be a bad choice. Furthermore, it is enjoyed by different groups on different levels: non-City people treat it as a send-up of City mores, City people treat it as an inside joke, line staff treat it as an example of the difference between managers and staff. Both cartoons are therefore used not only to defuse tensions and define images of particular groups, but to reinterpret, connect and define relationships between groups in a playful way.

Beyond a Joke: Discussion and Analysis

Jokes as Identity Markers

On the face of it, humour in the office seemed mainly to be a means of breaking tension in a high-stress job, in a manner that recalled Goffman's observations on surgeons (1961: 50, 122–24) and Law's on commercial researchers (1994: 120). This was borne out by the observation that dealing rooms, where people are constantly making split-second decisions, had a more raucous atmosphere than other bank divisions. Most of this humour, as noted, revolved around points of conflict between groups in the office. Joking thus could be seen as a way of expressing and dealing with intergroup tensions in an office with a hierarchy based on ethnic origin and degree of globalization.

Joking could, however, as Czarniawska notes, also be seen as a means of negotiating power relations within the organization (1997: 137). The fact that many of the jokes focused on Head Office suggests that this is the case here; the joking about Germans could also be seen as negotiating staff-manager relations, as they were mainly made by English staff members about German managers. Some jokes worked to bring Head Office into the domestic realm, for instance when one locally hired German department manager jokingly 'spoke' for Head Office using the 'Royal We', traditionally a UK monarchical form of speech. Joking thus can be a site of negotiating intergroup relations, not only – or even primarily – of dealing with workplace tensions. In the cases of joking, therefore, language and linguistic symbols are not used so much to define groups as to relate in different ways to the global and the local, causing the global to be locally interpreted and the local to become global.

Furthermore, the flexibility of self-presentation was also used as an escape mechanism to change the subject smoothly when the humour was approaching dangerous areas. A series of jokes about a 'wartime' film could thus segue into a series about the reputed business efficiency of Germans, into the other personal traits of the individual who was the butt of the joke, or into the set-up of the company. One rather clever sequence involved switching, through the metaphor of 'takeover as war', from joking about 'wartime' images to joking about the merger of two banks, one German, which had recently been in the business news (see Burrus 1997: 210 for a more in-depth discussion of warfare metaphors in business language). Frequently, when the jokes began to approach too-sensitive areas, it was a common occurrence for participants to change the subject of the joke to a less sensitive topic, or to 'turn the laugh onto' the joker by accusing them in jest of having something to hide themself (during which the above-mentioned episode of *Fawlty Towers* was frequently invoked). Furthermore, the joking sessions which referred to Nazis did not refer to real Second World War history so much as to images drawn from 'wartime' films or television programmes; other groups, most notably Americans, were also made fun of in ways which referred to 'wartime' film images of their ethnic group. Within ZwoBank, the image of Germans could be transformed from a negative into a positive one, thus saving face for participants in a possibly contentious conversation. The jokes are thus not exclusively about defining power relations, but are primarily about negotiations between groups in the organization.

In the case of Germans in business, then, it seems that positive and negative images blend into each other in deliberate and non-conscious ways. For instance, Warner and Campbell's jocular description of German business style as '*Technik über Alles*' may evoke English fears of German 'takeovers' (1993: 101). However, the same quality is used in the workplace to avoid, and even to actively pre-empt, the image of the German as Nazi from emerging in jokes, by deliberately situating the image of German-as-Nazi in a fictional context. In humour, then, the underlying meanings of a given discourse can change with startling rapidity.

The case of jokes in the workplace again gives us a pattern of a seemingly simple discourse with more complex operations going on beneath the surface. Joking appears to be a way of alleviating tensions, defining groups within the workplace and conveying messages about business practices to one's superiors or inferiors. However, which of these functions dominated depended on the context, and the nature of the jokes meant that they could also be used to blend roles with each other, and even to switch between topics and categories of discussion. This could be used in strategic ways, to actively control discourses within the office; however, the issue of who controlled the discourse depended on the situation. Like jargon and language crossing, then, humour defines a multiply linked, multi-layered series of interactions rather than defining solidary groups.

The ZwoBank case therefore suggests that humour does not so much form a site of conflict between groups or of tension release as a complex site of renegotiation and affirmation on different levels. This, once again, can form the basis for strategizing, both playful and more serious, in the financial sphere. This in turn suggests that relations in the business world are not so much a case of global versus local as of multiple forms of globalization and localization, linked through diverse forms of symbolic expression.

Implications for Research and Practice

The implications for anthropologists are, firstly, that greater research needs to be done into humour, not only in terms of its uses in defining identity of various sorts, but in other areas. Jokes, analysed as cultural objects, can be used to identify points of tension, unspoken taboos and anxieties, and the changing nature of jokes can indicate long-term developments in society; in the present case, for instance, jokes about Germany's role in the Second World War have become less and less taboo in mixed environments since this study was completed. For example, a trailer for the 2010 England-Germany World Cup football game humorously riffed on the above-mentioned chant by beginning 'England want revenge for the Blitz, Germany want revenge for the 1966 World Cup'. At the same time, the complex interweaving of images of Germanness with British popular culture, particularly as regards football, presents a multi-layered and complex image of national identity as defined against an equally complex Other.

The implications for international business specialists are that such qualitative items as jokes and comics can, in fact, yield valuable data into the culture of an organization, and into relations between ethnic groups within it, of the kind that is difficult to obtain through quantitative means, or even through qualitative interviews. As it has been noted (for instance by Hebert et al. 2005) that culture is one of the intangible factors which can be crucial to organizational change, the formation of a new organization after a merger, and the successful operation of a cross-cultural business venture, finding ways of assessing and understanding such factors is essential. The greater study of humour in a business context may provide one means of exploring these.

The implications for managers are that jokes, as well as providing indicators of tensions in the organization, can also play a more positive role; not only do they provide a means through which staff can express discontent or flag up crucial issues without actually challenging management (as in the case of the Dilbert cartoons), but they can also allow staff members to work through such tensions and negotiate issues between groups. An understanding of the humour of an organization can thus provide a valuable insight for practitioners.

Areas for Further Research

The study is arguably limited by its age and geographical range, and it would be interesting to pursue other studies among other groups in more recent times; indeed, it might be interesting to revisit the situation in Anglo-German banks as Germans become more confident in their own national identity. Outside of business, this study would suggest that there is great potential value in considering humour, jokes and cartoons in greater detail as means of expressing identity and presenting the self, and as a means of cross-cultural negotiation.

Conclusion

The conclusion which can be drawn from the ZwoBank case is that humour in the office forms a site of self-presentation and definition of identity, through the use of professional and ethnic humour. As a result of this, it also forms part of complex, ongoing negotiations between groups, not only relieving ethnic tensions but also acting as ammunition in inter-ethnic conflicts, as a means of expressing and working through problems which would otherwise be inappropriate in a work context, and as a means of defining and redefining ethnic, and other, identity in an international business context.

Appendix

Formal interviews were conducted on a periodic basis over the course of the six-month participant-observation period and the six months following it, with sixteen individuals at the London branch. Of these, six were expatriate Germans, five were Germans living permanently in the UK, two were English who had lived in Germany, and three were English with no German connection. The people interviewed were mainly junior and middle managers, with three members of top management and two non-managerial staff members also participating. In addition, formal interviews of this type were conducted at the bank's Head Office with six managers in the personnel department and one in a Front Office division; these were conducted during three trips to Frankfurt, in April, September and October 2000, with follow-up work done via telephone and email. Each participant was interviewed between one and four times, with interviews lasting approximately an hour apiece. Although a standard questionnaire was used to start the interview, it was normally abandoned early on, with the interests of the interview subject being allowed to shape the proceedings. Bilingual interviewees were given the option of being interviewed in English or German; although most at the London Branch chose English, and most at the Head Office chose German, no interview was conducted exclusively in one or the other language, as participants would occasionally drop into the other language for expressions that they felt unable to translate, or if they found giving an explanation in a language which was not their mother tongue too difficult. Rough demographic information regarding my sample can be found in Table 5.1.

These interviews were also complemented by informal interviews and conversations with about twenty other members of the branch's staff. These did not have

Table 5.1 Rough demographic information regarding author's subjects

Status	Gender	Ethnicity	Cohort	Department	Approx. Age	Branch
Manager	Male	German	Expatriate	Finance	32	London
Junior Manager	Male	German	Expatriate	Finance	28	London
Manager	Male	German	Expatriate	Finance	30	London
Manager	Male	German	Expatriate	IT	55	London
Manager	Male	German	Expatriate	Ops.	40	London
Manager	Female	German	Expatriate	H.R.	31	London
Manager	Male	German	Local Hire	Customer Service	48	London
Manager	Female	German	Local Hire	Sales	55	London
Front-Line Staff	Female	German	Local Hire	Sales	28	London
Manager	Male	German	Local Hire	Sales	50	London
Manager	Male	English	Germanophile	Trading	35	London
Senior Manager	Female	English	Germanophile	General Mgt.	40	London
Senior Manager	Male	English	Anglophile	Compliance	64	London
Senior Manager	Male	English	Anglophile	General Mgt.	55	London
Front-Line Staff	Male	English	Anglophile	Unknown	30	London
Senior Manager	Female	German	–	HR/General Mgt.	50	Head Office
Senior Manager	Male	German	–	HR	45	Head Office
Manager	Male	German	–	HR	32	Head Office
Manager	Male	German	–	HR	38	Head Office
Senior Manager	Female	German	–	HR	47	Head Office
Manager	Male	German	–	Investment Banking	34	Head Office

a formal schedule of questions (although I made certain to ask whether or not I could use the relevant part of the conversation in my study), but were guided by the research questions of the study and by the findings of the formal interviews, and were usually conducted over lunch or after work. Informal interviews of this sort were held with all but four of the formal-interview participants; of the other people with whom I regularly had conversations of this sort, five were Germans living permanently in the UK, six were non-Germans who had lived in Germany, and nine were non-German employees with no connection to Germany.

References

Adams, S. 1996. *The Dilbert Principle: A Cubicle's-Eye View of Bosses, Meetings, Management Fads & Other Workplace Afflictions*. New York: Harper Collins.

———. 1998. *The Joy of Work: Dilbert's Guide to Finding Happiness at the Expense of Your Co-Worker*. New York: Harper Collins.

Arthur D. Little Ltd. 1979. *The EEC as an Expanded Home Market for the United Kingdom and the Federal Republic of German*. London.

Beevor, Antony. 1999. 'Tommy and Jerry', *The Guardian*, 16 February 1999, 2.

Bloch, Maurice. 1974. 'Symbols, Song, Dance and Features of Articulation: Is Religion an Extreme Form of Traditional Authority?' *Archives Europaiennes de la Sociologie*, 15, 55–81.

Burns, T. 1992. *Erving Goffman*. London: Routledge.

Burrus, K. 1997. 'National Culture and Gender Diversity within One of the Universal Swiss Banks', in S.A. Sackman (ed.), *Cultural Complexity in Organizations: Inherent Contrasts and Contradictions*. London: Sage, 209–27.

Czarniawska, B. 1997. *Narrating the Organization: Dramas of Institutional Identity*. Chicago and London: University of Chicago Press.

Davies, C. 2000. 'Bus Driver Dubbed "Herman the German" Loses Racism Claim', *Daily Telegraph*, 6 July 2000.

Ebster-Grosz, D. and D. Pugh. 1996. *Anglo-German Business Collaboration: Pitfalls and Potentials*. London: Macmillan.

Goffman, E. 1956. *The Presentation of Self in Everyday Life*. Edinburgh: Anchor Books.

———. 1961. *Encounters: Two Studies in the Sociology of Interaction*. Indianapolis: Bobbs-Merrill.

———. 1963. *Behaviour in Public Places: Notes on the Social Organization of Gatherings*. London: The Free Press of Glencoe.

Hebert, L., P. Very and P. Beamish. 2005. 'Expatriation as a Bridge over Troubled Water: A Knowledge-Based Perspective Applied to Cross-Border Acquisitions', *Organization Studies* 26(10), 1455–76.

Hughes, T. 1994. *The Image Makers: National Stereotypes and the Media*. London: Goethe Institut.

Jenkins, R. 1996. *Social Identity*. London: Routledge.

Law, J. 1994. *Organizing Modernity*. Oxford: Oxford University Press.

Lawrence, P. 1980. *Managers and Management in West Germany*. London: Palgrave Macmillan.

Ramsden, J. 2006. *Don't Mention the War: The British and the Germans Since 1890*. London: Little, Brown Book Group.

Sperber, D. 1974. *Rethinking Symbolism*. Cambridge: Cambridge University Press.

Der Spiegel. 1998. 'Ich bleibe Deutscher', 7 September, 88–89.

Strecker, Ivo. 1988. *The Social Practice of Symbolization: An Anthropological Analysis*. London: Bloomsbury Academic.

Warner, M. and A. Campbell. 1993. 'German Management', in David J. Hickson (ed.), *Management in Western Europe: Society, Culture and Organization in Twelve Nations*. Berlin: Walter de Gruyter, 89–108.

Fiona Moore is a business anthropologist and Professor of Business Anthropology at Royal Holloway, University of London. She received her doctorate from Oxford University, Institute for Social and Cultural Anthropology. Her research on German multinational corporations, chiefly BMW, UK, was published in the *Journal of International Business Studies*, *Management International Review* and *Thunderbird International Business Review*. She has written a monograph, *Transnational Business Cultures*, on German expatriates in London. Her current research focuses on the development of international knowledge networks by Taiwanese professionals in the UK.

6

LAUGHING AT THE FUTURE
Cross-Cultural Science Fiction Films

Dolores P. Martinez

The Naming of Parts
To-day we have naming of parts. Yesterday,
We had daily cleaning. And to-morrow morning,
We shall have what to do after firing. But to-day,
To-day we have naming of parts. Japonica
Glistens like coral in all of the neighbouring
    gardens,
And to-day we have naming of parts.
(Reed 1942)

By way of introduction to this chapter's[1] attempt to weave together a variety
of topics – dreams, Hollywood films, science fiction and comedy – into an
anthropological analysis of a global filmic subculture, I begin with the 'naming
of parts'. The reference to Reed's Part I of the poem *The Lessons of War* is
intentional. The opening imagery of the poem contrasts the bewilderment of
training for the young soldier, who must learn how to use his weapon, with
the dream-like peace of nearby gardens. The poem is about the technology and
reality of death, which, by the end of this chapter, I will link to a discussion of
how comedy science fiction films, while asking us to laugh, speak to a certain
attitude towards both technology and death in post-modernity. In taking such
a line, I am making fairly large-scale assumptions about a global filmic culture
(Jameson 2006; Cazdyn 2003), but with some caveats. Both Jameson and
Cazdyn see the global dominance of Hollywood films as being part and parcel
of the spread of capitalistic ideology around the world. Taking this line also
involves, generally, a sense that audiences are passive receptors of films and that
somehow films have a tremendous power to inculcate and change belief and
attitudes in its audiences. I have argued elsewhere (Martinez 2009) that this is

far too simplistic a view of a process that many have already begun to question in relation to an anthropology/sociology of audiences (Ang 1991, 1996), which has documented how spectators are perfectly capable of reading film or television in a variety of ways, imbuing the narrative with their own meanings and symbols. In short, the process of viewing is dialogic (Bakhtin 1981) in a way that Benjamin (1973) understood early on, although his essay on the topic is often misread.

It would seem then, that to speak of a global culture shared by film audiences is oxymoronic, that the best we could do is to speak of global and local assemblages. While I accept current theorizing that sees the spread of global culture and technology as one which does not end in creating the same sort of societies worldwide (Sahlins 1981, 1989; Tsing 2005; Ong and Collier 2005), I agree as well with MacDougall (1998) that cinema is often transcultural because of shared human experiences. In this case, science fiction films as a form of fantasy can be seen as explorations into the fears and ambitions societies have about not just the future, but about a future based on the continuous spread of technology into everyday life. To put it in other words, no matter how underdeveloped a society might be (and 'untouched' Amazonian tribes aside), it has some engagement with the technology of modernity even though it may be as basic as a radio, an electric generator, modern medicine in some form, the mass print media of books and newspapers, and especially the existence of modern weapons. We take these technologies for granted and yet they are part and parcel of the post-industrial landscape. In short, there is no escaping the machines or science of the post-Enlightenment; even if they are rejected, an awareness of their existence is there. And accompanying this awareness is an anxiety about technology. I will return to this at the end of this chapter, but want to note here that given the evidence of shared transcultural concerns, anthropologists need to consider the conjunctures as well as the disjunctures in the global cultural economy (pace Appadurai 1996) and the fact that such combinations of cultural themes may coalesce in unexpected ways.

But first, the naming of parts. Dreams and dreaming are key themes that link film, science fiction and humour. By dreams I do not mean 'a series of thoughts, images and sensations occurring in the mind during sleep' (OED), although the structures of such unconscious activity will be elaborated on below, but define dreams 'as a cherished hope or ideal' (OED), in this case the hopes and ideals being seen as social, that are shared by a collectivity. In her 'how to' book on mutual dreaming, Magallon gives a definition that is useful: 'over time, people will develop a mutual bank of symbols from which they withdraw in order to create their dreams. The shared experience of powerful emotional, sensory, mental, and intuitive events will produce ideas and feelings that translate into similar symbols for each person involved' (1997: 66). This would appear to be a very Jungian, rather than Freudian, and communal rather than personal, approach to dreams, but it is one that is implicit in the work of Benjamin when he discusses dreams and politics: 'The collective, from the first, expresses the conditions of its life. These find their expression in the dream and their interpretation in the awakening' (2002: 392). For Benjamin the awakening is equivalent to conscious political action, in a Marxist sense, which ends in the making of history (2002: 390).

Benjamin's thoughts on dreams were part of his attempt to understand how the creation of the new spaces resulted in places within which collective dreams might be experienced; for example the display of products in the windows of nineteenth-century arcades represented novel lifestyles to which many consumers could only aspire. Paradoxically these new spaces also allowed for the consumption of older fantasies as in late night encounters with sex workers who sheltered in and used the arcades as places for their own 'displays'. Film and its related places also fall into this type of 'dreaming'; the movie theatres of the early twentieth century provided not just locations for the consumption of a new form of entertainment – the moving picture – but also presented audiences with glimpses of different lifestyles, and moreover became places that allowed for new forms of sociability such as 'dating'. Both examples are analogous to the sort of unintentional social changes, or history making, that Benjamin imagined as a by-product of creating the new. We might ask as well if science fiction, which by its very nature belongs to the realm of futuristic imagining and is another form of collective dreaming, actively makes history or if it only, in a symbolic way, represents[2] it, given that science fiction imagines the future but almost always wrestles with the concerns of the present. Csicsery-Ronay offers a useful exploration of this when he outlines what he terms the genre of science-fictionality:

> The attitude of science-fictionality is characterized by two linked forms of hesitation, a pair of gaps. One gap extends between the belief that certain ideas and images of technoscientific transformations of the world can be entertained, and the rational recognition that they may be *realized*, with ramifications for social life ... The other gap lies between belief in the immanent possibility (even the inexorability) of these transformations, and reflection about their possible ethical, social and spiritual consequences... SF thus involves two forms of hesitation: a historical logical one (how plausible is the conceivable novum?) and an ethical one (how good/bad/altogether alien are the transformations that issue from the novum?). (2008: 3)

Unlike many, but not all, forms of fiction then, science fiction is an active meditation upon, and even mediation between, what is and what might be. It has the potential to inform, explore and even prefigure important social changes and their consequences; in this way, the genre can often be read for its implicit political meanings. It is only necessary to think of how Mary Shelley's nightmare led to her writing *Frankenstein* (1994 [1818]), arguably the first modern science fiction novel: the written exploration of her dream was framed by what was, for a woman of her generation, a very broad education that included knowledge of advances in the natural sciences. She asked an age-old question: what would happen if men – and I will return to the use of the male here – were to play god and make another man? Her exploration of the consequences of such experimentation has been filmed in a variety of ways that have twisted her vision, but each version represents the concerns of the social moment that produced it. Filmic representations of her monster have run the gamut from modern Prometheus, strange yet articulate and handsome, to the grunting shambling giant who is feared not because of his superiority but for his brutality in *Frankenstein* (Whale 1931). In the second half of the twentieth century, his representation has moved into the realm of camp through its sequel *The Bride of Frankenstein* (Whale 1935), to a comic character that eventually was relegated to children's cartoons such as *Frankenstein, Jr. and the Impossibles* (Barbera and Hanna 1966), television situation comedies like *The Munsters* (Kayro-Vue Productions 1964–1966) and then re-imagined as a comical sexually suspect creature in *The Rocky Horror Picture Show* (Sharman 1975) or *Young Frankenstein* (Brooks 1974).

Attempts to reinstil her creation with a new gravitas in films such as Branagh's 1994 *Mary Shelley's Frankenstein*[3] have failed, although Ridley Scott's reimagining of the character as Roy Batty (Rutger Hauer), a replicant, in *Blade Runner* (1982) is the representation of the character that comes closest to the original monster. Such progressions would seem to mirror not only advances in technology, such as the fact that modern medicine has the potential to make cyborgs of us all with stents, artificial joints, etc., but also the fact that if we are going to make artificial life, we may well clone it before we try 'building' it. In most of the versions, however, some aspect of the politics of changing gender relationships surfaces. Thus, if science fiction is like a dream, it most resembles prophetic dreams that have the power to reflect contemporary concerns and to cause individuals to react,[4] but as technology advances, so does the nature of the dream. Nothing dates a science fiction film as quickly as the advances in technology that not only make the special effects look primitive, but also make the technology depicted obsolete.

It is necessary to consider a further point: that films may not only present and represent a form of collective imaginings, but that the language of films is like the 'language' of dreams. As Rascaroli (2008) argues in her extensive review of the oneiric metaphor in film theory, the idea that films are like dreams has had a long history. Generally, as she describes it, this has been premised on the idea that the dreamer and the film spectator enter similar states, that both films and dreams are deeply symbolic and can be subject to analysis, and both bear a complex relationship to the real. However, each of these suppositions can also be critiqued. More fruitful on the other hand is the approach just mentioned in passing by Botz-Bornstein in his discussion of the experience of the uncanny and the aesthetics of film dreams: 'Dreams cannot be produced through dissolves, fades or other devices taken from formal registers, but films follow a structure of experience proper to that of dreams and similar to that of the uncanny' (2008: 121). To put it another way, film narratives rely on a series of techniques that create an experience similar to that of dreams;[5] this is accomplished not just through the use of symbols that require post-film viewing analysis, but also through montage sequences that fold time; through the movement in space accomplished through a single edit; through the point of view of the camera that can make us spectator and put us in the shoes of a protagonist at the same time; through visual puns and, last but not least, through the way in which repressed fantasies may be played out publicly, particularly violent or sexual desires. Science fiction films therefore rely on two formal registers that relate to dreaming: first, the representation of the future, based on a form of collective hope about humankind's continued existence and, second, the use of narrative techniques common to all films that structure our viewing experience. Science fiction films move seamlessly between these dream registers and, in doing so, the political complexity of the written genre is simplified, more emphasis is given to the present and its concerns are imagined as continuing into the future, rather than in considering how our societies might change.

But what does it mean when our dreaming of the future becomes a series of jokes, black comedy or just plain slapstick, that is, the film shifts into yet another level of symbolic dream-like structures? Why and how does potentially serious science fiction descend into comedy? I come now to the most difficult of my parts to name – the comic, the humorous, or the joke – but I am entering the field by using dreams yet again as the glue that brings this all together. In this I follow Freud who begins his essay on *The Joke and its Relationship to the Unconscious* with an overview of previous theory on jokes and who quotes Kuno Fischer: 'The judgement which produces a comic contrast is *the joke*. It has already played a silent part in caricature, but only in judgement does it attain its distinctive form and the free sphere of its unfolding (p.49)... it is a playful judgement' (ibid., 51, in Freud 2002: 4). He adds from Jean Paul Richter: '"Wit is mere play with ideas" (p.24)' (in Freud 2002: 5).

In his analysis, which constitutes his attempt to understand how and why jokes are able to do all of this, Freud argues that we can only begin to understand the way in which jokes work if we think of how dreams work. That is, both dreams and jokes do similar things: they condense, invert, rely on symbolism, make odd juxtapositions and satisfy a desire in the face of an obstacle that stands in the way; they relieve tensions by expressing them, but while dreams are asocial and tend to be individual, jokes are meant to be shared and involve a shared collectivity; thus in contrast to dreams, they bring the unconscious into a shared consciousness, lifting inhibitions and subverting censorship (Freud 2002: 165–75). They can represent a rebellion against authority; here he builds on Bergson's (2008) ideas of the humorous being the occurrence or reminder of the flexible through the representation of inflexibility (Freud 2002: 203–204,

216–22). The social situation which restricts or an individual's behaviour that is unvarying can be poked fun at through the joke that reveals our vulnerability in the face of larger institutions or social conventions. Jokes rely, then, on shared experiences of repression and the release of tension that comes from playing with the concepts and resultant subversion of authority. In the anthropological and sociological elaborations of Freud's theory (cf. Apte 1985; Berger 1997; Billig 2005), the need for shared experience is taken to limit the extent to which a joke, or that which is humorous, is found to be funny. Not only might jokes only make sense within a given social context, but in more complex societies they may only be funny for various subgroups depending on age, ethnicity, gender and/or class.

Yet jokes have a further function according to Freud who adds that 'carica-ture, parody and travesty just like their counterpart in real life, unmasking, are directed against persons and things with a claim on authority and respect, and in some sense *sublime*"' (2002: 195). And by sublime he refers to large institutions that lead to the alienation of the ego from itself. In this sense, as Lukes also argues (1985), humour can be both a coping mechanism and subversive. My argument here is that some large-scale institutions are now globally shared – for example, the modern nation-state and its organs of government – and out of these com-monalities arises transcultural comedy. One film that travelled the globe in the era of the great depression may suffice to make my point: Chaplin's *Modern Times* (1936). His character's consistently difficult relationship with the technology of modernity was not only funny for those with an experience of industrialization, but almost worked as a science fiction tale for those societies which had not yet reached that level of technology. The film succeeded both because of its depiction of 'modern' machinery and because of Chaplin's vexed, slapstick relationship to it and to the legal system during the Great Depression (he keeps being arrested). Thus several institutions of modernity are mocked in this film.

This line of analysis is similar to Bakhtin's (2009) overview of Rabelais and the concept of carnival. Bakhtin is less interested in jokes as he is in the broader concept of humour, of what people find funny and what moves them to laugh-ter. His detailed analysis of the world of Rabelais offers an evolutionary over-view of how humour has changed within a European context since the middle ages. For the purposes of this chapter I am only going to use his concept of gro-tesque realism: the images, plays and ritual performances found in folk culture especially during carnival. Bakhtin distinguishes between grotesque realism and the Romantic grotesque found in Renaissance literature, which emphasizes the serious.[6] The former, being rooted in folk culture, finds its humour in the earthiest of jokes, puns and images while also relying on the parody and satire of mainstream culture; the latter expresses a 'fear of the world' and seeks 'to inspire their reader with this fear. On the contrary the images of folk culture are absolutely fearless and communicate this fearlessness to all' (2009: 39). Thus grotesque realism, far more than the Romantic grotesque, is liberating; it affirms regeneration and recognizes that while death is inevitable, there is always life: 'Terror was turned into something gay and comic' (ibid.).

Bakhtin's concept of grotesque realism is comparable to Csicsery-Ronay's definition of science fictional grotesque: 'The technoscientific grotesque is the inversion, and frequent concomitant, of the technosublime' defined as 'a sense of awe and dread in response to human technological projects that exceed the power of their human creators' (2008: 7). In inverting the technosublime, the technoscientific grotesque 'represents the collapse of ontological categories that reason has considered essentially distinct, creating a spectacle of impossible fusions' (ibid.). While Csicery-Ronay considers only the serious science fiction that results from these impossible fusions, I take his 'collapse of ontological categories' as being similar to the folk inversions of high culture through the parody, scatological humour, satire and libidinous performances that characterize grotesque realism in Bakhtin's overview of the history of humour. I will push this further by saying that 'serious' science fiction film is analogous to the Romantic grotesque which expresses 'fear of the world' and focuses on noble heroes, while comedy science fiction is as fearless as the folk humour that turned terror into something comic. To make my point clear, I turn to the films.

Laughing at Modern Masculinities

> Sometimes I have wondered whether
> life wouldn't be more amusing
> if we were all devils, no nonsense
> about angels and being good.
> (Dr Pretorius in *The Bride of Frankenstein*)

The topic of comedy science fiction films is rather broad and I have chosen to narrow it to a few films and television series from the 1970s onwards as well as a few topics that dominate them. These shared themes include amusement at new forms of masculinities that are imagined as the result of advances in science; related to this is an anxiety about understanding and using new technologies, as well as a fear of the experts who create them. Finally, these films question our ability to withstand the threatened destruction of humanity in the face of invading others, who are technologically more advanced. These are overlapping areas of representation as well as common themes in serious science fiction; however, they are often pared down or simplified in their film versions. It is their elaboration in a comic form that interests me most. First I need to elaborate somewhat on the problem of science fiction as a global mass media.

As a written medium, science fiction has until recently been dominated by writers from Anglo-American cultures as well as being generally the province of male writers and readers. Shifts in the worlds of publishing and marketing, plus the success of the genre when aimed at younger readers, have meant that science fiction audiences have expanded and changed their nature throughout the last decades of the twentieth century. Blockbuster science fiction films such as *Star Wars* (Lucas 1977) played a part in this changing audience demographic, although, as we shall see, science fiction films have a long history. What is worth noting, however, is that the written genre long had transcultural fans who read the works either in translation or in their original language,[7] forming a sub-culture of readers that has grown and fragmented into sub-universes of science fiction and fantasy audiences.[8] Also important were the science fiction themed children's television programmes that began to circulate globally, some as early as the 1960s such as *Astro Boy* (Mushi Productions 1963–1964), many of which were made initially in Japan and then dubbed or recut for foreign audiences. This led to a growing market in importing the related Japanese manga and toys while creating new generations of science fiction consumers. The fact that these often comic children's versions of science fiction seem to travel so well might explain the increase in comedy science fiction films aimed at older audiences. Moreover, as science fiction audiences grew, the narrative versions that mocked the conventions of the genre (Mähkä 2011) began to increase as well, appealing to the spectators who were the genre's main consumers; such intertextual[9] humour helped to reinforce and maintain their subculture's boundaries since one had to be familiar with the dominant tropes in order to get the jokes.[10] However, by the 1990s, as we shall see, comedy science fiction films had spread to a wider, global audience. A possible explanation is that the potential for comedy is always present in science fiction and that film as a genre was able to explore and exploit this to its fullest extent.

Consider, for example, one of the earliest silent short films which was Georges Méliès' *Le Voyage dans la Lune* (*A Trip to the Moon*, 1902), in which the spaceship crashes into the smiling face of the moon. Such comic moments often continue to appear in science fiction films of all types, often because a comic aside can relieve a moment of tension just before a scene of pure terror – and in this the genre reveals how it borders on and overlaps with the horror film genre. Such comic interludes apart, the question might well be how soon comedy and science fiction came together in a film that was meant to amuse and the best I can come up with is a 1934 short film by Chase entitled *Another Wild Idea*. I would argue, however, that much of what is now regarded as funny science fiction was initially produced as serious science fiction and has come, over time, to be seen as camp to the point of comic. A good example of this, aside from Whale's *Frankenstein*, to which I will return, is Universal's *Flash Gordon* (Stephani 1936) serial which has run the gamut from beloved comic book, to short film, to camp remake (Hodges 1980), to serious television serial in the twenty-first century (Flash Films 2007–2008). It is in the way that the original series held the potential for camp, with its melodramatic dialogue, hero in tight tights, clearly Oriental (and Orientalist) villain Emperor Ming and its mise en scène attempts to appear ultra-modern, that we can locate the camp. But how does the camp become comic? Like Sontag (1964) I can offer no concrete answer to such a query, but will pin-point the element of science fiction film that to me seems to have held the greatest camp, and later comic, potential: its portrayal of heroic masculinity.

The starting point is obvious: Mary Shelley's novel asked what would happen if men began to usurp the female prerogative in 'birthing' the next generation. She explored the philosophical dimensions of this, but it was left to the direc-tor James Whale to subtly, or perhaps inadvertently, insert the camp elements into his *Bride of Frankenstein* (1935), in which Dr Frankenstein's monstrous progeny is lonely and the proposed solution is to make him a woman with whom to share his monstrosity. For many, the film crosses the line into camp in many ways, but I think it also plants the seeds for a comic examination of a figure that was becoming of increasing concern in the public imagination: the scientist, in this case the 'mad' scientist (Dr Pretorius, played by Ernest Thesiger in the film), who had begun to haunt science fiction cinema in Lang's *Metropolis* (1927). Obsessed, often wild-haired, with suspect social and political agendas and almost always male, the mad scientist knows no moral or ethical limits and acknowledges no higher authority than the quest for knowledge. The mad scientist wants to play at, or even imagines himself to be, god. Serious con-cerns about scientists' inability to consider the widespread ethical ramifications of their inventions, most notably the atom bomb, began to be fictionalized in film in the late 1950s; however, the comic concern was explored earlier in such films as *Abbot and Costello meet Frankenstein* (also known as *Abbott and Costello Meet the Ghosts*, Barton 1948) in which the mad doctor is portrayed as a woman who is destroyed by her own creation. Gender change aside, the potential for laughing at some of the symbolic implications of a man making his own 'child' began to be explored more fully in the 1970s and 1980s, precisely the era when, hypothetically, western, particularly American, masculinity was seen to be under threat from the rise of feminism.

Two key comic representations of Dr Frankenstein make this point clear. First we have Dr Frank N Furter (Tim Curry) in *The Rocky Horror Picture Show* (1975), the alien scientist from outer space, who is also a bisexual transsexual, trying to build a perfect man for himself – with the emphasis on *for* himself.

Unfortunately his perfect creations have a habit of falling for women rather than for him, an inversion of the early film in which Frankenstein's bride falls in love with the doctor and not the monster.

Based on a cult musical, written by an Australian, first performed in London, this film was made for 1.2 million dollars and made nearly 140 dollars at the US box office alone, with another 112 million worldwide. Less successful globally, but a favourite amongst European as well as US audiences, was Mel Brooks' 1974

Figure 6.1: Peter Hinwood as The Creation and Tim Curry as Dr Frank N Furter in *The Rocky Horror Picture Show* (Twentieth Century Fox Film).

Young Frankenstein, in which Frederick (Gene Wilder), the grandson of the original Frankenstein, becomes obsessed with his grandfather's work and also decides to build himself a 'perfect' creature. This time, although henpecked by his apparently frigid fiancée and too timid to avail himself of the romance offered by his lovely blonde assistant Inga (Terry Garr), it is not his sexuality that is in question, but his masculinity. When, in desperation, he 'transfers' some of his intelligence to the mute monster, for whom he seems to have a parental affection, he receives in return something from his creation. What this might be is only alluded to by the cries of delight Inga makes on their wedding night, but is hinted at by this early exchange:

> Dr Frederick Frankenstein, reading from his grandfather's diary: '... I resolved to make the creature of a gigantic stature'.
> Then he says: 'Of course, that would simplify everything'.
> Inga: 'In other vords: his veins, his feet, his hands, his organs vould all have to be increased in size'.
> Dr Frederick Frankenstein; 'Exactly'.
> Inga: 'He vould have an enormous schwanzstucker'.
> Dr Frederick Frankenstein: 'That goes without saying'.

Figure 6.2: The doctor (Gene Wilder) prepares to give life to his creation (Peter Boyle) in *Young Frankenstein* (Twentieth Century Fox Film).

As Freud might say: that does not go without saying if you are making a joke.

The mad scientist whose manliness, if not sexuality, is in question reappears in the comedy trilogy *Back to the Future* (Zemeckis 1985, 1989, 1990) in which it seems that the young hero's lack of maleness is the problem: Marty McFly (Michael J. Fox) not only has to learn to stand up to bullies, but also travels back in time and teaches his father to stand up to his tormentors, transforming his parents' marriage and making home life happier for his family. Doc Brown (Christopher Lloyd), the trilogy's stereotypically mad and yet somehow benign scientist, is eventually also transformed by his relationship with Marty and through time travelling. A wild eyed and lonely figure, he, by the third film, finds a wife and has children after an adventure in the Old West, where he too learns to act in a more manly manner when he stands up to the town's bullies and learns how to handle a gun. The gun as phallic symbol is an often used comic device and requires no deep analysis, yet it is Doc Brown's mastery over and invention of new technologies that is also important: while we may fear the 'mad' scientist, there is also a grudging respect for the man of science who can change the world through his mastery of forms of knowledge that most of us cannot comprehend.

The humour lies in the fact that the mad and the totally rational scientist are but two sides of the same coin, as is so cleverly and globally represented in the television series *The Big Bang Theory* (Lorre and Prady). This hugely successful situation comedy, first broadcast in 2007, is shown in sixty-nine countries around the world and, I am assured in my impromptu surveys of viewers from abroad (whenever I encounter them), the jokes travel fairly well.[11] It may help that the jokes are not just about science, but also about how post-modern scientists are part of ordinary subcultures; they combine science fiction consumption and fandom with their professional expertise, and also have trouble finding romance. The four young protagonists of the series are almost adolescent and nerdy but mature in their chosen disciplines, socially inept but confident about their technical expertise, neither stereotypically handsome nor comfortable around females and yet somehow attractive because of their completely romantic attitude to women. If they are not confidently masculine in their everyday lives, they have enough intellectual capital to reign supreme in battles that require all sorts of wit. We might say that in the twenty-first century, we have made our peace with the mad scientist, having categorized him into one of several possible versions of what it means to be male. Perhaps, it could be added, this is evidence of the routinization of science, a system of knowledge that requires an active leap of faith on our part (Santayana 2009), in modern societies that are becoming more comfortable with new technologies, and with those who produce them.

However, in the 1990s the theme of modern man's emasculation, not necessarily because he was a scientist but in relation to long-term post-war social changes, dominated Hollywood science fiction films in general and the comic ones in particular. For example, in the supposedly serious film *Independence Day* (Emmerich 1996), the main characters fighting the alien invaders include a depressed because divorced scientist; a US president with low approval ratings because he seems, after a military career, to have become a man of cautious inaction; a fighter pilot who isn't promoted because, it would seem, of his relationship with a stripper, but perhaps also because he is black; and an alcoholic Vietnam veteran, who is believed by no one when he tells his tale of alien abduction. By the end of the film, all these characters have proved themselves heroic in totally masculine ways: the fighter pilot volunteers for the most dangerous mission, accompanied by the scientist who overcomes his fear of flying to do so, while the president suits up again to do what he loves best: flying. It is the Vietnam vet, however, who ultimately saves the day. Before this Earth-saving mission, President Whitmore (Bill Pullman) gives the following speech:

> Good morning. In less than an hour, aircraft from here will join others from around the world. And you will be launching the largest aerial battle in the history of mankind. 'Mankind'. That word should have new meaning for all of us today. We can't be consumed by our petty differences anymore. We will be united in our common interests.

Figure 6.3: President Thomas J. Whitmore (Bill Pullman) being applauded for his speech in *Independence Day* (Twentieth Century Fox Film).

Perhaps it's fate that today is the Fourth of July, and you will once again be fighting for our freedom ... Not from tyranny, oppression, or persecution... but from annihilation. We are fighting for our right to live. To exist. And should we win the day, the Fourth of July will no longer be known as an American holiday, but as the day the world declared in one voice: 'We will not go quietly into the night!' We will not vanish without a fight! We're going to live on! We're going to survive! Today we celebrate our Independence Day!

In comparison, the comedy *Mars Attacks* (Burton 1996), released the same year and with the same story line of alien invasion, has an ineffectual US president played by Jack Nicholson who is killed while giving the following speech: 'Why can't we work out our differences? Why can't we work things out? Little people, why can't we all just get along?'

The *Mars Attacks* invaders are finally defeated because they explode when they hear Slim Whitman's recording of 'Indian Love Call', a fact accidentally discovered by the rather ineffectual young hero, Richie Norris (Lukas Haas). When, aliens destroyed, he receives a medal for saving humankind, it is given to him by the only surviving representative of the government, the president's young daughter. His speech at the film's end is simple as well: 'I want to thank my Grandma for always being so good to me, and, and for helping save the world and everything'. In the end, it is not heroic action against the invaders that has mattered, but Norris' loving care for his family, most of whom ignore him for being a 'wimp', which has saved the world. This comic solution to the situation in which advanced alien technology threatens to destroy the Earth is one frequently used in comedy: it is not necessarily masculine violence, but something other, some essentially human attribute that will be the saving of us.

In *Galaxy Quest* (Parisot 1999) it is a combination of human capabilities and attributes that saves, not Earth, but a sweet alien race, the Thermians. The comedy in this film is much more complex than that of *Mars Attacks* and in its parodying of various subjects resembles the far more intertextual *Rocky Horror* and *Young Frankenstein* films. The initial satire is that of late twentieth-century science fiction conventions and the fan adulation of cult television series that have been cancelled. The reference is to Gene Roddenberry's *Star Trek*, another example of science fiction that descended into camp rather quickly, but which has, much more successfully than *Flash Gordon*, been resurrected and reincarnated in a variety of ways.[12] There is also a clear reference to Kurosawa's 1954 *Seven Samurai* (Martinez 2009) in that the actors of the television series *Galaxy Quest* are mistaken for 'real' heroes and are hired by the Thermians to defend them from another invading alien race. The central, and somewhat philosophical comic conceit, is that the Thermians do not understand the concept of fiction: they do not know how to lie. This allows them to create all the imagined technology depicted in *Galaxy Quest*, but disadvantages them in war. It is in the moment when their leader learns to tell an untruth, that he finds the courage to fight against his oppressors (not a Kurosawa solution), but this is only made possible because the young teenaged fans of *Galaxy Quest* can explain the real science behind the fictive science of the television programme and allow everyone to travel back thirteen seconds in time and change the immediate past.

We see, again, how the concern with masculinity is bound up with these comic reiterations of fighting off alien invaders; in fact, there is only one woman in the crew and the following exchange satirizes the role played by such characters in the earlier *Star Trek* series:

> Gwen De Marco: 'Fred, you had a part people loved. I mean, my TV Guide interview was six paragraphs about my BOOBS and how they fit into my suit. No one bothered to ask me what I do on the show'.
> Fred Kwan: 'You were... the umm, wait a minute, I'll think of it...'.
> Gwen: 'I repeated the computer, Fred'.

However, it is not just some form of being male that matters, but also other, more essential or ontological qualities of being human, in this case, the capacity to lie, that allow the heroes to vanquish the monstrous other. Besson takes a similar tack in his equally intertextual, but visually and narratively much more ambitious and subversive, *The Fifth Element* (1998) by giving us the hypermasculine Corben Dallas (Bruce Willis) as its apparent hero and then adding the totally female Leeloo (Milla Jovovich), a supreme being who is 'perfect', as Earth's saviour. The film stresses how unimportant Dallas' military know-how is in three

Table 6.1 Comparative Box Office Earnings

Box Office
Men in Black (gross):
- $250,690,539 (US)
- $338,700,000 (Worldwide; except US)

The Fifth Element (gross):
- $63,820,180 (US)
- $200,100,000 (Worldwide, except US)

Galaxy Quest (gross):
- $71,583,196 (US)
- $19,100,000 (Worldwide, except US)

Source: Box Office Mojo

ways: at several points in the story, Dallas' mother rings to nag him about his uncaring behaviour towards her; when Dallas fights the alien Magalores he needs a huge gun, but Leeloo, fighting a separate band of Magalores, defeats them in unarmed combat; and, finally, it is love not violence that saves humankind and Earth. The fifth element then is not only unexpectedly divine and female, but is also love, which is necessary for life together with the other four elements: earth, wind, water and fire. In tandem with the man trying to make his own progeny, with the wimp whose love leads to the accidental yet fortuitist destruction of the alien, and with the lie that makes for heroism, this is a collapse of ontological categories indeed.

My final example is the most successful of all the films discussed so far. While the examples given above may have their fans around the globe, they are often fans who see themselves as part of a sub-universe that includes those who like comedy, and who like science fiction and understand it well enough to comprehend the films' satire and parody at both a visual and spoken level. In contrast, the first of the two *Men in Black* films (Sonnenfeld 1997, 2002) appeared to appeal to broader audiences than any previous science fiction comedies, at least if we consider box office takings (see Table 6.1).

One obvious answer to the question of why *Men in Black* was so globally successful is that its themes resonated with human global experiences. The MiB is a secret NGO that polices the alien populations of the planet Earth, and staves off attempts at larger scale alien invasions. And although the parallel to the illegal human migrant is made right at the start of the film, the emphasis is on the joke that these are real aliens come to dwell amongst us. Not only are these aliens vetted and given permission to remain or not by the agency, the further joke is that all the strangeness of modern life, our urban myths in particular, can be explained by the presence of these extraterrestrials. Some of them pass for human – 'Elvis didn't die, he just went home' – while others work behind the scenes. Alien technology, confiscated as these beings migrate to Earth, makes up most of our modern machinery, which was thus not invented by humans. Moreover, the MiB survey the new immigrants through technology so advanced that it can focus in on any given individual anywhere in the world, keeping them and us safe from each other.

The jokes made about daily life in *Men in Black*, of all the films discussed, may seem more pertinent than the humour of other films that seem to derive so much hilarity from the transformations that modernity has wrought, and may yet bring about, in masculine identities and which often ask how we might survive an invasion by technologically advanced aliens. Through its focus on the experience of migration, legal and illegal, on the experience of life lived as an alien in all senses of the word, within a new society, on our experience of authority (although in this case it is imagined as a non-state authority) and on our fear that Big Brother may well be watching, *Men in Black* has an obvious transnational appeal. It also, perhaps like *Galaxy Quest*, raises questions about the nature of reality, although the MiB film literally imagines other realities, while *Galaxy Quest* hints at the fictions that form the social construction of our reality. If we add to this the two Men in Black protagonists, Agent J (Tommy Lee Jones) and Agent K (Will Smith), who like the knight errants of old 'just do their job', whether this involves diplomatic investigations or huge macho battles with monsters from outer space, we have a film of irrepressible imaginings, in which some very modern fears and myths are burlesqued for all they are worth. More than the other films discussed, the visual element of slapstick is used frequently: heads explode and grow back, there are chases that involve climbing up walls, and Agent K is shown to be creatively flexible in a world that appears inflexible. Finally, while *The Fifth Element* invites us to ponder the nature of the divine, MiB leaves us with the final image of Earth as seen from a huge distance. As small as a marble, it is then picked up by an alien, who literally uses it to play marbles, making it clear how our lives may well be nothing more than a game of chance when viewed from afar. Thus the ontological certainties relating to the male mastery of science and its technology are examined and deconstructed: what does 'to be' mean if existence is a matter of chance, a supreme being's whim, or an accident that grows out of love?

Conclusion: Tactics not Strategies

Strategy, to be quite frank, you will have no hand in.
It is done by those up above, and it merely refers to,
The larger movements over which we have no control.
But tactics are also important, together or single.
You must never forget that, suddenly, in an engagement,
You may find yourself alone.
(Reed 1950)

Serious science fiction films could be seen as narratives that help us to imagine strategies about how we will respond to events yet to come. As romantic fictions they often fall back on the oldest of mythic tropes: heroic men will rise to the challenges presented by the novum that technology will create and/or they will defeat the alien other. Even dystopic science fiction films often end with an optimistic hint at mankind's continuation into the future – often in contrast to the novels they might be based on, which end more ambiguously or pessimistically. Serious science fiction films fully encompass the hesitations that Csicsery-Ronay (2008) identifies as being characteristic of the genre, but generally focus on a noble hero whose attitude embodies the final lines of Whitmore's speech quoted above: 'We will not go quietly into the night! We will not vanish without a fight! We're going to live on! We're going to survive!' One of the successes, we might speculate, of science fiction as a serious genre is that it tends to confront and alleviate our uncertainties about the future simply by postulating the indefinite continuance of humanity. Not only does humanity continue to exist in these narratives, it also appears to continue to triumph, in one way or another, surviving to the bitter end. In the main science fiction offers us ways of understanding modern identities, at least as continuing ways of being human, into a barely imaginable future; as well as reassuring us that we will learn to live with the experiences created by our modern technologies.

In contrast, comedy science fiction films, while dwelling on similar themes, offer a different reflection: that whatever we imagine is no more than we already know and that any strategy we envisage in relation to the novum of the future is nothing more than a contemporary tactic, a method of coping with uncertainty. They also suggest a subversive possibility, basically comic, but also fundamentally serious: that whatever makes us human or civilized will not save us in the end: it is all a roll of the marble, the luck of the draw, or pure chance; that we may need the intervention of a god(dess); or that science, based on speculation, may mean nothing next to the ability to lie and be violent. We may have to release our inner monster, reveal our repressed animal selves, to win in the end. In short, these films allow us to laugh at our deepest anxiety: that the science in which we have come to trust will not/cannot save us from imminent disaster. In so doing they reveal a more anxious relationship to the real, one which acknowledges how unconvincing heroic confidence is. If science fiction is a form of dreaming, then the comedy science fiction film resembles dreams in three ways: (1) it examines our hopes about the future, shared by a collectivity that is alienated from the technosublime through (2) comic meditations on what *is* in the guise of asking what *might be*, (3) in a form – the movie – that plays with and reveals the deepest anxieties we share in relation not just to the present and future, but also critiques how this future is typically represented.

The comedy science fiction film has had a chequered history since 2001, revealing a sense that such films are somehow subversive. While serious science fiction films have been increasingly made and some have been hugely successful (*Avatar*, Cameron 2009), and comic science fiction films have continued to be produced for children only, perhaps because their anxieties must be both examined and then reassured through a form of humour that often is a gentle aside to the heroic action of the story, little has been produced in terms of comedy films aimed at adults. The example of *Men in Black II* (2002), already in production in 2001, highlights this point, since it had to change its ending to include the destruction of the twin towers and grossed less than the first film. The few, non-Hollywood, adult comedies that have been produced have been even less successful. Two British films – *The Hitchhiker's Guide to the Galaxy* (Jennings 2005), which begins with the destruction of Earth, and *Paul* (Mottola 2011), a parody of Spielberg's *E.T.* (1982) – have had lukewarm receptions and the third *Men in Black* was not released until 2012. This last film makes my point well: in order to continue to find humour in the concept of 'aliens' in New York, the film took its protagonists back to 15 July 1969, on the eve of Apollo 11's launch to the moon. I think the dates are no coincidence: since 9/11 the main producer of transcultural science fiction, Hollywood, has assumed that the audience will not – or perhaps should not – laugh at the dread we feel about the weapons of modernity which now include the apparently insignificant and innocent technologies (airplanes) that have been used in horrific ways with appalling consequences. However, we might relax and laugh at the jokes set around a space rocket's launching (albeit its potential as a weapon of mass destruction) set in an era now remembered with some nostalgia (Vietnam aside, of course).

Although the serious science fiction film as a form of the Romantic grotesque has flourished in this time of political uncertainty and growing state repression (the jokes about immigration in *Men in Black* no longer seem so outrageously exaggerated), the grotesque realism of the comedy film has not. Our twenty-first-century terror, to paraphrase Bakhtin, cannot be converted into something gay and comic, at least not yet. The truths that comedy science fiction films playfully reveal and conceal again with jokes – that there will be an end, that we will die and that we humans have no control over these facts, that no hero can save us, that we might well be alone and so we might as well take solace from the pleasure of living and the fun of dreaming – are too unpalatable to represent. If the comic can be a collective judgement, and, following Freud, a rebellion and liberation, then the passing of judgement on the future of science in the twenty-first century seems to be something we are no longer comfortable doing. We also no longer pass judgement on the relationship of technology to the modern nation-state nor do we laugh at the contemporary political world in which weapons of mass destruction are in the hands of both ordinary men and our own leaders, rather than in the claws of extraterrestrials. For the time being, although we still dream about it, we have stopped laughing at the future.

Notes

1   I must thank both David and Martin Gellner for their comments. I am also grateful
    to Lidia Sciama and Elizabeth Hsu for inviting me to participate in the seminar series
    at which I gave a first version of this chapter; the audience discussion was very useful
    in formulating this version. Finally, the SOAS students on 'The Other in Horror and
    Science Fiction Films' course heard me think through the key ideas in this chapter for
    six years and their patience and responses have been much appreciated.

2   I do not take the terms represent and representation as unproblematic: to re-present
    something is inherently to do some sort of violence to the original; see de Lauretis
    (1989).

3   This is but a brief look at the filmic representations of Frankenstein's monster; IMDB
    lists 127 titles relating to the creature (www.imdb.com).

4   See Jenkins (1995) on how many NASA scientists were influenced by their early
    engagement with science fiction and decided to take up research that would allow
    them to achieve such technologically advanced futures.

5   This is something that was well understood by surrealist film-makers and is common
    knowledge amongst in the contemporary film industry. The science fiction film
    Inception (Nolan 2010) played skilfully with the relationships, pleasing many a film
    critic and audience member for making obvious the links between dream language,
    film and, I would add, science fictionality.

6   Palmer discusses Bakhtin's ideas in relation to romantic comedies (1994: 120–34),
    which leads to a useful discussion of the distinction between serious and funny.

7   I can provide ethnographic evidence for much of this in quickly outlining the for-
    tunes of the shop *Forbidden Planet*, which went from being a tiny book-packed store
    on Neal Street to a huge shop off Tottenham Court Road that was franchised, and
    currently to a new shop on Shaftesbury Avenue which sells not just books, but comic
    books – including manga translated from the Japanese – graphic novels, DVDs,
    costumes, games and collectable action figures. When I first visited the shop in 1980,
    I was often the only female customer; later in the larger shop, I kept encountering
    foreign businessmen buying up large amounts of books in English; and finally, I
    stopped shopping there when the non-book items took over.

8   Berger (1997) uses this term, taken from William James, in his discussion of how
    Shutz's work might apply to a sociology of humour.

9   The way in which the interdependence of filmic texts, or intertextuality, is used in
    post-modern comedy is discussed by Rutter 1996.

10 For an elaboration on how jokes reinforce boundaries through ridicule, see Billig's
    discussion on the humour and the social order (2005: 200–35).

11 In fact an examination of clips from the programme posted on Youtube is inter-
    esting as viewers post them in whatever language they watch the programme, so
    it is possible to compare English versions with Russian, Portuguese or French
    translations. The popularity of the programme for a broad range of viewers (mixed
    genders and age groups) is testified to by the comments found on the IMDB
    website: discussions of the accuracy of the equations shown on the whiteboards
    in the background share space with women's discussions on whether or not one

of the main characters has Asperger's syndrome, often using their own sons as comparative examples.

12 The original television series ran from 1966 to 1969 before being cancelled because of the expense of producing each weekly episode. Despite an animated version being aired, fans began to protest and the first *Star Trek* conventions were held in the mid-1970s; eventually several films were produced and a whole new generation of television series based on the original were aired: *Star Trek: the Next Generation* (1987–1994), *Voyager* (1995–2001), *Deep Space Nine* (1993–1999), *Enterprise* (2001–2005) and *Star Trek, New Voyages* (2004–2011). *The Next Generation* series also spawned a series of feature films. There was a decade, beginning in the 1990s, when it seemed possible to watch a *Star Trek* programme on almost any night of the week. A series of novels has also appeared and the original television series appears to have given rise to the phenomena known as slash fiction in which, initially, same-sex relationships were imagined for the original series characters. Finally, the series has been 'rebooted' with a new film in 2009 simply entitled *Star Trek* (J.J. Abrams). It is an interesting measure of the series' cult status that certain of its fans have completely invented the language Klingon, spoken by the original villains of the series, and that this language is credited as one of two of the later series' languages. For more on the impact that the audience, as cult fan base, had on this version of futuristic space travel, see Jenkins and Tulloch 1995.

References

Ang, I. 1991. *Desperately Seeking the Audience*. London: Routledge.

———. 1996. *Living Room Wars: Rethinking Media Audiences for a Postmodern World*. London. Routledge.

Apte, M.L. 1985. *Humor and Laughter, an Anthropological Approach*. Ithaca: Cornell University Press.

Appadurai, A. 1996. 'Disjuncture and Difference in the Global Cultural Economy', in his *Modernity at Large: Cultural Dimensions of Globalization*. Minneapolis and London: University of Minnesota Press.

Bakhtin, M.M. 1981. *The Dialogic Imagination: Four Essays*, edited by Michael Holquist, translated by C. Emerson and M. Holquist. Austin: University of Austin Press.

———. 2009. *Rabelais and his World*, translated by Helene Iswolsky. Bloomington, IN: Indiana University Press.

Benjamin, W. 1973. 'On the Work of Art in the Age of Mechanical Reproduction', in Hannah Arendt (ed.), *Illuminations*, with an introduction by Hannah Arendt, translated by Harry Zohn. London: Fontana, 211–44.

———. 2002. *The Arcades Project*, edited by Rolf Tiedemann, Howard Eiland and Kevin McLaughlin. Cambridge, MA: Belknap Press of Harvard University Press.

Berger, P.L. 1997. *Redeeming Laughter, the Comic Dimension of Human Experience*. Berlin: Walter de Gruyter.

Bergson, H. 2008. *Laughter, an Essay on the Meaning of the Comic*, translated by C. Brereton and F. Rothwell. Rockville, Maryland: ArcManor.

Billig, M. 2005. *Laughter and Ridicule, Towards a Social Critique of Humour*. London: Sage.

Botz-Bornstein, T. 2008. *Films and Dreams: Tarkovsky, Bergman, Sokurov, Kubrick, and Wong Kar-Wai*. Lanham, MD: Lexington Books.

Cazdyn, E. 2003. *The Flash of Capital: Film and Geopolitics in Japan*. Durham, NC: Duke University Press.

Csicsery-Ronay Jr., I. 2008. *The Seven Beauties of Science Fiction*. Middletown, CT: Wesleyan University Press.

De Lauretis, T. 1989. 'The Violence of Rhetoric: Considerations on Representation and Gender', in N. Armstrong and L. Tennenhouse (eds), *The Violence of Representation*. London: Routledge, 239–58.

Freud, S. 2002 [1905]. *The Joke and its Relation to the Unconscious*, translated by Joyce Crick. London: Penguin.

Jameson, F. 2006. *The Political Unconscious: Narrative as a Socially Symbolic Act*. 2nd edn. London: Routledge.

Jenkins, H. 1995. 'How Many Star Fleet Officers Does it Take to Change a Light Bulb? Star Trek at MIT', in J. Tulloch and H. Jenkins (eds), *Science Fiction Audiences: Watching Star Trek and Doctor Who*. New York: Routledge, 213–36.

Jenkins, H. and J. Tulloch (eds). 1995. *Science Fiction Audiences: Watching Star Trek and Doctor Who*. New York: Routledge.

Lukes, S. 1985. *No Laughing Matter, a Collection of Political Jokes*. London: Penguin.

MacDougall, D. 1998. *Transcultural Cinema*, edited and with an introduction by L. Taylor. Princeton: Princeton University Press.

Magallon, L.L. 1997. *Mutual Dreaming*. New York: Pocket Books.

Mähkä, R. 2011. 'A Killer Joke? World War II in Post-war British Television and Film Comedy', in H. Salmi (ed.), *Historical Comedy on Screen*. Bristol: Intellect, 129–52.

Martinez, D.P. 2009. *Remaking Kurosawa*. New York: Palgrave.

Ong, A. and S.J. Collier (eds). 2005. *Global Assemblages: Technology, Politics and Ethics as Anthropological Problems*. Oxford: Blackwell.

Palmer, J. 1994. *Taking Humour Seriously*. London: Routledge.

Rascaroli, L. 2008. 'Like a Dream: a Critical History of the Oneiric Metaphor in Film Theory', *Kinema: a Journal for Film and Audiovisual Media*, online at www.kinema. uwaterloo.ca/article.php?id=141.

Reed, H. 1942. 'Naming of Parts', Part 1 of *The Lessons of War*, *New Statesman and Nation* 24(598), 8 August, 92.

———. 1950. 'Movement of Bodies', Part III of *The Lessons of War*, *Listener* 43(1106), 6 April, 609.

Rutter, J. 1996. 'Stepping into *Wayne's World*: Exploring Postmodern Comedy' in George E.C. Paton, Chris Powell and Stephen Wagg (eds), *The Social Faces of Humour, Practices and Issues*. Aldershot: Arena, 297–320.

Sahlins, M. 1981. *Historical Metaphors and Mythical Realities: Structure in the Early History of the Sandwich Islands Kingdom*. Ann Arbor, Michigan: University of Michigan Press.

———. 1989. 'Cosmologies of Capitalism: the Trans-Pacific Sector of "The World System"', *Proceedings of the British Academy* 74, 1–51.

Santayana, G. 2009. 'Knowledge is Faith Mediated by Symbols', in *The Essential Santayana: Selected Writings*. Bloomington, IN: Indiana University Press, 88–97.

Shelley, M. 1994 [1818]. *Frankenstein or, The modern Prometheus*. London: Penguin.

Sontag, S. 1964. 'Notes on Camp', online at http://www9.georgetown.edu/faculty/ irvinem/theory/Sontag-NotesOnCamp-1964.html

Tsing, A.L. 2005. *Friction, an Ethnography of Global Connection*. Princeton: University of Princeton Press.

Filmography

Abrams, J.J. 2009. *Star Trek*. USA/Germany: Paramount Pictures.

Barbera, J. and W. Hanna. 1966. *Frankenstein, Jr. and the Impossibles*. USA: Hanna-Barbera Productions.

Barton, C. 1948. *Abbot and Costello meet Frankenstein* (also known as *Abbott and Costello Meet the Ghosts*). USA: Universal International Pictures.

Besson, L. 1998. *The Fifth Element*. France: Gaumont.

Branagh, K. 1994. *Mary Shelley's Frankenstein*. UK: TriStar Pictures.

Brooks, M. 1974. *Young Frankenstein*. USA: Gruskoff Venture Films.

Burton, T. 1996. *Mars Attacks!* USA: Warner Brothers.

Cameron, J. 2009. *Avatar*. USA/UK: Twentieth Century Fox Film Corporation.

Chaplin, C. 1936. *Modern Times*. USA: Charles Chaplin Productions.

Chase, C. 1934. *Another Wild Idea*. USA: Hal Roach Studios.

Emmerich, R. 1996. *Independence Day*. USA: Twentieth Century Fox.

Flash Films. 2007–2008. *Flash Gordon*. Canada.

Hodges, M. 1980. *Flash Gordon*. USA: Dino de Laurentiis Company.

Jennings, G. 2005. *The Hitchhiker's Guide to the Galaxy*. USA/UK: Touchstone Pictures.

Kayro-Vue Productions. 1964–1966. *The Munsters*. USA.

Kurosawa, A. 1954. *Seven Samurai* (*Shichinin no samurai*). Japan: Toho Company.

Lang, F. 1927. *Metropolis*. Germany: Universum Film.

Lorre, C. and B. Prady. 2007. *The Big Bang Theory*. USA: Chuck Lorre Productions.

Lucas, G. 1977. *Star Wars*. USA: Lucasfilm.

Méliès, G. 1902. *Le Voyage dans la lune*. France: Star Film.

Mottola, G. 2011. *Paul*. USA/UK: Universal Pictures.

Mushi Productions. 1963–1964. *Astro Boy*. Japan.

Nolan, C. 2010. *Inception*. USA/UK: Warner Brothers Pictures.

Parisot, D. 1999. *Galaxy Quest*. USA: Dreamworks SKG.

Rodennbery, G. 1966–1969. *Star Trek*. USA: Desilu Productions.

———. 1973–1974. *Star Trek* (animated series). USA: Filmation Associates.

———. 1987–1994. *Star Trek: the Next Generation*. USA: Paramount Television.

———. 1993–1999. *Star Trek: Deep Space Nine*. USA: Paramount Television.

———. 1995–2001. *Star Trek: Voyager*. USA: Paramount Television.

———. 2001–2005. *Enterprise*. USA: Braga Productions.

———. 2004–2011. *Star Trek: New Voyages*. USA: Cawley Entertainment Company.

Scott, R. 1982. *Blade Runner*. USA: The Ladd Company.

Sharman, J. 1975. *The Rocky Horror Picture Show*. UK: Twentieth Century Fox Film.
Sonnenfeld, B. 1999, 2002, 2012. *Men in Black* trilogy. USA: Amblin Entertainment.
Spielberg, S. 1982. *E.T.: the Extra-Terrestial*. USA: Universal Pictures.
Stephani, F. 1936. *Flash Gordon*. USA: Universal Pictures.
Whale, J. 1931. *Frankenstein*. USA: Universal Pictures.
———. 1935. *The Bride of Frankenstein*. USA: Universal Pictures.
Zemeckis, R. 1985. *Back to the Future*. USA: Universal Pictures.
Zemeckis, R. 1989. *Back to the Future II*. USA: Universal Pictures.
Zemeckis, R. 1990. *Back to the Future III*. USA: Universal Pictures.

Dolores P. Martinez is an Emeritus Reader in Anthropology at SOAS, University of London and Research Associate at the University of Oxford. She is the author of *Remaking Kurosawa: Translations and Permutations in Global Cinema* (Palgrave Macmillan, 2009) and *Identity and Ritual in a Japanese Diving Village* (Hawai'i, 2004). She is also the editor of two major collections, *Modern Japanese Culture and Society* (Routledge, 2007) and *Gender and Japanese Society* (Routledge, 2014), as well as editor of *The Worlds of Japanese Popular Culture* (Cambridge University Press, 1998) and *Documenting the Beijing Olympics* (Routledge, 2010). Her current work is on science fiction and the anthropology of the imagination.

7

THE ENGLISH CHRISTMAS PANTOMIME
Toying with History, Playing with Gender, Laughing at Today

Shirley Ardener

English Vulgar Comedy

The English have had a long fascination with the grotesque and the vulgar. Formerly, for example, we found gurning (making ugly faces framed in a horse's halter) a highly comic form of entertainment. More recently, the knobbly knees competitions at holiday camps, and the risqué seaside postcards featuring large fat women and small skinny men, similarly play with exaggerated physicality. On British television we had the Benny Hill shows with their 'exaggeratedly built' scantily dressed girls; Eric Morecambe with his risible unfitting clothes and crooked spectacles; and the ludicrous cross dressing of the Two Ronnies, Barker and Corbett – they all raise a laugh. If we were to meet such oddities and inversions on the street, we might pass by with a giggle, but most likely would accord them 'civil inattention' from embarrassment or disgust.[1] In a bounded space, such as on stage with a captive audience, the likely responses are nervous titters, or hilarity. Such reactions underpin the success of farce – defined in the *Oxford Companion to the Theatre* as 'an extreme form of comedy in which laughter is raised at the expense of probability ...', and glossed by the great exponent, Brian Rix, as 'tragedy with its trousers down' (Rix 1995).[2]

This chapter deals with a theatrical discourse involving vulgarity and 'gender bending' in what Cookman (1998: 17) considers to be 'one of our only true British art forms: the Christmas pantomime', for which here I commonly use its popular short form, panto. For Michael Coveney (2001: 54–5), 'The whole ritual [of panto] is part of our national character and behaviour, at least since the "Victorian Times"'. As a small contribution to this study of humour, I attempt to look beyond the laughter to the skills and methods of the writers and actors, to various interpretations of audience loyalties, and at panto's changing contexts, themes and expressions over time.

So what is the English pantomime?[3] For Brandreth (1974: 7) it is:

> a phenomenal phenomenon ... a romantically farcical fairy tale set to music, peopled with men dressed as women, women dressed as men, humans dressed as animals, and packed with spectacle and slapstick, topical jokes and old chestnuts, community singing and audience participation ...

A famous actor in the genre, Roy Hudd (1998: 9), suggests the panto is:

> a bewildering mix of comedy, 'drag', audience participation and topical jokes. In the Panto, the man dressed as a woman is, of course, known as a Dame, while the young woman who dresses like a young man is The Principal Boy.

A notable feature of the pantomime is its popularity in the community, among all ages and across gender. Tamara Malcolm, when Director of the Theatre at Chipping Norton, also noted that 'the beauty of panto is that it cuts across the class system and is totally dependent on the audience' (2001). It is well known that, as children, Queen Elizabeth II and her sister Princess Margaret devised and acted in private pantos for the Court – just as local schoolchildren were performing for their parents. Of course, the costumes and productions reflect the actors' stations in life. Compare, for example, the dress of the St Joseph Players of Leigh village (see pages 147, 148 and 152) with that of the two Princesses.

Unfortunately, owing to escalating production costs, commercial panto is rarely found on London's West End stages, but it still flourishes in the London suburbs, and in many provincial towns. Its popularity in these venues is attested by the report that 'in 2000, two million people paid more than £20 million to see 27 Pantos, presented by the chief producing organisation, Qdos ...' (Coveney 2001: 54–5). Beyond that there are hundreds, perhaps thousands, of productions in schools, community halls and in hospitals, in which both amateurs and professionals are engaged. For groups in such venues, the earnings from panto help to finance the rest of their programmes throughout the year, including their aid to social welfare projects, be they local or overseas.

In one view, 'Pantomime is less likely to be performed at seats of higher learning [than elsewhere] as it is considered to be unworthy of academic notice' (Cookman 1998: 20). I must dispute this, not only because there are numerous Christmas pantos performed annually by students in English universities,[4] but because, as a manifestation of popular art, panto is obviously an eminently suitable topic for an anthropologist.

Commercial theatre often refurbishes old scripts and re-uses scenery. But in the run-up to Christmas new topical scripts are also written, with local and national allusions. In 1925, Disher (1925: 277) wrote that 'Pantomime was once

Figure 7.1: Queen Elizabeth when Princess Elizabeth and her sister Margaret in Pantomime, Windsor Castle, 1940s. Royal Collection Trust / © Her Majesty Queen Elizabeth II 2015.

the mirror of society', and in many ways it still is. Mothers are still found making costumes, while uncles paint scenery. There are numerous how-to-do-it books to guide them. Arguably, the oldest amateur dramatic group in England is the St Joseph's Players at Leigh, Lancashire, which is now absorbed in the conurbation of Wigan. The group was founded in the 1850s, or earlier, but only began pantomimes annually after the last World War. Linked to a Catholic church, its 60–70 members now come from all faiths. It competes with five other pantomime stagings in its catchments area, yet in 2005 it sustained eleven panto performances, drawing a total audience of about 3,000, which included the local MP, Bishop and Mayor – and provided useful income to support its other shows. In Oxfordshire, in 2001, among the local venues for pantos were: The Oxford Playhouse (*Mother Goose*); The Theatre at Chipping Norton (*Babes in the Wood*), which was attended by a party of social anthropologists and their children; The Old Fire Station at Oxford (*Peter Pan*). The 2015 panto at the Oxford Playhouse is *Aladdin*.

As an example of community theatre, the *Oxford Mail* (6 February 2002) recorded that:

> Parents, pupils and people living near Ducklington School in west Oxfordshire are to come together to stage their second pantomime after the success of their debut last year ... Director Sara Church said: 'The plan originally was that we would do one every two years because there is so much work involved. It's by public demand that we are doing one again just 12 months later'.

In 2003, the amateur Launton Village Players, who write, score and produce a new panto each year, complete with local allusions and 'special effects', presented *Red Riding Hood*, the male Dame being Countess Hairbrush, while a young woman represented Bramble the Mischievous Elf.

For those who have not seen a panto, it can be recommended as a true 'ethnic' experience. In a panto audience, hundreds of children and parents will 'cross the fourth wall' of the stage to boo and hiss the villains, and join in repartee with the players on stage. Unlike in other forms of theatre, through information secretly passed to the players before the performance, individuals and groups in the audience may be addressed by name from the stage. Indeed there is a sense of cosy complicity in the suspension of disbelief, between the players and the audience. Deborah Manley (personal communication) was amused when, at Christmas 2000, she was with 'two Dutch visitors, not warned of this tradition, who shushed the audience around them when they called out as the curtain went up on the Oxford Playhouse Panto!'

Despite panto's popularity, when in 2001 I began looking for material on pantos I encountered an interesting fact: despite the popularity of the genre, it was not possible to hire a commercial video of a complete on-stage pantomime. Such

videos just did not exist, perhaps because watching without being able to partici-
pate negates the point of it. I did find an interesting early (1982) video produced
and directed by Elizabeth Wood, compèred by, the then young, Victoria Wood
(now a high-profile comedienne), entitled *The Pantomime Dame*. I am indebted
to this video for the excellent interviews with performing Dames, some now dead,
whose comments I have drawn on. Private videos did exist; Gina Burrows kindly
lent me her copy of a pantomime performed at the charming theatre in Chipping
Norton. Although the West End theatres and videos shun this genre, each
Christmas radio broadcasts and television programmes present entertainments
that include in whole or in part seasonal pantomimes. In fact, in 2001, the only
video of a panto I might have obtained – by special application – was a TV panto,
with the comedian Paul Merton as the star. Indeed, panto makes its mark in many
TV and radio scripts which, like some stage shows, rely heavily on references to
broadcast programmes and on actors and comedians regularly seen on screen.
For example, the story lines of several of the regular soaps on British TV include
pantomimes. Likewise, the long-running radio saga of rural life, *The Archers*, has
its characters involved in a panto most years. And in real life the soap stars take
to the public stages, earning useful additional income over the Christmas period.
For example, in December 2014 Steve McFadden, a heavyweight actor in TV's
EastEnders, played the villain Captain Cook in *Peter Pan* at a provincial theatre.

A Potted History of Pantomime

The considerable literature on theatre history has found many intermingled
sources for the modern 'traditional' panto. Most agree that it owes something
to the Greeks and Romans. In a letter, Pliny describes the elderly matriarch of a
distinguished and wealthy Italian family – Ummidia Quadratilla – who passed
her later years as a fan of 'pantomime'; indeed she is reported to have what might
be called a small 'theatre empire'. The soothing of the masses with the enjoyment
of pantomime gave her control and thereby access to limited political power
(Sick 1999).

But as Brandreth (1973) notes, the Roman 'dumb-shows' were very different from modern panto. More relevant was the fusion of the Italian tradition of *commedia dell' arte*. This very popular Italian entertainment included
the Harlequinade, in which the actors assumed the roles of a familiar group of
characters – Harlequin, Columbine, Pantaloon, Scaramouche and others – who
improvised within a series of stock situations. According to Thelma Niklaus
(1956, quoted in Frow 1985: 21), in Europe:

> Every actor of experience had … a vast collection of phrases and speeches that could
> be drawn upon to fit any occasion. According to the type of role he normally played,

his *repertorio* would consist of reproaches, boasting, obscene jokes, angry tirades, declarations of love, challenges to mortal combat, protestations of despair, delight, or delirium, streams of wild oaths, soliloquies that were rhetorical, impassioned, or gibberish, all ready to spring to mind when required.

Thus pantomime has always been (and remains) formulaic – full of stock episodes, repetitive old jokes and so on, regardless of the story.

If the dating of 'the first' English panto, like the source of the River Thames, is problematic, despite contenders the first play to contain the ingredients of a proper English pantomime is said to be William Mountfort's 1685 adaptation of Marlowe's *Doctor Faustus* (Frow 1985). To Marlowe's plot Mountfort (1664–92) added the comic characters of Harlequin and Scaramouche and re-titled the drama *The Life and Death of Doctor Faustus made into a Farce* (Brandreth 1973).

In the theatre of Elizabethan England, as we all know, female roles were taken by boys and young men. This enabled Shakespeare to play many games involving transvestism. During the Commonwealth, public theatres were closed for political and moral reasons, but at the Restoration, when players followed Charles II and his court to London, French fairground entertainment brought continental influence to England. However, even after actresses entered the profession at the Restoration, the convention of a man playing a comic old woman continued (Frow 1985). Indeed, well into the eighteenth century some actresses *preferred* to see their male colleagues playing the unflattering parts of older or ludicrous women commonly found in high comedy and farce.

For a while the pantomime settled down as 'a one-act entertainment, divided into roughly eighteen scenes, which lasted perhaps two hours. The opening, which was always the shorter part of the performance, was usually based on a nursery rhyme or a classical myth, and invariably involved a pair of young lovers having to flee from the girl's disapproving father and unsuitable suitor' (Brandreth 1974: 141). The pantomime ended with a splendid transformation scene, with a happy resolution, especially of all love lives. By the 1860s and 1870s, with its comical Dame and glamorous Boy, with its rhyming couplets and verbal jocularity, with its lavish scenery and token harlequinade, the Victorian panto was a far cry from the pantomime of Regency days.

As for the modern period, the typical pantomime structure, as summed up simply by Cookman (1998: 39), has five main elements:

1. *Hero and Heroine under threat (financial or physical)*
2. *Introduction of further threat*
3. *Introduction of possible saviour*
4. *Battle between the forces of good and evil*
5. *Evil vanquished and hero and heroine united*

Story Lines

The origins of some of the stories used as themes for panto, and of the writers who adapt them, are fascinating, but space precludes much detail here.[5] Often the stories are a mixture of fact with fiction – such as in *Dick Whittington* in which the historical Sir William Whittington of Gloucester is linked with a cat. Almost all the more popular English panto subjects have long pedigrees, and many of them reached English shores from alien parts. For example, it is thanks to a seventeenth-century Frenchman, Charles Perrault, that we know the stories of *Cinderella, Sleeping Beauty, Red Riding Hood, Puss in Boots*, and *Bluebeard*, and it is due to *The Arabian Nights* that we were introduced to *Aladdin, Sinbad the Sailor* and *Ali Baba*. According to Gill Davies (1995), of all the panto stories, the two most popular are, and always have been, *Cinderella* and *Aladdin. Cinderella* reached the English stage in 1804 as a 'New Grand Allegorical Pantomime Spectacle', but it was not until Boxing Day 1860, that H.J. Byron presented *Cinderella* as 'a Fairy Burlesque Extravaganza'. Over four hundred versions of the Cinderella story have been traced and all of them differ slightly from the tale we have come to expect. The modern English version is very much as Perrault (1697) recounted it in his *Contes de Ma Mere L'Oie*, except that, in the original, Cinderella wore a *fur* slipper not a *glass* one; *en vair* (fur) was mistaken for *en verre* (glass) (Brandreth 1974: 8).

A great deal is owed to John Rich (c.1682–1761), the eighteenth-century Harlequin 'John Lun', who established pantomime in London. Harlequin, along with Columbine, Clown and Pantaloon, became a basic element in the popular theatre until comparatively recently, but he first emerged in sixteenth-century Italy as 'Arlecchino' (Frow 1985: 21). Indeed Arlecchino (as Harlequin) – one of the two stock servants, the other being Brighella (Frow 1985) – was to become the most important, most popular, and longest-lived character of the entire genre. In turn mime, acrobat, dancer and actor of many parts, he was a sort of cross between Figaro and Pagliacci in opera. He stood out due to his skin-tight spangled costume of multicoloured lozenges and triangles, derived from the coloured patches of his original servant's costume, which was introduced by James Burne in his *Harlequine Sheppard* (Disher 1925: 293).[6] Gilbert (of Gilbert and Sullivan fame), writing in 1868, recalls his childhood:

> To be a Harlequine, or Columbine was [then] the summit of earthly happiness to which a worthy man or woman could aspire, while the condition of Clown or Pantaloon was a fitting purgatory in which to expiate the guilty deeds of the miss-spent. (Gilbert 1868: 51)

In the nineteenth century there was great competition among the impresarios to dazzle the public with spectacular scenery and elaborate props, often supported by intricate mechanisms. The elaborate scene at the end became less extravagant, but nevertheless remains there today as a transformational climax to the evening's entertainment. As the pantomime shrank, the Harlequinade story itself began to disappear, and the panto opening became the panto proper.

Dames

The origins of the stock characters in pantomime who 'bend gender', and of those who have played them, can now be looked at in more detail. Again, authors offer various origins for the roles. The earliest English ancestors of the pantomime Dame are said by one authority, Frow (1985), to be Mrs Noah and Mac the Sheepstealer's Wife in the miracle plays of the Middle Ages. These had comedic elements, as when Mrs Noah flatly refuses to board the newly built Ark because she does not want to abandon the 'gossips' who are her friends (Frow 1985). Despite such possible ancestries, it is also said that the now 'traditional' role of the Dame, as we understand it, was not created until the part of the Principal Boy was well established.

Of Dames it was said:

> There's nothing like a dame: pantomime wouldn't be pantomime without her. *Cinderella* minus the Ugly Sisters, *Jack and the Bean-stalk* without Dame Trot (or Trott), *Aladdin* lacking Widow Twankey, would be like Christmas without Santa Claus – a contradiction in terms, and a dreary one at that. (Brandreth 1974: 21)

As a young child I grew up to think that the name of our feared next-door neighbour *really was* Widow Twankey, as she was known in my family! In fact, Widow Twankey, a character in Aladdin, was so-named in 1861 when Twankay was a tea, popular in London, which came from Tuan Kay Province of China (Ellacott and Robbins undated).

Men can get away with things, as women, that they could not as men. Thus, of the Dame role, Douggie Byng says: 'You can be more saucy as a woman than as a man. "What he did to me" is very different from "What I did to her". She's on the *de*fensive. A man's on the *off*ensive' (quoted in Frow 1985: 184). Kwame Sintim Musa (KSM), 'the only man doing stand-up in Ghana', who was trained in the United States, as part of his act has 'donned a dress to become Afia Siriboe, the four-times divorcée with a passion for flirtatious clothes and ruby red lips'. He is quoted as saying 'There are advantages to playing a woman'. For one thing, 'in a dress he can talk candidly about men – particularly their relations outside marriage' (Simpson 2003).

Given the role's long history, there have been too many famous Dames to mention all of them here. Grimaldi nevertheless deserves note. He was born in

1778 and retired from the stage in 1828. He played several female roles in various pantomime 'openings' before being 'transformed' into a great, and still remembered, nineteenth-century Clown (Frow 1985). He became a popular hero; an actor with versatile skills he is credited with having made the pantomime a national cult. Also outstanding in the role was Dan Leno (1860–1904) – 'A legend in his own lifetime' (Brandreth 1974: 22) – whose house is dignified by a commemorative blue plaque. 'When he died the nation mourned. The three and a half miles of his funeral route were lined with people standing three-deep all the way' (Brandreth 1974: 22). Leno was adept at conveying what some think of as an essential quality in the portfolio of Dames – pathos. Max Beerbohm wrote:

> I defy anyone not to have loved Dan Leno at first sight. The moment he capered on, with that air of wild determination, squirming in every limb with some deep grievance that must be outpoured, all hearts were his… The face puckered with the cares of the small shopkeeper or the landlady or of the lodger; that face so tragic, with all the tragedy that is writ on the face of a baby monkey, yet ever liable to relax its mouth into a sudden wide grin and to screw up its eyes to vanishing-point over some little triumph wrested from Fate, the tyrant; that poor little battered personage, so 'put upon' yet so plucky, with his squeaking voice and his sweeping gestures; bent but not broken; faint but pursuing; incarnate of the will to live in a world not at all worth living in – surely all hearts went out to Dan Leno with warm corners in them reserved to him for ever and ever. (Quoted in Brandreth 1973: 148 and Brandreth 1974: 22)

Leno's appeal to the public's sympathy is paralleled by the fact that, according to tradition, it should only be the Dame, with the occasional exception of the servant Buttons, who may address the audience directly – thus breaking the 'fourth wall' of the stage ('Dame' Stirling Roberts, personal communication, 2003). George Robey (of the expressive bushy eyebrows) became another national institution. Born in 1869, he is described by Ivor Brown (in the *Dictionary of National Biography* as 'bonneted and bridling, at once grotesque and genial, creating out of a termagant's tantrums a fountain of hilarity'; before he died in 1954 he was given a knighthood.

For over a hundred years, Dames were drawn from the variety stage and the music hall, until the impresario Augustus Collins introduced musical comedy stars into the Drury Lane pantomimes (Frow 1985). Since then, as noted above, radio and television have also provided a number of notable Dames, including the late Arthur Askey, Cyril Fletcher, Terry Scott and John Inman (1935–2007). Stirling Roberts is among those Dames who can be seen on the boards at Christmas. The above are all experienced comics; in recent years, various so-called TV celebrities – programme presenters, anchormen, newsreaders and the like – have appeared on screen in pantomimes. Even the London boxer Frank Bruno (World WBC Heavyweight titleholder in 1995, whose family was of West Indian origin) has taken to the pantomime boards, including at the Wolverhampton

Grand in 2001. And the much honoured cricketer, Sir Ian Botham, OBE, on retirement took to the stage in Dick Wittington.

Although stories and characters are pretty stock, the panto usually manages to reflect everyday culture. Today pantos may include 'soap' characters, and refer to popular concerns of the moment. 'Instead of entering with a large basket on her arm, the Dame is more likely to be seen pushing a supermarket trolley' (Frow 1985: 1). She might well make a topical joke about someone in the news.

Victoria Wood (Wood 1982) echoed Laidlaw when he described a Dame as a 'fellow in a frock with truth', when she said 'if comedy isn't true it's not funny'. And, indeed, many stress that Dames are based on real life – on the mother-in-law, the daft maiden aunt (Laidlaw, in Wood 1982), the aunt who has never had sex (Terry Scott, in Wood 1982), but above all they are based on the mother (Wood 1982). Thus, Billy Dainty (1927–1986) claimed to have picked up many of his jokes from his mother's unwitting malapropisms ('I have a stimulated mink in my cupboard') (Wood 1982). Jack Tripp said he would reject lines not life-like, and claimed he got more like his mother as he aged. For Paul Laidlaw, who still performed as Window Twankey in Stevenage in 2014, 'Dames are mums, and usually elderly. They are The Third Sex ...' (in Wood 1982). If Dames are mums, then typically they are neither happily married, nor as well behaved as one would wish one's mum to be. As a widow she is likely to be depicted as over-eagerly seeking a husband or, if unmarried, as a frustrated spinster.

Some Dames play the roles of the Ugly Sisters in *Cinderella*. Like other characters, the Sisters have changed their names and clothes frequently to keep up with fashion. Originally Clorinda and Thisbe, they have been Daisy and Buttercup (names associated with cows), Hysteria and Hydrophobia (Ellacott and Robbins, undated) and, at the Theatre in Chipping Norton in 2001, Euphoria and Aphasia. But it has occurred to me that, given the age of many actors playing Dames, they must be the mums, not of the *children* in the audience, for whom they more resemble grandmothers, but of the *accompanying parents*. Perhaps that is why pantomimes attract adults as much as children.[7] It is a time to laugh at the older authority figures, just when they are becoming a burden. Nevertheless, although Dames are grotesque and outrageous, they must be gentle and kind, as they must not offend. For Gill Davies, she should be seen as 'a nice man being a nice lady' (Davies 1995: 108). In fact the Dames must be naughty but nice.

Dainty stated, on video, 'I don't play sexy – I play vulgar. I show my knickers'. Thus, the Dame must not be too crude, and although 'she' may be ridiculed, she is not usually subjected to gross violence. At the end of the performance, like the Principal Boy, she usually ends up happily engaged to be married to one of the characters.

Figure 7.2: Dandini and two Ugly Sisters from Cinderella. Courtesy St Joseph's Players, Leigh, Lancaster.

Dress and Make-up

Make-up is very important. Dames usually put on their own cosmetics. But, except for the glamorous Dames like La Rue, the make-up is usually applied deliberately crudely; lipstick overflows the lips; rouge appears as bright red circles, false hair is piled outlandishly high. Nevertheless, it seems that it is largely the make-up that changes the man into the Dame. George Lacy (1904–1989) claimed, 'I begin to smile like a woman' (in Wood 1982). The late Terry Scott (in Wood 1982) said much the same. He saw the Dame as an extension of himself, reflecting his feminine side: 'How could anyone feel masculine with all this makeup on?'

Figure 7.3: Dame Buckle-me-Shoe from Babes in the Wood. Courtesy St Joseph's Players, Leigh, Lancaster.

Traditional Dames wear many layers of outrageous clothes which, as the evening warms up, they discard, sometimes down to their long-johns in a sort of strip-tease, with appropriate music. The preposterous sight of these ugly old Dames behaving sexily brings out the titters. Strip-tease itself is thus mocked. The aged are reminded of their proper place and appropriate behaviour. After many quick changes, Dames usually end up in an over-the-top glamorous outfit, covered in jewels and crowned by feathers – a dress suitable for the grand finale of the pantomime – when they all live happily ever after.

Women, Drag and Female Impersonators

Although most Dames have been played by men, there have been some female Dames. For example, in Covent Garden's 1826 and 1836 versions of Aladdin, the Widow Ching Mustapha was played by women. And one of the greatest of Dames was Nellie Wallace, the music-hall artiste, who also made a robust Principal Boy (see below). Nevertheless, it has been suggested that no woman is ever as convincing as a man playing the part of Dame. Indeed, Clinton-Baddeley (Frow 1985) has pointed out that for a woman to play a Dame is to attempt to make sense out of nonsense.

It follows that, if women do not make good Dames, men who are too success-ful as imitators may also be thought to fail in the role. In 1982 the late Arthur Askey (who went into pantomime in 1924) believed Dames must be 'butch men ... His trousers must show'. He went on to say 'Recently a little touch of effeminacy has been coming in' (in Wood 1982). Askey, who never wore make up but always played himself, with his own voice, regretted when people were not quite sure whether they were watching a man or a woman. It has been said that those whose 'disguise' is so good that you cannot really tell that the wearers are 'not what they seem', should be regarded as 'transsexuals', not actors. The distinc-tion is an important one, pacé Germain Greer – who equates the two and even refers to transsexuals as pantomime Dames who should not be allowed to delude women into accepting them as true sisters (Lezard 2000).

Again, according to Brandreth, 'To some panto-enthusiasts, glamorous drag queens don't count as Dames; they are seen more as female impersonators' (1974: 23). The late Danny La Rue, OBE, who performed as a drag entertainer all year round, and who starred in more than sixteen pantomimes, appeared in December 2002 in *Cinderella* at the Wycombe Swan Theatre, as Countess Voluptua. Such a role suited his normal glamorous stage persona better than had he taken the role of Principal Boy (perhaps difficult for him to get away with) or played a preposterously dressed hag-like Dame.

Those who are unfamiliar with the traditions of panto might fail to see the significance of the stage name of Barry Humphries, CBE, when he plays 'Dame

Edna Everage', whose make-up and flamboyant eyeglasses and clothes seem to be clear referents to the English panto. Like panto Dames (and some other drag [or cross-dressed] entertainers, including Hinge and Brackett[8]), part of his joke is that he is not what he claims to be – and we have to know that. Humphries' act also has implicit, if not explicit, references to the honorific title of Dame (the counterpart today, for a female member of an Order of Chivalry[9]) which the Queen of England bestows on notable worthies – hence, no doubt, his frequent suggestions of intimacy with the Queen. The ambiguous gender identities portrayed by male stage transvestites nevertheless draw our attention, for we are often uncomfortable with uncertainties. When the uncertainties are resolved, we have the pleasure of relief.

Principal Boys

The eighteenth-century practice of having women play young men's parts in opera is a precedent for female Principal Boys. However, possibly in contrast to opera, it is a heresy to suppose that Principal Boys are concerned with male impersonation. They merely assume postures that are meant to be recognized as manly, and are 'not trying to create an illusion of manhood' (Frow 1985: 90).

The role of the Principal Boy has been a star part ever since it was introduced by the actress Peg Woffington early in the nineteenth century (Brandreth 1974). Even though the girl playing the role of Principal Boy may be junior and less well-known than the other stars, she still comes on last, bringing the Principal Girl with her. The Principal Boy should always have the last word, the valedictory couplet which, according to theatrical custom, he must not speak before the first night, for fear of bringing bad luck (Brandreth 1973; Davies 1995).

A notable Boy was Madame Vestris. In 1815, she made her London début (as an opera singer) at the King's Theatre in the Haymarket, when her husband put her on in his own benefit performance. She was a considerable success, and was thus launched upon a stage career.

> Born Lucy Elizabeth Bartolozzi (her grandfather was the eminent engraver Francesco Bartolozzi) into the London of 1797. Her father was a commercially indolent Italian with a passion for music and a talent for the tenor violin; her mother a German, vain and tending to corpulence, who indulged a liking for flowered hats and provided for the family by giving piano lessons. When she was sixteen, Lucy entered into a short-lived marriage to a French dancer, ballet-master and rake named Armand Vestris. (Frow 1985: 90)

Vestris was described as 'remarkable for the symmetry of her limbs'. She had her numerous admirers, one saying 'She is the best bad young man about town, and can stamp a smart leg in white tights with the air of a fellow who has an easy heart and a good tailor' (Frow 1985: 91). The buxom Madame Vestris, 'a highly gifted performer in all manner of parts and a noted singer and impresario', was still playing breeches parts when she was fifty. She is referred to here as 'impresario', as she became the first woman ever to manage a London theatre when she took over the Olympic Theatre in 1830 (Frow 1985).

But many other distinguished ladies of the theatre have cut dashing figures in the role of Principal Boy across the years. James Agate, the dramatic critic of the *Sunday Times* from 1923 to 1943, described the Boys of the Victorian pantomimes as of 'the big-bosomed, broad-buttocked, butcher-thighed race'. He thought them examples of 'walking definitions of what the scientist means by "mass" and the Victorians by the "statuesque"' (quoted in Frow 1985: 183). Augustus Harris who managed Drury Lane Theatre in the 1880s was one of the impresarios of that time who insisted on having Principal Boys with 'opulent curves'. Harriet Vernon, one of his favourites, was 'a magnificent creature of ample figure' (Brandreth 1973: 43). Of course, not everyone cheered the Boys. One critic said that 'This theatrical system of putting the female sex in breeches is barbarous and abominable' (Frow 1985: 91).

There are a number of children's plays performed at Christmas, often, but not always, based on fairy stories, but without all the comic features associated with panto. J. M. Barrie's (1904) play *Peter Pan*, about a boy who can never grow up, was instantly successful on stage. Savage (1993: 25–6, quoting Gaber) states that, from the beginning, Peter was played by a young woman, because 'a woman will never grow up to be a man'.

For a period from 1912, the impresario Arthur Collins, who took over Drury Lane Theatre after Harris at the end of the nineteenth century, gave the role of Principal Boy to a man. And in the 1950s and 1960s in particular, the Principal Boy role fell into the hands of male pop stars. It remained for Cilla Black to reclaim Aladdin's breeches at the London Palladium in 1971 (Frow 1985).

An interesting twist is when a 'gay' performer, who habitually dresses on stage in exotic gender-indeterminate clothes, and adopts a high camp manner, takes the role of Principal Boy – as Julian Clary[10] did as Dandini in Cinderella, in Richmond, in December 2000, a role he still repeats.

Commentary

According to Christine Yousseff (undated), in her commentary 'Pantomimic Convention in the Plays of Peter Nichols', the cross-dressing in Victorian pantomimes legitimately subverted the principles of Victorian morality. She writes, 'All symbolic inversions define culture's lineaments at the same time as they question the usefulness and absoluteness of its ordering'. For Yousseff, the

Figure 7.4: Dandini and Prince Charming from Cinderella. Courtesy St Joseph's Players, Leigh, Lancaster.

nineteenth-century pantomime depicted 'the moment of upturning' and 'the world turned upside down'. For her it was a silent protest against oppression, both against the State and its mechanisms. Pantomime, unlike real life, permitted a girl, as Principal Boy, 'to assume a primary role in influencing the other [pantomime] characters' behaviour'. The audience accepted that, for the limited period of the performance, life could be different from reality.

Yet we must ask, 'how realistic is this alternative persona?' Davies, in advising the amateur girl on how to play the Principal Boy defines him as 'thigh-slapping, jaunty, chivalrous, brave, and in love with the heroine' (1995: 109). Wishful thinking perhaps, as it is a long time since a young man has habitually slapped his thighs – if he ever did – or bears those other fine qualities! No wonder that, in fiction, the young leading male is sometimes referred to as Prince Charming. Perhaps, rather, we meet in this idealized role the interpretation of a former Principal Boy, Dorothy Ward, who saw the Boy as 'an attractive woman's version of how a man behaves in romantic circumstances' (quoted in Frow 1985: 184).

Youssef, quoting Bakhtin (1968: 7), links pantomime to Carnival where there are no barriers of caste, property, profession, age or sex. Many others, including Simon Trussler (1994: 30), have noted that panto offers space for 'Rabelaisian topsy-turveydom' traditions, commonly found at Christmas or carnival, when authority and class structures are (temporarily) reversed. Examples include when junior clergy swapped places with senior brethren at the Feast of Fools, and when army officers serve Christmas dinners to 'Other Ranks'.[11] Further, in opera we find maids and mistresses changing places, in fairy stories a prince may (temporarily) transform into a toad or a beast, while the impoverished Aladdin becomes rich, and downtrodden Cinders becomes a princess. In such an ideal world people were 'reborn for new' (Bakhtin 1968: 7). This renewal and revival can also be seen in the transformation scenes at the end of the pantomime, with the union of the lovers who start a new life.

Sometimes we see an overlap between the stage identities and theatrical devices of pop stars and pantomime characters. Peter Pan (who we know was characteristically played by a girl) has been described by Jon Savage (1993: 25–6) as a 'founding text of the 20th Century pop culture'. One of the attractions of the evergreen Cliff Richard, who has for long apparently defied time, has, perhaps, been his identification as 'the Peter Pan of Pop'. Savage (ibid.) likewise argues that the pop singer Michael Jackson 'enshrines the Peter Pan principle within his own body. In transcending the boundaries of age, race and gender, he epitomises one pop paradigm: the unity of apparent opposites'. Can we see this denial of natural laws of maturation, as with the reordering of gender-bending, as a triumph of man's will over nature? Do these real special cases, and the fictional possibilities, give us pride and the hope that we can change the world, if we will?

I have quoted the views of comics that when in 'drag' they can say things that as men dressed in their normal male attire they could not. Is it also possible that such transvestite comics also fill a gap, by talking on behalf of women about men, when conventions inhibit comediennes from doing so? In England today, women (including Victoria Wood who when young compèred the video I have drawn on) have entered fields of humour, including that involving sex, that they had not heretofore explored. Have such females changed the scripts for drag comics in England? Will KSM be in competition with Ghanaian comediennes one day? If so, will it change his stage material in the future?

The flexibility possible within the panto frame attests to the vitality of the form, reflecting, among other things, our current multi-ethnic society. In 2001 Stratford Theatre in East London put on *Snow Black & Rose Red; a tale of two babes in the wood*. This 'musical Christmas fable'[12] is described as a magical and intoxicating blend of African, Caribbean and Asian myth and legend. Moreover, it was said that:

> If you go down to the woods this Christmas … in the forest, anything goes. Girls can be boys and boys can be girls. Drink the blood of two young maidens and [the spider] anansi will live forever and be always beautiful. Snow Black and Rose Red are alone in the wood. Trapped in a spider's web. Only with Kali's help can they discover the secret of true love and be free once more …

Another example of innovation was in the version of Cinderella performed by the children of St John's Primary School in Wallingford, near Oxford. It appears that Cinderella 'made it seem that the shoe was too small for her so she didn't have to marry the prince because he wasn't very charming at all' and Prince Charming ended up marrying one of the Ugly Sisters.[13] Another variation in 2001, by the Oxford Youth Theatre, was entitled *The Sanity Clause: A Pantomime in Disguise*. The title is, of course a variation on Santa Claus. Based on *The Pied Piper of Hamlyn* story, the hand-out ominously said 'the rats are back, and this time they're not alone …'

Nowadays, with the familiarity of drag shows on TV, and since the outrageous costumes and coloured wigs which used to draw a laugh can be seen at night club raves, or even on the street, Dames are wondering where their next laughs will come from. The licence for Dames to use mild innuendo which, it was once assumed, passes to adults over the heads of young children, may have a different reception from them today. Stirling Roberts reported (verbal communication) that on one occasion when the Principal Boy embraced the Principal Girl, he distinctly heard a young child call out 'Lesbians!'

Savage (1993) noted that 'playing with Gender Roles can take many forms. The most common is cross-dressing which, for many people, is a sign of homosexuality (though often not true) and is somewhat shocking…' He goes on: 'after a period when men have been men, and women women, gender-bending is back on the pop scene'. Writing of the pop group The Manic Street Preachers, he notes that, in 1991, 'all heterosexual, they were coming over extremely camp, both as a provocation, and in an implicit understanding of the transformational possibilities inherent in pop'. They transformed themselves by use of women's make-up, and by wearing 'cheap white women's blouses manhandled with stencilled slogans like Death Culture and Generation Terrorists'. Savage suggests that, 'for a long time now, popular culture – whether by pantomime Dames or pop stars like Boy George – has provided a space within our morally restrictive societies for sexuality and gender in all its forms to be discussed, rehearsed, and changed. Within popular culture we can see what we are not, but what we could be'. But, despite his defence of cross-dressing, and his recognition of its roots in English tradition, Savage also recognizes it as potentially dangerous. He states 'there is something threatening and disturbing' about it. It is a 'refusal to take the world at face value, a refusal to accept things as they seem' (ibid.).

Danger, in a controlled setting, like a thrilling ride on a roller-coaster, has its attractions for many – even for children. Perhaps it is fear stimulated by danger that compels us all to laugh, as a coping strategy – and the comics know and exploit this. In a long discussion of laughter, Disher (1925: xiii–xiv) noted the strong link between emotion and laughter: 'loss of control over the one is accompanied by outbreaks of the other... in normal emotional disturbances, internal conflict causes grim laughter'. Moreover, for him laughter 'tends to take away fear and anger' (1925: xiv). Disher also claims that 'to know what is ridiculous we must know what is sublime' (1925: xiv). Presumably the reverse is also true: when we laugh at panto's ludicrous distortions of normal life, perhaps we more clearly perceive, and become more contented with, the charms of our daily lives. Fortunately, the panto always ends reassuringly 'happily ever after'. Good triumphs over evil and disaster; villains are outwitted; anxiety is followed by the satisfaction of relief. Following the subversion of conventional life, normality, even be it of a theatrical kind, returns. We can leave the theatre happy.

When I began my research on this topic, I was told by a community theatre manager that pantomime should not be analysed by academics – its ephemeral, transitory nature could not, should not, be captured by them. Disher (1925: xii–xiv) also piles scorn on 'the professors', who analyse humour (in this case the psychologists[14]). Lord Brian Rix, now a Baron sitting in the House of Lords, but previously known as a performer of farce, which is a large component of panto, said trying to define it was 'like trying to catch feathers in a gale force wind' (1995: 43). Echoing such sentiments, I agree that there is no easy way for writers to express the meaning panto has for all involved in such a complex and varied, ever evolving, annual event. Panto is multivalent, and has many possible meanings, not necessarily all of which are shared by everyone. I therefore warmly recommend readers, if they have not already done so, to experience the English Christmas Panto for themselves. May the other contributions in this book, as well as this chapter, make that all the more interesting and enjoyable.

Notes

A version of this chapter was first published as 'Male Dames and Female Boys: Cross-dressing in the English Pantomime', in A. Shaw and S. Ardener (eds), *Changing Sex and Bending Gender* (Oxford and New York: Berghahn Books, 2005).

1 This apt phrase I borrow from Hilary Callan when she referred to the attitude of male Oxford dons towards wives of fellow dons with whom they supped recently in College (verbal communication; see Ardener 1984).

2 Farce: a dramatic work (usually short) which has for its sole object to excite laughter (OED). The term derives from the action 'to stuff' or interpolate, in this case jokes and impromptu buffoonery.

3 Pantomime's original meaning of dumb show, or voiceless mime, is poorly represented in its modern realization.

4 For example, at Oxford University, every year since 1923 the first year students at Nuffield College have put on a winter panto, often based on traditional fairy stories. Their 2002 panto was based on the Harry Potter books, and in 2003 it was a spoof on the Mafia. Their 2015 production is *Peter Panto in Nufferland* (The College Porter and Rob Forde, personal communication). Wadham College also presents pantos in the Moser Theatre; their 2003 panto was put on by the College Medical Society (College Porter, personal communication).

5 An early writer, Aphra Behn who produced some twenty plays, essayed a Harlequin farce called *The Emporor of the Moon* (spelling *sic*) 1686. Mrs Behn (the 'incomparable Astraea'), the first Englishwoman to earn a living from writing, was, even in her own uninhibited day, famous for her robust dialogue and indelicate situations (Frow 1985: 30).

6 A. E. Wilson (1934, 1974) gives Harlequin four colours: yellow (for jealousy), blue (for truth), scarlet (for love) and black (for invisibility). According to Wilson (1974), James Byrne, in the play *Harlequin Amulet* (1800), introduced a much-copied costume of three hundred coloured pieces attached to a silk base, with thousands of metal spangles that sparkled wonderfully. The dress of many coloured lozenges (the motley) still appears on stage occasionally (e.g. in *Salad Days*); it is more often found at Christmas in advertisements, and at children's fancy dress parades (viz. 'Charlotte Bull, who wore a colourful clown's costume', *Oxford Mail*, 18 January 2003).

7 Michael Coveney (2001) suggests that children over eight might prefer other forms of entertainment to panto.

8 Other examples of cross-dressing in popular culture include the play *Charlie's Aunt*, the film *Some Like it Hot*, and the Monty Python television shows. In none of these is the illusion of womanhood meant to be successful; the portrayals are grotesque.

9 Some wives and widows of Baronets and Knights are formally described as Dame in legal documents. Dame may also be the formal address of a nun in her final vows, but this is now uncommon (*Debrett's Correct Form* 1999).

10 Clary is described in the *Cambridge Illustrated History of British Theatre* (Trussler 1994: 371) as 'high-camp but low-intensity', who responded with an outgoing and often outrageous humour to his situation. One is reminded of the Shakespearean

'twist' in *As you Like It* of having a youth pass himself of as a girl impersonating a youth, who then reveals 'herself' to be a girl.

11 In our less deferential society ritualistic cross-classing is becoming something of an embarrassment, and is dying out.

12 The text of the handout was in a different font to that given here. The text was by the award-winning writers Valerie Mason and John Aka Queenie.

13 According to the report in the *Oxford Mail*, eighty children between ages seven and eleven made up the choir; Cinderella and the Ugly Sisters were all aged eleven. The infants were given an early performance and 'they all understood the difference from the original story'.

14 William McDougall (1908) is among the psychologists Disher (1925) quotes.

References

Ardener, S.G. 1984. 'Incorporation and Exclusion: Oxford Academics' Wives'. In *The Incorporated Wife*, Callan, H. and S. Ardener (eds). London: Croom Helm, 27–29.

———. 2005. 'Male Dames and Female Boys: Cross-dressing in the English Pantomime', in A. Shaw and S. Ardener (eds), *Changing Sex and Bending Gender* (Oxford and New York: Berghahn Books, 2005).

Bakhtin, M. 1968. *Rabelais and his World*. Translated by Helene Iswolsky. Cambridge, MA: MIT Press.

Brandreth, G. 1973. *Discovering Pantomime*. Aylesbury: Shire.

———. 1974. *I Scream for Ice Cream*. London: Eyre Methuen.

Cookman L. 1998. *Writing a Pantomime*. Plymouth: How To Books.

Coveney, M. 2001. *Daily Mail*, London, 7 December.

Davies, G. 1995. *Staging a Pantomime*. London: Black.

Debrett's Correct Form. 1999. London: Headline.

Disher, M.W. 1925. *Clowns and Pantomimes*. London: Constable.

Ellacott, N. and P. Robbins. Undated. *Its-behind-you* [http://www.its-behind-you.com]

Frow, G. 1985. *Oh Yes It Is!* London: BBC Publications.

Gilbert, W.S. 1868. *Getting Up a Pantomime*. London: London Society.

Hudd, R. 1998. 'Foreword'. in L. Cookman *Writing a Pantomime,*. Plymouth: How To Books.

Lezard, N. 2000. 'Greer Uncut', *The Guardian*, 26 February.

Malcolm, T. 2001. *Oxford Mail*, 20 March.

McDougall, W. 1908. *An Introduction to Social Psychology*. London: Methuen.

Niklaus, T. 1956. *Harlequin, Phoenix; or the Rise and Fall of a Bergamask Rogue*. London: Bodley Head.

Perrault, C. 1697. *Contes de Ma Mere L'Oie, ou, Histoires ou contes du temps passé: contes en vers*. Strasbourg: Brocéliande.

Rix, B. 1995. *Life in the Farce Lane or Tragedy with its Trousers Down*. London: André Deutsch.

Savage, J. 1993. 'Oh You Pretty Things', *The Times*, 3 April. [www.thisisyesterday.com/int/pretty.html]

Shaw, A., and S. Ardener, eds. 2005. *Changing Sex and Bending Gender*. Oxford and New York: Berghahn Books.

Sick, D. 1999. 'Ummidia Quadratilla: Cagey Businesswoman or Lazy Pantomime Watcher?' *Classical Antiquity*, 8, 2, 330–48.

Simpson, S. 2003. *West Africa*, 3–9 March, 27.

Trussler, S. 1994. *The Cambridge Illustrated History of British Theatre*. Cambridge: Cambridge University Press.

Wilson, A.E. 1934. *The Christmas Pantomime: The Story of an English Institution*. London: Allen & Unwin; Reprinted in 1974 as *The Story of Pantomime*, with a foreword by Roy Hudd. Wakefield: E.P. Publishers.

Wood, E. 1982. *The Pantomime Dame*. Video, a Woodfilm Production.

Yousseff, C. Undated. *Pantomimic Conventions in the Plays of Peter Nichols*. [http://members.tripod.com/~warlight.christiney.html]

Shirley Ardener (BSc(Econ) London, MA status Oxford, OBE), has carried out many years of fieldwork (until 1987 with her husband, Edwin) in Nigeria and in Cameroon, where she is still involved with the University of Buea and the National Anglophone Archives. She was the Founding Director of the Centre for Cross-Cultural Research on Women (1983–1997), now International Gender Studies at Lady Margaret Hall, where she is a Research Associate. She is also an AR at Oxford's Institute of Social and Cultural Anthropology. Ardener has edited and contributed to many books including *Perceiving Women* (1975), *Women and Space* (1981), *Swedish Ventures in Cameroon* (2002), *Changing Sex and Bending Gender* (2005) and *War and Women Across Continents* (2016).

8

THE FUNCTION OF SATIRE IN ITALIAN POPULAR SONG

Glauco Sanga

Satire, irony and sarcasm are very prominent in Italian folk songs, so much so that in collections of folk songs satire is treated as a stable semantic and functional category, because it does not have an exclusive metric form of its own, and is generally composed in the forms of poetic dialogue (*contrasto*) and of simple one-strophe lyrical or satirical song (*strambotto* and *stornello*) (Sanga 1979a).

Satirical songs have a function of social critique and control: on the one hand, they stigmatize every difference, and every deviation from normal commonly shared behaviour; on the other hand, they signal tensions that may challenge such 'normality', indeed from that point of view they may be most valuable for anthropologists.

Satire in folk songs has crystallized around a series of traditional stereotypes and themes: those satirized are mountaineers, priests, spinsters, women, family relations. From peasants' point of view, the mountaineer, with his customs, takes on the role equivalent to that of the villain in urban culture. Indeed in the past mountaineers were well-known to peasants because coal pedlars, haberdashery sellers, tinkers, grinders, chair makers, chimney sweepers, umbrella repairers, as well as shepherds, and so forth, used to spend the winter in the countryside (Sanga 1977 and 1997, Carissoni 1978).[1]

Peter from the mountains
Wanted to find a wife
He wanted to wed Rosina
She is slim at the waist
But her shoulders are wide
In the fashion of mountaineers

The ring he gave her
Was a nice ring
It was not gold nor silver
But it was made of brass
In the fashion of mountaineers
(Parre, BG, in Anesa-Rondi 1978: 212–213)

Satires against Catholic priests and friars, rooted in ancient origins and enjoying constant popularity, traditionally represent them as lewd and homosexual:

And the maid is on the fig tree
And the priest below is laughing
Do pull down [your skirt] Teresa
For the priest is in a rut
(Ponte in Val Tellina (SO), in Bergomi-Lavagnino 1995: 468)

They were at the end of the barnyard
The parson and the farmer's wife
They were at the end of the lawn
The parish priest and the divine
(Val San Martino (BG), in Tiraboschi 1977: 450)

Satire that aims at the priests, because they shouldn't have sexual relations, is directed against 'spinsters' for the contrary reason; because they should, and would like to, be married, but they do not succeed:

Merry spinsters[2]
Straw is very cheap
Go get a pair of breeches
And 'make' yourselves a man
(Parre (BG), in Anesa-Rondi 1978: 233)

Naturally, also love is among the themes privileged by satire. Courtship is an object of irony, and self-irony, sometimes affectionate and nostalgic:

See, here he comes
With a cigarette in his mouth,
swaggering like a fool.
The first love is so lovely
The second is better still
(Cerignola (FG), in Sanga 1979a: 52)

Also the warnings to the girl keen to get married are ironical

O little girl with your ardent little heart
Don't be in a hurry to take on a husband
Consider how you take him, before you take him on

He is not a loaf of bread borrowed then given back
(Villanova Monferrato (AL), in Nigra 2009: 861)

The husband in bed, the baby in the cradle
That is the end of freedom – the fate of married girls

The husband always away, to eat and drink at the pub
The wife with little children always at home to sigh

Be careful girls not to dwell on such dreams
Because married young women always suffer and grieve
(Pezzaze (BS), in Pianta 1976: 117)

Marriage itself is a subject of open satire: whatever the wife may be like, she is never right:

If you marry a thin woman
That is not a good thing
She may be well dressed
But there's nothing to feel

If you marry a widow
That is not a good thing
'Cause she always remembers
The kisses of poor Jim
(Cigole (BS)m in Sanga 1979b: 145)

In traditional peasant culture, marriage was first of all an economic transaction; therefore the economic implications of marriage, especially the efforts of fathers to marry off their daughters and give them a dowry are often subjects of satire and ridicule:

There was once a father who had seven daughters
And of seven he married just one
For a dowry he gave her a cart:
And that was already too much
(Cigole (BS), in Sanga 1979b: 145–146).

Also the family is an object of satire. Sarcasm directed at the difficult relations in the traditional peasant family is particularly meaningful:

The mother and her daughter
Eat risotto
To me, daughter-in-law,
They show the pot

The mother and her daughter
Eat salami
To me, daughter-in-law,
They show the string

The mother and her daughter
Drink good wine
To me, daughter-in-law,
They show the empty flask
(Vittuone (MI), in Hertel 1985: 344)

That song relates to the traditional conflict (*contrasto*) between the mother- and her daughter-in-law, and it refers to the favouritism that took place in the peasant household, when various generations, especially the father with his married sons and grandchildren, or several married brothers with their sons and their off-spring, lived together under the rule of the family head.

Let us play music, let us sing and dance, that the she-ass
Has given birth to a cub: that pleases uncle,
It pleases uncle and grandmother
The she-ass has produced a little donkey that will carry the load
(Bergamasca, in Tiraboschi 1977: 445)

Give uncle [*barba*] a drink
He will buy you new clogs
Get him completely drunk
He'll buy you better ones
(Bresciano, in Brunelli 1976: 402)

Barba is the uncle who remains unmarried and becomes the head of the family (Sanga 1988: 4), the ruler (*regiù*); the grandmother (*nona*) is the old woman (*regiùra*) who rules over the family's women. The head of the peasant family is always represented as a hard, mean despot whose only concern is the success of the family's farm (*azienda*) and who therefore is absolutely reluctant to allow any expense for his sons, his daughters-in-law and his grandchildren.

The first song alludes to that characteristic of his: the birth of a donkey cheers the uncle and the grandmother only because it will carry the burden and thus increase the family's labour force; implicitly that hints that a similar attitude, characterized by narrow interest, would be typical on the birth of a child.

The second song shows ironically what one must do to obtain the economic favours of the *barba*: if you give him a drink he will give you money for new clogs; he will give you more if you get him drunk.

Control and social criticism may progress from satire to open invective, explicit enough to report both the name and surname of the culprit, according to the well-known model of public denunciations (*bosinate*) and of the mock-trials staged at carnival:

> Here I am, singing a long-winded yarn (*tiritera*)
> And [I wish] trouble to those who take offense
> Because those who take offense
> Are people of no worth
>
> Carletto Zirla's wife
> Is lovely and is proud
> She also has an aviary
> And keeps blackbirds by turns
>
> Carletto Zirla pretends that that is nothing
> With this music and song
> He, undisturbed and green
> Spends all day at the inn
> (Caslino d'Erba (CO), in Leydi 1978: 500–501)

Satire is of special anthropological and historical interest when it documents on-going transformations and changes in mentalities and social roles. Let us see some examples: a form of behaviour stigmatized in traditional culture is ostentation, and desire to appear different and to rise above one's social status:

> Just look there, see that 'character'
> The way he struts about
> He wears a straw hat
> Not his own
> He wears shoes
> That have no soles
> He seeks a fiancé
> And he can't find one
> (Milan, family tradition – Alessandra Sanga)

Ostentation is an urban phenomenon that follows the development of a cash economy – the economy of those who earn their living by a salary, or in any case through cash. For that reason it is particularly hateful to those still totally involved in a 'natural' peasant economy, based on production-consumption.

> Hat makers and cap-makers
> Don't know where to hang out
> They stroll in the arcades
> In their Persian lamb furs
>
> They look to right and left
> They speak Italian

Behind them is their father
Who is without a coat

Hat makers and cap makers
They are full of self-importance
They hire out their bod
To pay for all their whims

Hat makers and cap makers
They are all full of aspirations
And to indulge their fancies
They go walk on the bastions
(Alessandria, in Castelli 1984: 101)

The song above, about the women workers at the Borsalino hat factory [bor-saline], is a good example: just because they earn money, they are represented as prostitutes: they stroll in the arcades instead of staying at home: they earn impudently, they are full of self-importance and ambition, indeed they do not show a modest demeanour. They speak Italian – not the dialect like everyone else – and they display their luxurious clothes and their furs, while their father has no overcoat at all. In fact they waste their money, earned by prostitution, on unnecessary things.

The condition of factory worker exposed women to accusations of pros-titution, and the fact itself of their receiving money in exchange for labour suggested a great openness to venal relations. Undoubtedly the condition of factory worker did favour free love, and in that way a break away from tradi-tional culture especially in the area of sexuality (Kuczynski 1967; Shorter 1978). The increasingly central role of money as a measure of value, not only material and social but also moral, is immediately signalled in satirical songs, always extremely sensitive in revealing cultural changes.

Look at him properly
Look at the whole of him
The penniless man
How ugly he is
(Milan, family tradition – Alessandra Sanga)

In their open, mocking polemic with peasant morals, the songs of salaried workers, overturn traditional values, they assert that getting in debt is quite lawful and they claim the freedom to drink wine and eat white bread, the food of the rich and of invalids:

Long live those who are in debt
And down with those who are not
Debts do comfort us
They keep us healthy and well

Long live bread made with fine flower
It is as sweet as balm
If it is not quite balm
It will be still desired

I've had a lot to drink
It didn't do me harm
It is water that harms
But wine just makes us sing
(Pezzaze, in Pianta 1976: 122–123)

Satirical songs also capture the crisis in male roles. It is not only the women, but also the men who find it difficult to marry, because they are faced with women who refuse to get married, and then the men drown their misery and frustration in wine:

And also this year
I thought I would marry
But by dint of half litres
We get from here to the end of the year

And on come my thoughts and down go the glasses [of wine]
And as sadness rises down go the litres
And I think no more of my fiancée
(Vico di Capovalle (BS), in Leydi 1976: 332)

Those who do marry, then regret it, so that both men and women face an unstable and unsatisfactory home life:

How many are there of those who eat *ricotta* (shepherds)
Who take a wife and then they wish they hadn't
And zac and tac the girls end up in the sac (badly)

How many are there of those who eat polenta (peasants)
Who take a wife, then wish they were without her
And zac and tac the girls end up in the sac
(Pezzaze (BS), in Pianta 1976: 119)

The women abandon their traditional submission. The first signs are already present in the songs of the unhappily married woman (*malmaritata*): the young woman laments for having been forced to marry a rich old man and she claims her right to sexual satisfaction:

> At midnight on the dot the beautiful wakes up
> The beautiful wakes up
> With her handkerchief wet[3]
> She quickly quickly quickly
> Goes to look for her dad
>
> Father, my dear father, you have done me a great wrong
> You have done me a great wrong
> Yes, a great wrong
> To make me marry an old man
> Who sleeps all night and day
>
> Daughter, my dear daughter
> One must and needs have patience
> Must and needs have patience
> That the old man will die
> And you will be the mistress
> Of the whole estate
>
> Father, my dear father what will I do with so many possessions
> What will I do with so much inheritance
> While I am still very young/ and I long for my freedom
> (Parre (BG), in Anesa-Rondi 1968: 165)[4]

Satirical songs represent this historical phase as characterized by a refusal of wives to work hard and by the vanity and idleness of girls:

> Labour, poor man
> And do not waste your time
> You have a lovely wife
> And she can't do a thing
> Work? She does not want to work
> Sewing? She does not want to do it
> The sunshine of the countryside
> She says it does her harm
> (San Colombano (BS), in Bignami 1976: 349)

Under the pretext that she must feed her baby daughter, the wife stays home and rests all day, and claims the best food for herself:

> It is the stroke of noon
> And he finds me still in bed
> I would have got up earlier
> But if I rise the baby girl will cry

My dear Mariettina, please, dilute the wine (with water)
The barrel is near empty
We must thin out and ration it
Because we'll have to buy some

Dear husband, add some water
I'll drink it as it is
If I have it with my soup
The child will suck good milk
(Canavese; personal communication by courtesy of Amerigo Viglierno and Gian
Carlo Biglia from Baio Doria (TO))

To avoid going out to draw water from the fountain, lazy girls will eat their greens
without washing them:

The girls of Carmagnola
Have no desire to work
And rather than fetch water
They'll eat their greens unwashed

Have some, father; have some mother
Eat cauliflowers, they are so good
So, while they ate their food
They swallowed some large snails
(Castelnuovo Nigra (TO), in Leydi 1973: 225–226)

The new life style of the working class, and free love, were aggressively
vindicated by the salaried agricultural workers (*mondine*), who migrated away
from home in Piedmont and in Lomellina to work at the winnowing of rice
for forty days each year. On returning they brought about radical transformations in peasant society, because they were women who had earned money
and had adopted the modes of behaviour of factory workers, also in the area
of sexuality (Sanga 1990). *Mondine* would take sexual initiatives, and 'use'
the local men, making love with them and then abandoning them without
marrying them – in the traditional lexicon, they 'betrayed' and 'deceived'
them:

Good-bye rice-field, good-bye handsome young men
We shall no more make love[5] on little bridges

I have loved you for forty days to spend a few hours
Now the time has come [to leave] I send you to the devil

Forty days I have loved you, forty lies I have told you
Next year when I return I'll tell you forty more

You thought you were deceiving me, instead I cheated you
I have enjoyed your sweets and I have drunk your wine
(Ripalta Nuova (CR), in Mantovani 1979: 194)

There also developed competition between the mondine, who were available for
free love, and the local girls who were more reticent, because they were concerned
with marriage.

Young women, young women of Cozzo
Leave your jealousy
The rice weeders are leaving
Your lovers will return
(Cozzo Lomellina (PV), ricefields' area. Sanga 1990: 642)

The *mondine* were only a diversion, not a real danger for the local women

And the love of the Lumelina
Did not last for very long
Once the winnowing was finished
'T was the end of making love
(Ripalta Nuova (CR) in Mantovani 1979: 193)

To end, also the phenomenon of emigration did not escape satire: let us see this
example of a peasant who migrated from Puglia to New York, and who goes to
Broadway and is shocked by the city lights:

One day I felt a wish
To go to Broadway
I had never been there
And I wished to see

The thousand lights
Turning round here and there
My head gets all mixed up
I don't know where I am

Take me to my home
I want to go to sleep
I could have gone there yesterday
I don't know where I am

That last glass [of wine]
Yesterday it harmed me
Oh, kind sir, by your courtesy
Take me back to my home.

Appendix

The texts are presented in their original spelling. Note that *ṡ, ś* indicate voiced *s*, *ź* voiced *z*, *ṅ velar n*, *č* indicates palatal *c*.

For the sake of simplicity repetitions are omitted and some of the songs are not complete, as only the basic strophe and the relevant parts are included.

Pierìn di la montagna
l'völéa tö miér
vülìa spusà Rośina
l'è strécia de itìna
l'è larga de spalù
a la móda di montagnù

l'anèl che lü l'gh'è dac
sì che l'éra ün bèl anèl
nó l'éra gnè òr gnè arśént
ma l'éra de utù
a la móda di montagnù

Pierino della montagna
voleva prender moglie
voleva sposare Rosina
è stretta di vita
ma larga di spalle
alla moda dei montanari

l'anello che le ha dato
era un bell'anello
non era né oro né argento
ma era di ottone
alla moda dei montanari

***

E la serva l'è là sül figh
e 'l pret l'è sot che 'l rid
tira śü Teréṡa
che 'l pret l'è inamura

la serva è sul fico
il prete è sotto che ride
tira giù (la gonna) Teresa
che il prete è innamorato (= in calore)

***

L'éra l'éra in fond a l'éra
ol preòst e la masséra
l'éra l'éra in fond al pràt
ol preòst e 'l sör cöràt

Era in fondo all'aia
il parroco e la massaia
era in fondo al prato
il parroco e il signor curato

***

alégre pötaège
l'è bù mercàt la pàia
ciapì öna strasa d'braga
fì sö 'l vòst umasì

allegre zitelle
la paglia è a buon mercato
prendete uno straccio di pantalone
e fatevi il vostro ometto

***

E u vì u vì u vì ca mo së në vënë
ch'la sëgarètt a mmòch facènn u scëmë
ucc' e bèllë lu prìmm ammò
u śëgònd e cchiu mmègghj angò

eccolo che se ne viene
con la sigaretta in bocca facendo lo scemo
quanto è bello il primo amore
il secondo è meglio ancora

***

O fiolina dal curén ardito
non aver pressia de pié marito
prima da pial guarda come lo prendi
l'è mija come 'l pan presté e rendi

O ragazzina dal cuoricino ardito
non aver fretta di pigliar marito
prima di prenderlo guarda come lo prendi
non è mica come il pane prestato e reso.

***

Giü 'n dal lèt e giü 'n de cüna l'è finida la libertà
chèsta ché l'è le fertüna dèle s-cète de maridà

e il marito all'osteria sempre a bere ed a mangiar
e la moglie coi piccini sempre in caśa a sospirar

stighe atente ragasine di no aver de sti pensier
che le s-cète maridade le gh'à semper dispieśer

Uno nel letto e uno nella culla è finita la libertà
questa qui è la fortuna (= il destino) delle ragazze da maritare

il marito all'osteria sempre a bere e a mangiare
e la moglie coi figli piccoli sempre a casa a sospirare

state attente ragazzine di non avere questi pensieri
perché le ragazze sposate hanno sempre dispiaceri

***

Se spuśì 'na donna màgra
l'è 'n afàre che va nnò
ben vestìta che la sìa
de toccà non gh'è negòt

se spuśì 'na donna védova
l'è 'n afàre che va nnò
perché lé la gh'à sempr' em mènt
i baśì del por Lorèns

Se sposate una donna magra
è una cosa che non va bene
ben vestita che sia
non c'è niente da toccare

se sposate una donna vedova
è una cosa che non va bene
perché lei ha sempre in mente
i baci del povero Lorenzo

***

Gh'érà un pàder che 'l gh'ìà set fiöle
e de sèt el n'à maridat giönà

e per dòtå 'l gh'à dat la cariölå
l'è 'm po tròp l'è 'm po tròp l'è 'm po tròp

C'era un padre che aveva sette figlie
e di sette ne ha maritata una
e per dote le ha dato la carriola
è un po' troppo

***

La mama e la fiöla
lur mangian al riśòt
e mi che sum la nöra
me fan vidé 'l baślòt

la mama e la fiöla
lur mangian al salàm
e mi che sum la nöra
me fan vidé 'l ligàm

la mama e la fiöla
lur bévan al vin bon
e mi che sum la nöra
me fan vidé 'l pistón

La mamma (= suocera) e sua figlia
mangiano il risotto
e a me che sono la nuora
fanno vedere la pentola

la mamma e sua figlia
mangiano il salame
e a me che sono la nuora
fanno vedere il legaccio

La mamma e sua figlia
bevono il vino buono
e a me che sono la nuora
fanno vedere il bottiglione

***

Cantèm, balèm, sonèm, che l'à fač l'asna
l'à fač ü somarì che 'l piàs al barba
al piàs al barba e a la nóna
l'à fač ü somarì che 'l porta sóma

cantiamo, balliamo, suoniamo, che l'asina
ha fatto un asinello che piace allo zio
piace allo zio e alla nonna
ha fatto un asinello che porta la soma

***

Daga de bif ul barba
'l te comprarà i söpei
faga ciapà la bala
'l te comprarà i piö bèi

Dai da bere allo zio
ti comprerà gli zoccoli
fagli prendere la sbornia
te li comprerà più belli

***

Mé canti sö una tiritéra
e guài a chi sa la ciàpa
perchè chi sa ufént
in gent ca var un àca

La dona da Carlètu Zirla
l'è bèla e süstignüda
la gh'à un üelànda
la met i mèrli in müda

Carlètu Zirla al fa gna finta
perchè con sta sunàda
bèl fresch a l'usc-terìa
ài pasa la giurnàda

Io canto una tiritera
e guai a chi se la prende
perché chi si offende
sono gente che non vale niente

La moglie di Carletto Zirla
è bella e altezzosa
ha un'uccelliera
e mette i merli in muta

Carletto Zirla fa finta di niente
perché con questa suonata

bello fresco all'osteria
passa la giornata

***

Ma guarda lì chel magia
cum'el se stima
el gh'à la magiustrina
l'è minga sua
i scarp che lü el gh'à
inn sensa söla
el cerca la muruša
e nun la tröva

Guarda lì quella macchietta
come si pavoneggia
ha la paglietta
non è sua
le scarpe che ha
sono senza suola
cerca la fidanzata
e non la trova

***

Caplèri e bunetèri
i san pì 'ndo purtè 'l cü
i spasigiu suta i pòrti
col giachi 'd caracü

i uàrdu a dricia e snistra
i parlu l'italiòn
e adrera i an so pari
ch'l è sensa monfarlòn

caplèri e bunetèri
i son peñi d'impurtansa
s'i voru alvèsi i visi
is fan gratè ra pansa

caplèri e bunetèri
i son peñi d'ambision
s'i voru alvèsi i visi
is van ans i bastion

cappellaie e berrettaie
non san più dove portare il culo (= vanno sempre in giro)
passeggiano sotto i portici
con la giacca di caracul

guardano a dritta e a manca
parlano italiano
e dietro hanno il padre
che è senza soprabito

cappellaie e berrettaie
sono piene d'importanza
se vogliono levarsi i vizi
si fanno grattare la pancia

cappellaie e berrettaie
sono piene d'ambizione
se vogliono levarsi i vizi
vanno sui bastioni

***

Ma guardel ben
ma guardel tüt
l'òm a buleta
cume l'è brüt

Guardalo bene
guardalo tutto
l'uomo in bolletta (= senza soldi)
come è brutto

***

evìva chi gh'à i débiti
e crèpa chi non à
e i débiti consolano
manténgon la sanità

evìva 'l pan di sémola
l'è dolce come 'l bàlsamo
se non sarà di bàlsamo
sarà di véro amór

e gh'òi bevuto tanto
e non mi à fato male
l'è l'aqua che fa male
el vin fa ben cantar

evviva chi ha i debiti
e crepi chi non li ha

i debiti consolano
mantengono la sanità

evviva il pane di semola
è dolce come il balsamo
se non sarà balsamo
sarà vero amore

ho bevuto tanto
e non mi ha fatto male
è l'acqua che fa male
il vino fa cantare bene

***

E anche chest'àn
credìe de spuśàm
e a fórsa de mes lìter
ném de chì a la fì de l'àn

e sö pensér e śó bicér
e sö pasiù e śó litrù
e a la moróśa non si pensa più

e anche quest'anno
credevo di sposarmi
e a forza di mezzi litri
andiamo da qui alla fine dell'anno

e su pensieri e giù bicchieri
e su passione (= tristezza) e giù litri
e alla fidanzata non si pensa più

***

quài che ghi n'è che stà a mangià pu-ìna
e i töl mu-ér e pòi s'ingùra prima
e śach e tàch le s-cète le va 'n del sach
e śach e tàch le va 'n del sach

quài che ghi n'è che stà a mangià pulénta
e i töl mu-ér e pòi se ingùra sénsa
e śach e tàch le s-cète le va 'n del sach
e śach e tàch le va 'n del sach

Quanti ce ne sono che mangiano ricotta (= i pastori)
prendono moglie e poi si augurano (di essere come) prima
e zac e tac le ragazze vanno nel sacco (= finiscono male)

quanti ce ne sono che mangiano polenta (= i contadini)
prendono moglie e poi si augurano (di essere come) senza
e zac e tac le ragazze vanno nel sacco

***

a meźźanotte in punto la bélla la si riśveglia
la bélla la si riśveglia col fassolìn bagnà
e lèsta lèsta lèsta va in cerca del suo papà

padre mio caro padre mi ài fatto un grand'intòrto
mi ài fatto un grand'intòrto di un grande intòrto sì
farmi spośar quèl vècchio che dòrme la nòtte e 'l dì

figlia mia cara figlia biśògna avér passiènsa
biśògna avér passiènsa   che 'l vècchio morirà
e tu sarai padróma di tutta l'eredità

padre mio caro padre che ne faccio di tanta róba
che ne faccio di tanta róba di tanta eredità
son giovinètta ancóra mi piace la libertà

***

Laùra póer òm
E tè a mà 'l tò temp
Te gh'ét la fómna bèla
L'è buna de fa gnient

Laurà nó la öl laurà
Cöser no la öl fa
E el sul de la campagna
La dis che 'l ghe fa mal

Lavora pover'uomo
e non sprecare il tuo tempo
hai la moglie bella
e non è capace di far niente

lavorare non vuole lavorare
cucire non vuole farlo
e il sole della campagna
dice che le fa male

***

Suna mesdì turna 'l marì
e se mi trova ancura cugià

saria ausame an poch pi bunura
se m'ausu mi la cita piura

Cara Maìn, mës-cia 'n po 'd vin
che 'l butalin l'è prest a la fin
tuca mës-cielu e regulelo
che la fin 'd l'an toca cumprelu

Caro marì mës-ciatlu ti
che mi lu beivu bele cusì
se mi lu beivu ansema la supa
fa crëse 'l lait la cita pupa

Suona mezzogiorno
e mi trova ancora a letto
mi sarei alzata prima
ma se io mi alzo la bambina piange

cara Mariettina allunga il vino
che la botticella è quasi finita
bisogna allungarlo e dosarlo
perché poi bisognerà comperarlo

caro marito allungatelo tu
che io lo bevo così
se io lo bevo insieme alla minestra
fa aumentare il latte e la bambina poppa

***

E le fie 'd Carmagnola
l'àn nèn vöia 'd travaié
e pütost d'andé pi-è l'aqua

mangiu i còi-le da lavé
mangia pare mangia mare
mangia i còi ca sun tant bun
e in tal mentre ca mangiavu
traundìu i limassùn

Le ragazze di Carmagnola
non hanno voglia di lavorare
e piuttosto di andare a prendere l'acqua
mangiano i cavoli senza lavarli

mangia padre mangia madre
mangia i cavoli che sono così buoni
e mentre mangiavano
ingoiavano i lumaconi

***

addio riśaia addio giovanotti bèlli
l'amor sui ponticèlli non la faremo più

t'ò parlato quaranta giorni per passare una qualche ora
e adès l'è giunta l'ora mi ta mandi a fas ciaà

quaranta giorni t'ò parlato quaranta balle t'ò raccontato
l'an che vé quan végni amó quaranta balle ta cünti amó

tu credevi d'ingannarmi et invece t'ò ingannato
caramèlle t'ò ciüciato e vin bianch che t'ò bevü

Addio risaia addio giovanotti belli
l'amore sui ponticelli non lo faremo più

t'ho parlato (= amato) quaranta giorni per passare qualche ora
e desso che è giunta l'ora (di andare) ti mando a farti fottere (= ti abbandono)

quaranta giorni ti ho parlato (= amato) quaranta bugie ti ho raccontato
e l'anno prossimo quando tornerò quaranta bugie ti racconterò ancora

tu credevi di ingannarmi e invece io ti ho ingannato
caramelle ti ho succhiato e vino bianco ti ho bevuto

***

Signorine signorine di Cozzo
mettete via la gelosia
che le mondine vanno via
i vostri amori ritorneran

***

E l'amor de Lümelina
la g'à fai pòca dürada
l'è finida la mundada
l'è finì de far l'amor

***

Nu iùrnë më vënèttë
de scì a Vrudu-èttë
non gh'érë stàtë màië
vulèttë i a veré

mëliàië de lambadèllë
gëràvënë dë ccà e dë llà
s'ëmbròlië la capuzzèllë
non żàccë cchiu à ddo sta

e pùrtëmë a càsa mìë
më vòglië i a culcà
më n'ass ascétë aìrë
non żàccë cchiu à ddo sta

m'a ffattë màlë aìrë
quill'ultëmë bëcchìrë
signòrë per cortesìë
purtàtëmë a càśa mìë

Un giorno mi venne voglia
di andare a Broadway
non c'ero mai stato
volli andare a vedere

migliaia di luci
giravano di qua e di là
mi si imbroglia la testolina
non so più dove sono

portami a casa mia
voglio andare a dormire
potevo andarmene ieri
non so più dove sono

mi ha fatto male ieri
quell'ultimo bicchiere
signore per cortesia
portatemi a casa mia

***

Notes

1 The poems, in their original dialects and Italian translation by Galuco Sanga, are
   included in Appendix. Translation into English is mine.
2 *Pötaègia* 'spinster', literally 'old girl': *pöta* = girl, *ègia* = old.
3 Her handkerchief is wet with tears

4   A woman laments an equivalent, but inverse situation in an English folk song:
O father, dear father
I've feared you've done me harm,
You've married me to a boy
And I fear he is too young.
O daughter, dearest daughter,
And if you stay at home, and wait along of me
A lady you shall be while he's growing.
(Renwick de V., R. 1980: 99. Editor's Note)
5   In traditional folk song *Amore*, love, is feminine.

References

Anesa, M. and M. Rondi.1978. 'Cultura di un paese', in A. Carissoni, M. Anesa and M. Rondi (eds), *Cultura di un paese. Ricerca a Parre*. Milano: Silvana, pp. 79–665.

Bergoni, E and A. Lavagnino. 1995. 'Ventiquattro canti raccolti a Ponte', in O. Lurati, R. Meazza and A. Stella (eds), *Sondrio e il suo territorio*. Milano: Silvana, pp. 425–477.

Bignami, G. 1976. 'La collezione inedita di musiche popolari bresciane di Giovanni Bignami', in R. Leydi and B. Pianta (eds), *Brescia e il suo territorio*. Milano: Silvana, pp. 342–389.

Brunelli, V. 1976. 'Canti popolari bresciani raccolti e trascritti da Vittorio Brunelli', in R. Leydi and B. Pianta (eds), *Brescia e il suo territorio*. Milano: Silvana, pp. 391–455.

Carissoni, A.1978. 'Aspetti di vita tradizionale a Parre', in A. Carissoni, M. Anesa and M. Rondi (eds), *Cultura di un paese. Ricerca a Parre*. Milano: Silvana, pp. 13–78.

Castelli, F. 1984. *Ballate d'Amore e d'ironia. Canti della tradizione popolare alessandrina*. Alessandria: Il Quadrante.

Hertel, P. and Vittuone Alpine Choir. 1985. 'Canti popolari raccolti a Cisliano, Corbetta, Vittuone, in *Milano e il suo territorio*, in F. Della Peruta, R. Leydi and A. Stella (eds) vol. II. Milano: Silvana, pp. 317–395.

Kuczynski, J. 1967. *Das Entstehen der Arbeiterklasse*, München, Kindler, trad. it. *Nascita della classe operaia*. Milano: Il Saggiatore.

Leydi, R. 1973. *I canti popolari italiani*. Milano: Mondadori.

———. 1976. 'Per la conoscenza della musica popolare bresciana', in R. Leydi and B. Pianta (eds), *Brescia e il suo territorio*. Milano, Silvana, pp. 285–341.

———. 1978. 'Per la conoscenza della musica popolare comasca', in R. Leydi and G. Sanga (eds), *Como e il suo territorio*. Milano: Silvana, pp. 467–530.

Mantovani, S. 1979. 'La cultura della cascina cremasca. Le sorelle Bettinelli', in R. Leydi and G. Bertolotti (eds), *Cremona e il suo territorio*. Milano: Silvana, pp. 25–195.

Nigra, C. 2009. *Canti popolari del Piemonte*, F. Castelli, E. Jona and A. Lovatto (eds). Torino: Einaudi.

Pianta, B. 1976. 'La lingera di galleria. Il repertorio della famiglia Bregoli di Pezzaze e la cultura dei minatori', in R. Leydi and B. Pianta (eds), *Brescia e il suo territorio*. Milano: Silvana, pp. 75–127.

Renwick, deV. R. 1980. *English Folk Poetry. Structure and Meaning*. America Folklore Society: University of Pennsylvania Press.

Sanga, G. 1977. 'Il gergo dei pastori bergamaschi', in R. Leydi (ed.), *Bergamo e il suo territorio*. Milano: Silvana, pp. 137–257.

———. 1979a. *Il linguaggio del canto popolare*, Milano, Me/Di Sviluppo. Firenze: Giunti/Marzocco.

———. 1979b. *Dialetto e folklore. Ricerca a Cigole*. Milano: Silvana.

———. 1988. 'Introduzione', in 'Famiglie alpine lombardo-venete 2', in G. Sanga (ed.), *La ricerca folklorica* 38, pp. 3–4.

———. 1990. 'La cultura della cascina pavese', in R. Leydi, B Pianta and A. Stella (eds), *Pavia e il suo territorio*. Milano: Silvana, pp. 629–653.

———. 1997. 'Un modello antropologico dell'emigrazione alpina', *La ricerca folklorica*, 35, pp. 121–128.

Shorter, E. 1975. *The Making of Modern Family*. New York: Basic Books. Italian transl. 1978. *Famiglia e civiltà*. Milano: Rizzoli.

Tiraboschi, A. 1977. 'Canti popolari bergamaschi, La raccolta inedita di Antonio Tiraboschi', in B. Foppolo, *Bergamo e il suo territorio*. R. Leydi ed. Milano: Silvana, pp. 425–515.

Glauco Sanga is professor of Ethnnology and Ethnolinguistics at Venice University, Ca' Foscari. He has conducted research on Italy's popular cultures; alpine anthropology; popular oral literature (songs and fairy tales); ethnolinguistics (jargon, the origin of language, ethnoscience); the anthropology of writing; italian dialectology and the history of Italian language. He has taught at the Universities of Pavia, Bergamo, Zurich and UCLA. He is the Director of *La ricerca folklorica* and member of the Editorial Boards of *Quaderni di semantica, Quaderni di filologia romanza* and *Rivista italiana di dialettologia*. His main publications are: *Premana. Ricerca su una comunità artigiana* (Milan 1979); *Dialettologia lombarda* (Pavia 1984); *La rima trivocalica* (Venice 1992). He has edited *Nature Knowledge* (Oxford 2004); *Animal Names* (Venice 2005).

9

LAUGHING AT THE PAST AMONG VENETIAN ISLANDERS

Carlo Goldoni's *Scuffles in Chioggia*

Lidia Dina Sciama

Figure 9.1: *Le Baruffe Chiozzotte.* First Act, Scene XII. Le Commedie di Carlo Goldoni, G.B. Pasquali ed. 1774, Vol. 14. Venice: Pasquali. Courtesy of the Library of Casa Goldoni. Venice.

Mother [to Polo, a young boy who found a purse she had lost, with
three and a half meters of ribbon]: Do you want a penny?
The boy Polo: No, I don't
Mother: Do you want two pennies?
The boy Polo: No, I don't
Mother: Do you want three pennies for the finding?
The boy Polo: I don't want a penny, or two pennies, or three pennies
for the finding, I want your daughter for my wife.
Mother: Three fields and a cottage; take my Catineta. Take her, Polo,
for she is a clever girl ... she washes the floor, and she scrubs the walls. ... Three chairs
and a canapé, a small table and a cake, and we shall have a wedding, all us three!
(Nardo 1998: 65)[1]

Introduction

The short Buranello dialogue I have quoted above is an ironical comment on
the extreme poverty and the poor expectations of women in Venice's peripheral islands. Self-mockery here seems to echo the ridicule sometimes visited on
inhabitants of the islands, who in the past have often been at the receiving
end of teasing and humour by urban Venetians. In this chapter I aim to show
that feelings about being comically portrayed have greatly changed in time and
under different economic and cultural conditions. I shall first describe attitudes to laughter and ridicule among inhabitants of Burano, where I conducted
my fieldwork in the 1980s, then consider changes in responses of the citizens
of Chioggia to their own portrayal in a comedy by Carlo Goldoni, *Scuffles in
Chioggia*, written and performed over 250 years ago, but, to my mind, still
relevant to preoccupations of my informants and to themes I discussed in my
work (Sciama 2003).

Chioggia and Burano, respectively at the southern and the north-eastern
ends of the Venetian lagoon, are in some ways comparable, although different
in other ways, and especially in the eyes of their inhabitants. Chioggia's is a con-
siderably larger and more complex and stratified society, and its fishing boats are
more powerful than Burano's. But inhabitants of the two islands do share some
common traits: their dialects, although by no means identical, are similar, especially in their accents and cadence. Above all, as I found both in my fieldwork
and from Goldoni's comedy, there are similarities in their attitudes to Venice,
their capital city, and in relations with Venetians, often characterized by a mixture
of resentment and antagonism with mutual loyalty and affection.

The Fieldwork

I conducted fieldwork in the island of Burano in the 1980s, which, given the dynamic change of the last thirty years, now seems a very long time ago! One of the issues I was studying at the time was that of relations between inhabitants of Venice's peripheral islands and those of the city centre, or in general with outsiders. Much debate was focused on the islanders' need for housing, as well as social services and improvements in medical care. Traditionally, Burano's rulers, as well as all specially qualified personnel – the doctor, midwife, priest, policemen and teachers – came from outside, while, to carry out any bureaucratic practice, the islanders had to apply to the Venice town hall – and relations were not always smooth and cooperative. Buranelli were stereotyped as 'a community of fishermen and lace makers'; that is how they are still described in much tourist literature, although they are now employed in a variety of trades and professions.

Most Buranelli said they were happy and proud to be Venetian, and to know that their island is an integral part of the Venice Commune. However, resentment against the centre often came up, especially in our conversations about the past: throughout the nineteenth and early twentieth centuries, the islanders suffered great poverty and received little help from the dominant city; both fishermen and lace makers were grossly underpaid. Now, with Burano's economy greatly improved, some people are still bitter at the memory of their parents and grandparents' suffering. Many are angry and irritated at the strict conservation laws and the bureaucratic complexities that slow down much needed improvements to their homes, applications for medical care, employment, pensions, and so forth.

Another long-standing cause of Buranelli's resentment was, as for the Chioggiotti, the Venetians' tendency to ridicule their dialect. Indeed, although it is just a variant of Venetian, the Buranelli tend to double their vowels, and speak in a characteristic sing-song that has long been a source of merriment for Venetians at the centre, as have their past illiteracy and their habitual use of nicknames (Sciama 2003: 102–115). Like the Chioggiotti, Buranelli used to be teased on account of their readiness to take offence and have loud quarrels and feuds that could last a few years, till they finally ended with jolly reconciliations over a good meal and abundant drink.

All of that has been a basis for comic treatment, ever since the sixteenth century, when in Renaissance plays fishermen and sailors were parodied in comical rhymes and cast as the Venetian equivalents of country bumpkins, while a grotesque odd-speaking Carnival mask, the 'Gnaga', was associated with Burano. As we shall see, the aspects of life parodied in the comedies were frequently those of conflict between affines or between different generations, as plots usually concerned the early stages of courtship – by all anthropological accounts, a time of caution and ambivalence for the families involved (Silverman 1975: 309).[2]

When I arrived in the island, Buranelli had not yet encountered an anthropologist and they were puzzled at my attempts to find some lodging and live in their island for a while. As I found it difficult to explain clearly what I was hoping to do, I just offered what then seemed the simplest explanation, that is, to say that I had come to study their history, to learn about their customs and to record as much as I could of their dialect, so they readily pigeonholed me in a category they ironically defined as that of 'doctors, professors, lieutenants-colonels' and they embarrassingly referred to me as 'la professoressa'.[3] That put me in a position which I feared would undermine my hope to establish complete equality with my informants, who, I already knew, often referred to their poor schooling and their 'ignorance'. But that was one of the paradoxes of fieldwork, where an aspiration to equality so very often proves vain, if not somewhat hypocritical!

The fact was that several of the persons I talked to actually said they did not have, or did not know, any history. They pointed out that Burano was hardly ever mentioned in books on the history of Venice. One response was 'we do not have much history because we have been so poor that no one deigned to write about us'. In that view, history was to be found in books written by scholars and was regarded as a luxury that only the rich and well educated could afford.[4] However, it was just in our conversations about history and the past that I first experienced Buranelli's humour when, to make up for their supposed lack of historical knowledge, some of my informants gave me their own imaginative answers, providing 'just so' stories, some improvised, others already known and well-established, for example, on the colour of their houses, the street names, the origins of lace, and so forth. At that time, I perceived their self-deprecating irony, but I was far too busy collecting genealogies and studying housing problems to appreciate it fully.

On a second visit, I realized that while some people wished to ignore the problem of their island's history, others were engaged in collecting and recording memorials of their past; a strong distinction was made between history and memory, and the islanders, as they saw it, were going through the process of turning memories into 'history'. Schoolchildren were asked by their teachers to record their grandparents' accounts of archaic fishing techniques and to write up any narratives, puzzles or jokes the old people might have remembered.[5] Their work to recapture and record the past was tied up with a need to reaffirm, or at least not to lose, their identity at a time of intense social and economic change. Memories, however bitter, were an essential basis for their 'sense of who they were', which they felt it was important to maintain – and sometimes even to laugh at.

I shall leave Burano for the moment and turn to Goldoni's life and his comedy, *Scuffles in Chioggia* (*Baruffe Chiozzotte*), which takes us back over 250 years, to the Carnival season of 1762. But, because much teasing and laughter are focused on the Buranellis' and Chioggiotti's dialects, I shall first briefly discuss relevant aspects of Venetian speech.

Language and Dialect in Venice's Theatrical Tradition

'My boy, why don't you speak the way your mother taught you!'
(A woman in Burano, 1982)

Language differences often are both the sources of humour and the butts of ridicule. Therefore, without entering into the vexed question of the relative status of Venetian and Italian, I must explain that their definition respectively as 'dialect' and 'language' has frequently been challenged, both on linguistic and on historical grounds. Some critics, mindful of the fact that 'language' is associated with knowledge and power, while 'dialect' conveys ideas of cultural backwardness and subaltern positions, tend to look down on its use, with its potentially derogatory implications. Here I prefer to follow Crystal's view that in reality we all speak some dialect, and that therefore 'to see dialects as substandard varieties of a language, spoken only by low standard groups' is just an error (1988: 24).[6]

Arguments in favour of a definition of Venetian as a language are based mainly on the fact that, while Venice was an independent city state, its aristocracy and administrators all spoke Venetian. But, since 1866 when Venice joined Italy, Tuscan Italian, previously used mainly in literary writing, has also been the language of administration, education and officialdom (Sciama 1992: 361–362). Venetian nonetheless fully retains its expressive power and cultural importance. As an Italian linguist writes,

> Only in the late twentieth century are dialects beginning to be seen not as a weed to be extirpated … but as a living repository of the centuries' old experiences of the populations 'without history' … for whom history was entrusted to the vernacular expressions, common to all and yet different from place to place. (Cortelazzo 1996: 19)

What is of relevance here is that Venetian has been, and for many people still is, the idiom of intimacy and of humour.[7] Its variety offers rich opportunities for parody and laughter, as in addition to different local accents and vocabularies, there are an upper-, a middle- and a lower-class Venetian. Burano and Chioggia, long isolated in the lagoon, have maintained some archaic lexical and phonological features, in particular their descending tonic stresses that urban Venetians tend to find very funny!

Indeed, the presence of different Italian dialects, as well as local variation, has traditionally been excellent material for the writers and performers of comic dialogues. For example, among the characters in the *commedia dell'arte*, Pantaloon spoke Venetian, Doctor came from Bologna, and Harlequin and Brighella, mainly represented as comical servants or porters, were almost invariably from Bergamo and always spoke the dialect of that city (Goldoni 1951: 289 and ff.; Padoan 1982: 55).[8]

In a passage that clearly agrees with Bateson's and Douglas's views of humour (see above) as liberating from narrow and oppressive conventions, Cortelazzo (1996: 18–25) defines the Italian used in literary and erudite circles since the fifteenth and sixteenth centuries as strictly formal and 'controlled' by anxious purists. By contrast, he describes the dialect as 'creative, rich and uncontrolled'. He also notes that, just as Italian, the national language, was increasingly being used, there was at the same time a new impetus to writing in dialect; comedy lent itself to this most readily.

As we shall see, for Goldoni, dialect was above all an instrument in his aspiration to get close to social reality. In the preface to an early edition of his plays, he writes: 'I have intended what is proper to comedy, that is the simple and the natural, not the academic or the elevated ... the sentiments should be true ... this is the great art of the comic poet: to attach himself entirely to nature.'

Goldoni's Life and Work

Carlo Goldoni was born in Venice in 1707 and died in Paris in 1781. He produced, and later published, 150 comedies, some in verse, some in prose, in Italian and in Venetian, as well as opera librettos for Haydn, Galuppi, Vivaldi and other composers. As he wrote in his *Memoirs*, when his early attempts to write tragedies proved quite unsuccessful, he was soon persuaded that his real talent was a comic one. However, bearing out many a philosopher's and psychologist's observation that humour is often a counterpart to sadness, he frequently refers to his suffering from depression: 'I was cheerful by nature, but since childhood I have been subject to some hypochondriacal or melancholy vapours that darken my spirit with gloom' (1951: 32).

In his autobiography he nonetheless presents a comic vision of the picaresque existence and adventures of his younger years and he narrates his youthful escapades with a strong sense of their comic sides. As he recalls, only the life of the theatre could lift him from a state of apathy and utter wretchedness. Theatrical entertainments were part of his life since childhood, when his grandfather organized performances in his country villa and his father amused him with puppet shows. But by the time he was growing up their fortune had dissipated. His father was a doctor or apothecary, who was not earning enough to support the family in Venice, so they lived in Chioggia for about ten years. Sent to a school in Rimini, at that time part of the Papal states, Carlo found the large doses of Latin and scholastic philosophy taught there quite unbearable, but he soon managed to befriend a company of touring Venetian actors, who offered him a passage on their boat due to sail for Chioggia. He escaped from his boarding house, and he enjoyed the four-day journey with the actors as a time of infinite amusement and delight. It was from that time, he writes, that he developed a strong predilection for the 'little stage maid-servants' (ibid.: 32).

In Chioggia, all was well while the actors were there, but, as soon as they left, he was again attacked by 'a violent access of [his] lethargic illness … . I tried to find some diversion, but there was no way … '. His father wanted to make him a doctor and forced him to join him on his visits to patients, but Carlo found medicine disgusting. 'Feeling the pulse, looking at urine, examining spits and many other repulsive things …' was not for him. At last his good mother thought the boy should be trained as a lawyer, so Carlo was sent to help at the practice of an uncle in Venice, and his tedium immediately lifted: the city had no less than seven main theatres! Sent to complete his legal studies at a prestigious college in Pavia, he was expelled for writing a satire against that city's women. Thinking over his sins, in an attack of melancholy, he decided to enter a Capuchin monastery, but, once more, after a few convivial dinners and visits to the comedy theatres, the depression was overcome and the friary forgotten. 'My hypochondriacal vapours disappear; reason returns. After all [to avoid sin], it was not really necessary to entirely renounce the world' (ibid.: 78).

While Goldoni's account of his life seems to reveal a rather light-hearted, if artistic, personality, he was in fact a dedicated writer, driven by a strong sense of purpose. His lifelong aim, as he writes in the *Memoirs*, was to reform the theatre of his country. In his view, the *commedia dell'arte* that still dominated Italy's theatres had become repetitive and sterile; when actors were given only the plot for their performance, very few had enough skill to provide their own original and amusing lines. They used clichés or set pieces, referred to in the trade as their 'dowry', so that often the audience 'already knew what they were going to say, even before they had opened their mouths' (ibid. 13 and passim).

In contrast, Goldoni's idea was that dialogue should be written by the author, because very few actors – only rare geniuses – could rise to the challenge of improvization. Moreover, he thought that comedies should represent human nature and character in all their variety, and not be limited to the basic stereotypes of the masked 'arte' comedians, Pantaloon, Columbine, Doctor, Harlequin and Brighella. Therefore, to portray different social classes – the Venetian aristocracy, as well as the bourgeoisie and the working population – in their comical interactions, language was of primary importance, and indeed Goldoni was well aware that within the supposed unity of Venetian as the dominant language, there was great variety of registers and styles, all of them expressive of social differences and apt to produce some really hilarious dialogues when different people met – a linguistic richness which he excelled in using for comical effect.

Baruffe Chioggiotte

While he found Venice with its lively social life and its theatres invigorating, Goldoni never liked living in Chioggia, except for a time when his ever-forgiving father at last found him an occupation he enjoyed. At that time, like Burano and other peripheral areas, Chioggia was ruled by a Venetian noble and a Chancellor for Criminal cases with his assistant. Carlo, then a law student, was taken on as a second assistant and it was his task to write reports of hearings and trials. He was not paid but he enjoyed social privileges, concerts, parties, fine dining and balls. Because his superior did not like the work involved, Carlo, then twenty-one years old, was often trusted to take on difficult cases. 'Criminal procedures', he writes, 'are very interesting lessons for the knowledge of man' (1951: 79).

Like many playwrights, stand-up comedians and critics who emphasize the importance of the cognitive content of humour, that is, the need for all comic art to contain some essential insights into social realities, Goldoni writes that his fundamental aspiration was that his plays should above all be truthful. He explains in his *Memoirs* that his comedy was entirely based on observation and experience:

> In my youth I was in Chioggia as an aid to the criminal chancellor. Therefore I was dealing with that numerous and noisy population of fishermen, sailors and women, who have no place for their conversations other than the public streets. Observing their habits, their speech, their liveliness, their brio and their characteristic malice, I was able to describe them. In the capital [Venice], which is no more than eight leagues away from Chioggia, my 'originals' were perfectly well known: the comedy, *Scuffles in Chioggia*, was a splendid success. (1951: 355)

As he explains in his introduction to an eighteenth-century printing of his works:

> *Baruffa* is an Italian as well as Venetian word, which means quarrel, confusion, scuffle, affray of men or women, who shout and beat one another up. Such quarrels are frequent among the common people and they abound in Chioggia more than elsewhere, because of sixty thousand inhabitants, at least fifty thousand are of poor and low extraction, most of them fishermen or sea people. Indeed it was 'especially composed for the taste of ordinary people'. (Pasquali 1774: 10–11)

The play opens with a scene, familiar to me from my work in Burano: two women, Donna Pasqua and her husband's sister, Lucietta, are sitting on rush chairs before their front door, making lace. Not far, a group of three women, Donna Libera and her younger sisters, Orsetta and Checca – almost a mirror image of the first – are busy working at their lace in front of their house. They are neighbours and soon to become related through the marriage of Donna Libera's younger sister, Orsetta, to Donna Pasqua's son, Beppo. While they are waiting for

Figure 9.2: Island women (Filippi Archive. Venice).

their men to arrive back from fishing, they consider the weather: Donna Pasqua, the more experienced, says that the wind is favourable, 'if our men are coming, they have the wind behind them'. A young man, Toffolo, joins them, and, although he has an incipient liking for Donna Libera's daughter, Checca, through a strange whim he will later regret, he first chats to Lucietta who is engaged to one of the workers on her father's boat, Titta Nane. Toffolo offers the women slices of warm baked pumpkin, a popular treat on Chioggia's cool afternoons. As the men arrive, Toffolo's intrusion causes general disapproval and jealousy, while the young women all accuse one another of having been the main recipient of Toffolo's attentions. This leads to a loud confrontation, first verbal then physical, between the women, each pushing and striking their rivals. Because of the two women's mutual accusations, which anger and worry their prospective bridegrooms, the two engagements (Beppo–Orsetta and Titta-Nane–Lucietta) are broken. The men also get into a fight; they all turn on Toffolo, who, feeling threatened, decides to bring charges against them. Here then we meet the 'aid for criminal cases', Isidoro, a figure based on Goldoni's memory of his early experiences in the justice system.

Through patient, and very funny, interviews with each of the people involved, Isidoro will show that Toffolo's approach to the women was entirely innocent; his chat with Lucietta had been just a whim; in fact he really fancied young Checca, a feisty girl, only seventeen but very determined to find herself a husband. So the play ends with loud cheers, dancing and refreshments, and all relationships are happily restored.

Figure 9.3: Eugen von Blaas, 1905, *Conversation.* A painter's romantic vision of life in Venice's islands. (Photograph from: Dorotheum Vienna, auction catalogue 31 May 2007. Reproduced with kind permission of Macconnal-Mason Gallery, London).

As Goldoni recalled in his *Memoirs,* 'the basis of the comedy … is really a nothing, but the picture it presents is based on truth'. What then, we may ask, was the comic force of *Scuffles in Chioggia*? If I try to imagine how a late eighteenth-century Venetian audience might have responded to Goldoni's play, I think that the fun must have come, in the first place from the staging of Chioggia's street life, as a contrast to Venice's more restrained behaviour in public (although things were probably not too different in the city's popular quarters). But much amusement must have come also from the characters' speech, the women's colourful repartee, and in particular their accent and singsong lilt, with which Venetians were already familiar and had always treated as a well-established comical trait. The use of archaisms, and of a few robust insults, threats or endearments, well understood but not used any more at the centre, would certainly have evoked a pleasant sense of old intimacies.

The audience may also have been amused at the transparent irony in Goldoni's representation of the characters' resentment at their comical nicknames – as we shall see, a sore reality also for Buranelli – and at their reticence in admitting to them before the young clerk, Isidoro, who used them deliberately to tease and irritate them. Indeed, as the action develops, irony creates an understanding between writer and audience, especially through the skillful representation of a contrast between the characters' obstinate refusal to overcome their hurt pride, and their desire to see peace restored between the erstwhile fiancées and good relations among the affines to be.

Social Realism, Humour and Subversion

Baruffe was a great success on the Venice stage, but it also attracted sharp and malicious criticism that apparently divided the theatre-going public. Goldoni's main antagonist, and rival playwright, was Count Carlo Gozzi (1720–1806), an impoverished aristocrat and 'man of letters' in all ways different from and hostile to Goldoni's artistic and social persona. Indeed, the two men's characters and their views on humour and comedy cast an interesting light on the social and political realities of their time. In their life styles, as well as their art, Gozzi and Goldoni seem to embody the contrast between formality and freedom discussed by Mary Douglas (1975: 95–96 and see this volume's Introduction): as a strenuous defender of all things traditional, Gozzi abhorred all Enlightement ideals, he lamented the passing of the good old times when women were kept at home, ignorant of reading and writing, and, while many Venetian men were abandoning their wigs and their severe black cloaks, he never changed his *ancien régime* style of dress.

By contrast, Goldoni was a dedicated modernizer, both in his views about the theatre and in his genial use of Venetian, in all its variety, as well as Italian and French; he was in all ways a representative of the bourgeoisie, open and cordial, at ease with people of all social classes. Although he was not a political writer, his comedies inevitably reflect the social change and enlightenment ideologies then beginning to spread in northern Italy. A political dimension is therefore implicit in his choice of subjects, his use of dialect and his sense of humour, which inevitably reveal his moral and social judgments. Above all, Goldoni was a professional writer and man of the theatre who worked to earn his living, while Gozzi was convinced that to write for money was undignified, and, as a strict purist and strenuous defender of Dante's Tuscan, he described Goldoni as 'un-cultured' and he thought that 'his need to write too many works in a servile manner ... killed his talent'. At the heart of Gozzi's animosity was a feeling that Goldoni could not be forgiven for ridiculing 'some true nobles', and for making 'the plebs better than other social classes ... to win over the common people, who are always disdainful of the necessary yoke of subordination' (Gozzi 1914: 10750). In fact, Gozzi was well aware of the potential of comedy and humour for subversion and he perfectly understood that Goldoni's realism and his use of everyday language were strong threats to conservative values (Lunari 1985: 21–22; Gozzi 1914: 10750–80).[9]

Goldoni was not indifferent to Gozzi's criticism, which probably played a part in his decision to move to Paris. There his ideas on comedy and laughter are clearly expressed in his *Memoirs*. Reflecting on his past works, he again defends his use of dialect, and answering those who disapproved of his choice of 'vulgar subjects', he recalls that he wrote his popular comedies after many other works, like *Pamela*, *Terence*, *Tasso*, *Le Persiane*, 'that could satisfy the most serious and delicate spirits' (1951: 14). But in writing his popular comedies, he was mindful of the tastes and needs of his public. Italian theatres, he continues, 'are frequented by all orders of persons. The cost is so mediocre that, in Italy, unlike France, where cost is 12 Paoli or 2 standing, the shopkeeper, the servant, the fisherman may take part in this public entertainment'.

He had taken away from the simple people their ever-present Harlequin, and they were hearing about the reform of the comedies, so he felt he had to offer them something suited to their understanding – something with which they could identify and recognize their own faults and their virtues. What is more, even the most grave and noble members of his audiences had been highly amused and had laughed out loud at his dialect comedies. Anything true had the potential to arouse laughter, and it was one of his rules that before he could turn anything to comedy, he had to find it humorous and funny himself (1915: 10750).

Touching on a problem much discussed by moral philosophers and sociologists, from Plato and Aristotle to Billig (see the introduction to this volume) – the danger that humour and jokes may turn into cruel derision – Goldoni writes,

> Some will say that comedy should imitate *beautiful* nature, not that which is low and defective. I, on the contrary, say that everything is susceptible of comedy, except for the defects that sadden and the vices that offend' (1978: 86). A man who speaks fast and eats his words (like the *commedia dell'arte* stammerer, Tartaglia) has a ridiculous fault which becomes comical when it is used economically. For example, Vincenzo [a character in his Baruffe with a ridiculous speech habit] may be difficult to understand, but I did not want to change anything, because I believe and maintain that a merit of comedy is the exact imitation of nature. It would not be the same for someone lame, blind or paralysed; those are defects that demand compassion, and they must not be shown on the stage, unless the defective person may her/himself render the defect amusing or playful.

I think we would all agree with that but, as we shall see, Goldoni did, perhaps unintentionally, cause offence. Throughout the late eighteenth and nineteenth centuries, productions of *Baruffe* mainly emphasized its comical and picturesque aspects. Goethe saw it in 1786, and he wrote in his diary that he 'enjoyed the play immensely'. He actually summarized the plot, which he completely misunderstood, and he ended 'I have never in my life witnessed such an ecstasy of joy as that shown by the audience in seeing themselves and their families so realistically portrayed on the stage. They shouted with laughter and approval from beginning to end' (1962: 100–101). He had not understood that the people in the audience had not laughed at themselves, but at the unfortunate Chioggiotti! For him, as for many travellers on their Grand Tour, the play represented a typical example of the exuberance and vivacity they were seeking in the Mediterranean.

More recently, readers have given greater attention than in the past to the serious implications of Goldoni's humour. In a famous 1962 production, Giorgio Strehler, a very distinguished director, obviously influenced by Italian neo-realism, stressed the many passages that describe the hardness of the fishermen's lives, the dangers of their work and their exploitation by the wholesalers. For example, asked by his wife if the journey had been good, Toni replied,

> How can you talk of *journey*! When we are on land, we don't remember any more what we've been through at sea. When the fishing is good, the journey is good; and if we make a good catch, we don't think of the risk to our lives … we bring back the fish and we are all merry! (1978: 101)

Strehler's production also showed how Goldoni understood the dullness in the lives of women, for whom gossip was the only form of amusement and diversion, while the men's absence imposed a severe code of behaviour. As Lucietta protested, commenting on her fiancé's jealousy,

> Can't we even talk? Can't we laugh? Can't we have a good time? The men are out at sea for ten months [out of twelve] and what about us? Do we have to sit here, all stale and cheerless, to potter and fribble over those darned lace bobbins? (ibid.: 116)

They knew that marriage involved hard sacrifices, but life was not easy for single women who were almost servants in the homes of their married siblings. And, while feisty seventeen-years old Checca, certainly a very amusing character, states her firm determination to get married – as in the very first scene of *Baruffe*, she declares, 'Yes, yes, I do want to marry, even if I had to take one of those poor wretches who go about collecting crabs [for bait]' – her resolution actually shows that marriage was the only future she could contemplate. Or, as Lucietta answered her sister's husband, who had ordered her to go indoors,

> What manners! What am I? Your housemaid? Fear not, I don't want to stay with you. As soon as I see Titta Nane [her fiancé], I'll tell him: either he marries me at once, or, by Diana, I'd rather go into service. (ibid.: 103)

Hence the anxiety of the young women in *Baruffe* to save their endangered engagements. Like Brecht, Strehler thought that the theatre should stimulate awareness and debate and that, in his production of the comedy, the humour and laughter should not exclude Goldoni's references to the harsh realities of life in Chioggia.

Much could be said about the fortunes of Goldoni's works, but now, to turn to the reaction of Chioggia's people, tradition has it that they took the comedy as a bitter offence, they strongly resented it and they were angry and hurt on hearing about its enthusiastic applause by the Venetian audience. Over a hundred years later, a critic, Urbani de Gheltof (1883), claimed to have found in Venice's archives Goldoni's transcript of a trial that would have been his inspiration for *Baruffe*. De Gheltof also maintained that in Chioggia's city library he had found a number of anonymous letters and sonnets hostile to *Baruffe* and its writer, as well as a letter by Goldoni himself, trying to explain to the then governor of Chioggia that he had meant no harm. De Gheltof was not taken seriously, and it was suggested that he wanted to make fun of his readers. However, if his alleged archival discovery was a joke, the story certainly had a great deal of similitude. Without being able to ascertain the truth, on comparable evidence from Burano, the suggestion that *Baruffe* would have angered the Chioggiotti and hurt their feelings is very likely to have been quite correct.

The comedy was banished from Chioggia for over 150 years, till at last in 1919 a very popular and well-liked actor and producer, Cesco Baseggio, with his company of actors, dared to perform it in an old derelict theatre. To remove the offending implication that affrays and fisticuffs only took place in Chioggia, the title of the comedy was changed to *Scuffles in the Street* (*Baruffe in Calle*). In a later film production, it was called *The Village without Peace* (1943). At last, in 1948, a brave headmaster organized its performance by local actors in the school's courtyard, and it was a great success.[10]

To go back to Burano, as I mentioned in my introduction, its past life is in some ways comparable to Chioggia's. I also (perhaps predictably) find interesting similarities in their attitudes to social change and their good-natured responses to the fact of having been teased and sometimes ridiculed by Venetians in the past. For example, as one of my informants related in a very lively and high spirited report, a short time before my arrival in Burano, a group of friends had planned to revive the island's carnival that had lapsed for many years.

As part of the fun, they decided to collect all the islanders' nicknames and record them for posterity. As well as those still in use, they wanted to include those that were already forgotten, so in order to find them they were inspired to do some research in the old account books of shops where the impoverished Buranelli used to buy their necessities on credit. The recording of the long list of nicknames would then be broadcast, as loud as was possible, from the village square, with some added comical or salacious comments. The performance was meant to be a surprise, really just a joke, but its organizers were not at all sure how people might react; they feared some of them, particularly those who had

had to live with some thoroughly scurrilous and disagreeable nickname, might take offence.

That evening the Buranelli were all out dancing and having a good time, some wearing a masquerade, some in their everyday clothes; as the music stopped, and they heard the loud recorded voice reel off their nicknames, sometimes accompanied by the carnival organizers' witty quips and comments, they laughed and laughed and no one took offence. At long last, on that carnival night, the Buranelli, who had long been the butts of others' laughter, had become its initiators and that, they felt, was an important transition from passivity to agency.

As for the Chioggiotti, who now act in Goldoni's comedy, and at last have adopted it as their own, resentment at being represented as ridiculous by outsiders is now regarded as part of the past, as are the circumstances that occasioned it: indeed, their extreme poverty, their isolation and the feeling that their difference was a grave disadvantage, are over – now part of the past. But it is a past they certainly do not want to forget and abandon. Nor do they really wish to abandon their dialect. They still take exception at those who laugh at their speech, and, as they leave the island in the morning to go to work, they change to a more Venetian accent, but, as soon as they take the boat back at dusk, they go back at once to their lovely cadence and singsong.

What is at issue is their sense of identity as a separate island community. While some answered my questions on their history, in ironical self-mockery, with little stories and folk etymologies that they know very well are fruits of their imagination and humour, others are busy collecting testimonials of their past, in order to fight a sense of anomie and a concern that, due to their impressive social and economic change, they may be going to become just like any other Venetians.

Conclusion

In his discussion of laughter and humour, Critchley quotes a passage by Max Frisch:

> Which do you think is the more humorous,
> a) if we laugh at a third person;
> b) if you laugh at yourself;
> c) if you succeed to make another laugh at himself?

The answer is obvious for Goldoni: with his comedy, *Baruffe*, he has succeeded in making the people of Chioggia laugh at themselves – but only 'themselves' as they were in the past – and it has taken almost 200 years!

Notes

1 All translations are mine.
2 A type of comedy, popular in Italy in the fifteenth and sixteenth centuries, was the '*mariazo*', or rude marriage, which represented the loves of peasants for the amusement of urban and aristocratic audiences.
3 In Italy 'professor' designates a secondary school or A level teacher. It took about two years for the women who became my friends to address me by first name.
4 That was due to the formal and conservative attitudes of Italian teaching. At that time 'memory' had not yet entered the school curricula, although it did, and with a vengeance, from the 1970s and 1980s (Biondi, Rabitti and Torricelli 2004).
5 In a poster spread throughout the village, people were encouraged to lend any documents they might possess to the Neighbourhood Council, then planning to put together an archive.
6 As Crystal writes, 'In this encyclopedia, as is standard practice in linguistics, dialects are seen as applicable to all languages and all speakers … everyone speaks a dialect – whether urban or rural, standard or non-standard, upper class or lower class. And no dialect is thought of as "superior" to any other, in terms of linguistic structure – though several are considered prestigious … Standard English [read Italian] is as much a dialect as any other variety' (1988: 24). (But see Ferguson 2007: 165.)
7 It is reported that when, in the eighteenth century, a pompous senator addressed the Major Council in perfect Tuscan Italian, the whole house broke into laughter. Many Venetians did not know Italian until well into the nineteenth century. At present, Venetian is the most used of Italian dialects, spoken by people of all social classes, many of whom tend to alternate dialect and language phrases in a kind of ironical diglossia (Pellegrini 1996: 270). Because the city is often invaded by tourists, speaking Venetian is valued evidence that one is a native.
8 Bergamo was part of the Venetian Republic from 1428 to 1797.
9 Gozzi's plays, based on old fables, also used as frames for sarcastic attacks against his rivals, were escapist fantasia.
10 It is performed regularly in Naples and Rome, but most frequently in the Venice area, where people understand and love the dialect.

References

Biondi, L., S. Rabitti and P. Torricelli (eds). 2004. *La Rete della Memoria. Pesci, Pescatori e Merletti a Burano. Racconti di Aldo Vitturi*. Scuola Media Statale Baldassarre Galuppi di Burano. Venice: Arti Grafiche Venete.

Cortelazzo, M. and T. Agostini (eds.). 1996. *Sussidiario di Cultura Veneta*. Vicenza: Neri Pozza.

Crystal, D. 1988. *Cambridge Encyclopedia of Language*. Cambridge: Cambridge University Press.

Douglas, M. 1975. *Implicit Meanings. Essays in Anthropology*. London: Routledge.

Ferguson, R. 2007. *A Linguistic History of Venice*. Florence: Leo Olshki.

Goethe, J.W. 1962. *Italian Journey*, transl. W.H. Auden and E. Mayer. London: Harmondswoth Penguin.

Goldoni, C. 1907–1915. *Opere Complete nel Secondo Centenario della Nascita*, ed. G. Ortolani. Venice: Istituto Veneto di Arti Grafiche.

———. 1951[1787]. Tr. C. Signorelli, *Memorie. Per servire alla Storia della sua Vita e a Quella del suo Teatro*. Milan: Signorelli.

Gozzi, C. 1914 [1797]. *Memorie Inutili*. Bari: Laterza.

Lunari, L. 1985. Introduction to *Memorie di Carlo Goldoni*. Trans. P. Bianconi. Milan: Rizzoli.

Molinari, C. 1985. *La Commedia dell'Arte*. Milan: Mondadori.

Nardo, G. 1998. *Studi sul Dialetto di Burano*. Venice: Ateneo Veneto.

Ortolani, G. 1948. *I Capolavori di Carlo Goldoni. Sier Todero brontolon, Le baruffe chiozzotte, Il ventaglio*. Milan: Mondadori. Padoan, G. 1982. *La Commedia Rinascimentale Veneta*. Vicenza: Neri Pozza Editore.

Pasquali, G.B., ed. 1761–1778. *Delle Commedie di Carlo Goldoni*. Venice: G.B. Pascuali.

Pellegrini, G.B. 1996. 'Breve storia linguistica di Venezia e del Veneto', in M. Cortelazzo and T. Agostini, eds, *Sussidiario di cultura veneta*. Vicenza: Neri Pozza.

Sciama, L.D. 1992. 'Bembo Acknowledgement of Tuscan Superiority in Language', in D. Chambers and B. Pullen (eds.), *Venice, a Documentary History*. Oxford: Blackwell.

———. 2003. *A Venetian Island. Environment, History and Change in Burano*. Oxford: Berghahn Books.

Silverman, S. F. 1975. 'The Life Crisis as a Clue to Social Function: The Case of Italy', in R.R. Reiter (ed.), *Toward an Anthropology of Women*, 309–21. New York: Monthly Review Press.

Strehler, G. 2004. *Intorno a Goldoni: Spettacoli e Scritti*. Edited by F. Foradini. Milan: Mursia.

Urbani de Gheltof, G.M. 1883. 'Carlo Goldoni a Chioggia', in *Atti e Memorie dell'Archivio, Letter ed Arti*, vol. 2, 323–31. Veneto: Rivista Mensile di Scienze.

Lidia Dina Sciama studied English Literature in Venice at Ca' Foscari University and Cornell University in the US. She received her doctorate from the Oxford Institute of Social and Cultural Anthropology. She has lived in Italy, Israel and the US, where she taught Anthropology and Comparative Literature. She is a former Director, and currently a Research Associate of Oxford's International Gender Studies Centre (IGS) and a member of Venice's Ateneo Veneto. Her publications include articles on women's crafts, 'Academic Wives' and Sport and Ethnicity. With Professor Joanne Eicher, she edited a book on *Beads and Beadmakers* (Berg 1998). Her monograph, *A Venetian Island: Environment, History and Change in Burano* (Berghahn, 2003) is based on long-standing fieldwork.

INDEX

www.ingramcontent.com/pod-product-compliance
Lightning Source LLC
Chambersburg PA
CBHW070925030426
42336CB00014BA/2542